Religious Identity
and Cultural Negotiation

American Society of Missiology
Monograph Series

Series Editor, James R. Krabill

The ASM Monograph Series provides a forum for publishing quality dissertations and studies in the field of missiology. Collaborating with Pickwick Publications—a division of Wipf and Stock Publishers of Eugene, Oregon—the American Society of Missiology selects high quality dissertations and other monographic studies that offer research materials in mission studies for scholars, mission and church leaders, and the academic community at large. The ASM seeks scholarly work for publication in the series that throws light on issues confronting Christian world mission in its cultural, social, historical, biblical, and theological dimensions.

Missiology is an academic field that brings together scholars whose professional training ranges from doctoral-level preparation in areas such as Scripture, history and sociology of religions, anthropology, theology, international relations, interreligious interchange, mission history, inculturation, and church law. The American Society of Missiology, which sponsors this series, is an ecumenical body drawing members from Independent and Ecumenical Protestant, Catholic, Orthodox, and other traditions. Members of the ASM are united by their commitment to reflect on and do scholarly work relating to both mission history and the present-day mission of the church. The ASM Monograph Series aims to publish works of exceptional merit on specialized topics, with particular attention given to work by younger scholars, the dissemination and publication of which is difficult under the economic pressures of standard publishing models.

Persons seeking information about the ASM or the guidelines for having their dissertations considered for publication in the ASM Monograph Series should consult the Society's website—www.asmweb.org.

Members of the ASM Monograph Committe who approved this book are:

Michael A. Rynkiewich, Retired from Asbury Theological Seminary
Bonnie Sue Lewis, University of Dubuque Theological Seminary

RECENTLY PUBLISHED IN THE ASM MONOGRAPH SERIES

Keon-Sang An, *An Ethiopian Reading of the Bible: Biblical Interpretation of the Ethiopian Orthodox* Tewahido *Church*

Haemin Lee, *International Development and Public Religion: Changing Dynamics of Christian Mission in South Korea*

Juliet Lee Uytanlet, *The Hybrid Tsinoys: Challenges of Hybridity and Homogeneity as Sociocultural Constructs among the Chinese in the Philippines*

"This is a carefully researched book which is an important contribution to the field of migration studies. The reader will find their own identity challenged as they consider the construction of Christian identity alongside identities of departure, belonging, and displacement as experienced by the migrants whose stories are told here. I warmly commend this book for its creative use of the lens of migration to crack open questions of identity."

—CATHY ROSS

Tutor in Contextual Theology, Ripon College,
Cuddesdon; MA Leader, Church Mission Society;
Author of *Mission on the Road to Emmaus*, with Steve Bevans (2015)
and *Pioneering Spirituality*, with J. Baker (2015)

"Globalization and the fluidity of migration have both enriched our world as well as challenged it. In this reflective interdisciplinary study, Jenny McGill navigates the complexity of migration and cultural identity specifically with regard to the theological training of internationals. Her arguments are nuanced, her research thorough, and her conclusions judicious. This is a much-needed contribution to a growing area of discussion."

—MALCOLM GILL

Lecturer in Greek, New Testament, and Preaching,
Sydney Missionary and Bible College, Sydney, Australia

"This work explores the important phenomenon of educational migration and religious identity formation of evangelical minorities outside of North America. The author takes an imaginative, multidisciplinary approach to integrating extensive social science research, weaving rich theological conversations, and stimulating deeper understanding of changing religious minority identity in the context of multiple cultural and transnational experiences. A welcome, timely contribution!"

—JENNY PAK

Associate Professor, Fuller Theological Seminary, School of Psychology

"This genre-bending book, drawing from social science and theology, considers the identity construction of Christian immigrants who straddle continents and cultures. Grounded in rigorous research spanning multiple countries, it is a cogently argued and theologically profound meditation on how disoriented religious actors rewrite their identities within faith communities."

—DAVID R. SWARTZ

Associate Professor of History, Asbury University

"Dr. Jenny McGill notes that one in thirty-five of us will identify as a migrant at some point in our lives, making this work highly relevant for our increasingly migratory and global society. She masterfully integrates philosophical, theological, and psychological insights on identity development in her study of evangelical seminarians who have studied abroad - but she doesn't stop there. Migration becomes, for her, a metaphor of any Christian's growth in Christ. This is an insightful and helpful read for those of us working with international populations in non-profits, churches, and education, or anyone who desires to glean wisdom on Christian identity development through the metaphor of migration."

—**LISA IGRAM**

Associate Dean of Spiritual Development, Biola University

Religious Identity and Cultural Negotiation

Toward a Theology of Christian Identity in Migration

JENNY McGILL

PICKWICK *Publications* · Eugene, Oregon

RELIGIOUS IDENTITY AND CULTURAL NEGOTIATION
Toward a Theology of Christian Identity in Migration

American Society of Missiology Monograph Series 29

Pickwick Publications
An Imprint of Wipf and Stock Publishers
199 W. 8th Ave., Suite 3
Eugene, OR 97401

www.wipfandstock.com

PAPERBACK ISBN: 978-1-4982-9012-8
HARDCOVER ISBN: 978-1-4982-9014-2
EBOOK ISBN: 978-1-4982-9013-5

Cataloguing-in-Publication data:

Names: McGill, Jenny.

Title: Religious identity and cultural negotiation : toward a theology of Christian identity in migration / Jenny McGill.

Description: Eugene, OR: Pickwick Publications, 2016 | Series: American Society of Missiology Monograph Series 29 | Includes bibliographical references.

Identifiers: ISBN 9781498290128 (paperback) | ISBN 9781498290142 (hardcover) | ISBN 9781498290135 (ebook)

Subjects: LSCH: Emigration and immigration | Group identity

Classification: JV6033 M2 2016 (paperback) | JV6033 (ebook)

Manufactured in the U.S.A.   08/01/16

To Kevin, whose surname means son of the stranger or foreigner
To my international friends around the world
To all those who journey and one day will find who they are
(1 Cor 13:12)

Contents

List of Tables | viii

Acknowledgments | ix

Part I. Introduction

1   Background | 3

2   Precedent Literature | 16

Part II. Approaches toward Self and Identity

3   Theological Contribution of Miroslav Volf | 35

4   Psychological Contribution of Jenny Pak | 55

5   Theo-Ethical Contribution of Stanley Hauerwas | 78

6   A Theology of Christian Identity | 100

Part III. Sociological Research on Identity in Migration

7   Research Methodology | 121

8   Field Research on Identity in Migration | 138

Part IV. Toward a Theology of Christian Identity in Migration

9   Transformation: Identity in Migration | 183

10 Applications and Conclusion | 235

Appendix 1 | 247

Appendix 2 | 249

Appendix 3 | 252

Bibliography | 261

Tables

Table 1. Ethnic Identity Interpretations

Table 2. Estimate of Percentage of Christian Population by Country (2010)

Table 3. Percentage Christian Population by Country and Tradition (2010)

Table 4. Percentage Estimate of Evangelical Population by Country (2010)

Table 5. Means, Medians, and Standard Deviations for Strength of Religious, Ethnic, and National Identities

Table 6. Frequencies and Percentages for Location after Graduation by Religious Reasons

Table 7. Migration as a Metaphor for Theology and Christian Identity

Acknowledgments

THIS BOOK, LIKE ALL of life, has been a social act among numerous actors. This international project would not have been possible without the approval of Dr. Robert Garippa, the support of scholarship bodies (King's College London Theological Trust, Sir Richard Stapley Trust, and Alexis Trust) and Doreen and Albert Johnson, my dear host family in England. I credit my doctoral supervisors, Drs. Clemens Sedmak and Marat Shterin, whose kind encouragement and academic rigor kept me working steadily.

I thank Drs. Jerry Park, Jerry Wofford, Holly Ruhl, Roman Williams, and Margarita Mooney for their evaluation of this project at crucial stages. Special appreciation goes to my editors: Sharon Duncan, Dr. Herbert Jarrell, Kevin McGill, and Fiona Claridge. To the *many* who supported me in guidance and prayer (librarians, staff, friends, Debbie, and the Mag 7), thank you. Most of all, I am indebted to the international students and graduates, as friends and colleagues, whose life stories first motivated me to pursue this topic.

I am grateful to my mother and father for demonstrating the authentic pursuit of a virtuous life and for enlarging the boundaries of my world. Mum, your prayers, friendship, and encouragement bolstered me. Dadi, you first showed me love and the curiosity and keenness of learning. To my husband, your wisdom, humility, humor, and feedback, over hours of conversation and pages strewn on the floor, sustained me. Most importantly, I thank the triune God.

I

Introduction

1

Background

EVERY BOOK HAS ITS story, the narrative of how it came to be. My motivation to study identity and migration from a theological and sociological perspective has much to do with my own life experiences and identities. My personal interest in migration and identity was shaped by several factors, and, as is often the case in psychological narrative analysis, one starts from childhood. By the age of thirteen, I had moved five times and had lived in three different U.S. states. Secondly, to my parents' credit, international visitors were consistently entertained in our home, which exposed me at an impressionable young age to a world outside of the United States. During my first eleven years in the Midwestern United States, I recall knowing only one African American (who also happened to be my friend). In high school, however, my family moved to a predominantly Hispanic community, and I became a member of a white minority. My experience as a newcomer and an outsider—though still in a position of ethnic power—formatively prepared me for my future career and field of research.

I first traveled overseas in my second year of university and have since volunteered, studied, researched, or vacationed internationally twenty-three more times. My university friends were also predominantly foreign students. While my daily interaction with differing religious beliefs and cultural patterns was an education in itself, my university studies included a major in psychology and a minor in sociology. My subsequent master's degree included a combined study of theology and culture. Finally, my doctoral research is a culmination and interdisciplinary application of my previous studies. To this end, I completed an additional eighteen graduate hours in psychology and counseling, which equipped me to conduct in-depth personal interviews.

On a professional level, I served four years as a social services coordinator at a crisis agency during which I further developed my skills in working with those from diverse backgrounds. Concurrently, I began working in the international office of the graduate school I was attending and directed this office from 2004 to 2014. My prolonged engagement with international students from over sixty countries largely led to my choice of this research project. I enjoyed an unusual level of access to this constituency, and I became increasingly curious about how they navigate their various identities in migration.

My marrying interracially also greatly impacted my perspective on the subjects of ethnicity, culture, nationalism, and racialized identities. Lastly, since 2010, I have experienced a transnational identity of sorts as I continued my employment in the United States while also commuting to the United Kingdom as an international student at King's College London.

This most recent international venture has catapulted me routinely into markedly different ways of life: altered vocabulary, health care structures, currency, cultural mores, and patterns of thinking, etc. I am continually reminded what it feels like to be an international student by my limited freedoms, restricted employment, and different rules by which to abide. Daily, in my personal life, work, and travels, I consider the negotiation of national, ethnic, and religious identity in differing cultural contexts, and this crossing of borders has enriched my understanding of the processual forces involved in migration and identity construction. As much as transition and diversity have made me who I am, I have also made them my own by seeking out new opportunities for exploration and bringing them to bear on my research. To be sure, this work will bear the marks of the Christian tradition that I follow—Protestant and, more specifically, evangelical.

Given increasing global migration and the importance of positive cross-cultural relations across national borders, this book offers an interdisciplinary exploration of identity formation in migration, namely, with theological, psychological, and sociological lenses. To this end, I consider the views of three—Drs. Miroslav Volf, Jenny Hyun Chung Pak, and Stanley Hauerwas—to form a theology of Christian identity (chapter 6).

Part III summarizes my international research on the examination of the social construction of religious, ethnic, and national identities among foreign-born evangelical migrants who entered the United States to pursue advanced academic studies. From eighteen interviews and 405 surveys from graduates, I investigated how these participants understood their identities in their migration experiences. I combine the theoretical and social research to offer an initial theology of Christian identity in migration, the primary conclusion of which is that migration is integral to Christian identity (chapter 9).

RESEARCH QUESTIONS

This book seeks to define identity from a theological perspective as well as describe a theological understanding of identity in migration. To accompany this theological project, I conducted social research to gather related data and draw conclusions. This research attempts to address the following questions.

Qualitative

RQ1. To what degree do religious factors and aspects of personal faith relate to identity construction in the migration experiences of international theological graduates?

RQ2. Does, and if so, how does religious faith affect their migration after graduation?

RQ3. How do these graduates negotiate their multiple identities in different contexts?

RQ4. Does, and if so, how does international migration affect these graduates?

Quantitative[1]

RQ1. Relating to qualitative RQ1 above, which of their identities (e.g., religious, ethnic, national) do international theological graduates consider to be the most important?

RQ2a. Relating to qualitative RQ2 above, based on the perceptions of international theological graduates, to what extent does one's religious faith play a role in determining one's geographic residence after graduation?

---

1. After two thirds of the interviews were completed, I assessed the qualitative data prior to formulating the questionnaire. This allowed for refined questions targeting the subject areas that had surfaced in the interviews.

RQ2b. Relating to qualitative RQ2 above, are individuals who name religious reasons as the primary factor in determining their location more likely to leave the U.S. after graduation?

RQ3. Are there significant differences in individuals' assessments of their religious, ethnic, and national identities?

RESEARCH DESIGN AND CONTEXT

A mixed methodology was employed, using quantitative and qualitative measures to analyze the ways in which evangelical leaders who are educated abroad negotiate their religious, ethnic/cultural, and national identities. Participants were individuals born outside of the United States, from a variety of ethnic and national backgrounds, who migrated for a temporary period of graduate study in Texas.[2]

A multiple case study of eighteen semi-structured interviews, incorporating ethnographic direct observation, was completed through field research in several geographical areas: Catholic and former Communist Europe and South and Southeast Asia. Nine nationalities are represented. All of those interviewed had returned overseas and serve as international theologians, laymen, and religious workers in their respective countries. Transcribed interviews were analyzed using NVivo 10.

The group of 405 international alumni from 1983 to 2013 completed a questionnaire, thus representing a larger graduating body of internationals and a larger set of migration outcomes than the interviews alone. Sixty-four nationalities are represented. All participants attested to an evangelical Christian faith and a period of theological graduate education outside of their country of origin. Data were compiled and analyzed with SPSS version 18.0.

The questionnaire surveyed respondents from sixty-four countries, some of whom remained in the U.S. after completing their studies. The interview respondents were located in Eastern Europe—Poland, Hungary, Albania, Romania—and South/Southeast Asia—India, Singapore, and China (Hong Kong)—with two exceptions: Italy and Spain. All of the interviewees were return migrants to their country of origin upon completion of studies. Even within the two regional groupings of formerly communist Europe and South/Southeast Asia, individual experiences varied widely. For example, even though both countries were communist, the experiences and identity

---

2. Texas ranks third in the U.S. for international student enrollment, after California and New York. Chow and Bhandari, "Open Doors 2014."

construction for someone who identifies as an evangelical in Hungary is strikingly different from their counterpart in Poland. Space does not permit a thorough consideration of the historical and political context of each locality.[3] A modest attempt to survey individuals from two more distinct areas of the world—Asia and Europe, East and West—was made in order to demonstrate the potential commonalities various migrants might share. In addition, I interviewed representatives from multiple countries within these two major groups in order to gather how the process of identity construction varies among local contexts.

ASSUMPTIONS AND DELIMITATIONS

As both theology and sociology attempt to explain human behavior, each is engaged for the study of identity. In considering the epistemologies of positivism, realism, and constructivism (also called interpretivism), critical realism offers the best philosophical framework for this study.[4] The central presuppositions of critical realism are 1) that an *ontological reality* exists, with a nature and structure that exists apart from human construction, 2) *epistemological perspectivalism*, which claims that human knowledge is "incomplete and historically situated" and results in multiple explanations for events, and 3) *judgmental rationality*, which posits that the plausibility of differing accounts can be assessed.[5] Reality is singular and only "imperfectly and probablistically apprehendible."[6] Critical realism is elsewhere associated with postpositivism, and its nature of knowledge is claimed by others to be foundational.[7] Its proponents, however, claim its antifoundationalism.[8]

Critical realism accepts the strengths of and place for positivism and social constructionism and yet differs significantly from both views on the nature of reality, ontology, and epistemology. Critical realism does not hold to the reductionism of positivism and the human passivity of social constructionism. Both positivism and a radical social constructionist view share a common weakness: determinism. In positivism, biological determinism drives all human activity, and, in social constructionism, social structural determinism suggests a flaccid, underdeveloped sense of human

---

3. "Compare Nations".
4. Bryman, *Social Research Methods*, 28–30.
5. Smith, "Critical Realism."
6. Lincoln et al., "Paradigmatic Controversies," 100-102.
7. Ibid., 114.
8. Smith, *What Is a Person?*, introduction.

agency. Although genetics and society do forge a great deal of human reality, neither force serves as the sole conduit of knowledge.

Critical realism is not left however at the door of humanism, which posits a different weakness: unabated human potential. On the contrary, critical realism recognizes that genetic material and society limit human potential. Critical realism offers a way forward in considering the validity of each of these paradigms. To this end, this study presents an interdisciplinary approach that is informed by a mixed methodology in order to recognize and explore the complexity of human behavior.

Several assumptions are made in this study. That the conceptualization of identity is socially constructed, based on relational and contextual conditions, is assumed. For this theological study, that the Christian Scriptures—the Hebrew and Greek Testaments—constitute the revelation of God to humanity is assumed. Methodologically, that identity construction can be studied is assumed. Qualitative and quantitative methods have been used to consider the experiences of foreign-born citizens who entered the U.S. to pursue academic studies. I gathered descriptive data from graduates who returned overseas as well as from those who remained in the U.S. Further, that language can reflect and be used to identify the mechanics and social forces of religious identity and cultural involvement is assumed. Additionally, human memory is assumed as sufficient to recall past events and experiences for participants with no known cognitive disorders. Participants are analyzed according to their self-reported perceptions. I do not presume to portray the participants' voices, but to "elucidate the experience that is implicated by the subjects in the context of their activities as they perform them, and as they are understood."[9]

In considering the impact of faith on identity and migration, I delimit my discussion to the perspective of primarily non-North American evangelicals. I showcase the Judeo-Christian religious identity but plan to expand my scope in future research. The participants of this study, who migrated from various regions of the world to the United States on temporary student visas for a period of academic study, represent a limited cross-section of the population. The qualitative portion of this study focuses on return migrants functioning as religious minorities in several regions of Europe and Asia while the quantitative portion considers a broader set of individuals from sixty-four countries, including both those who returned overseas and those who remained in the United States.

I delimited my discussion to this particular group for several reasons. Firstly, in the areas where Christianity represents a majority of the

9. Altheide and Johnson, "Reflections," 592.

population, namely in Latin America and Africa, much research has already been conducted. This study, by contrast, highlights Christians in minority contexts. Secondly, for ethical reasons, I chose countries that I could visit without having to feign another reason for my legal entrance or endanger the participants for their attestation to the Christian faith. Thirdly, by their previous and current adherence to a similar character of evangelicalism, a group study could be accomplished. Fourthly, my unique access to this group of return migrants proved to be unusual and valuable for study.

Methods for studying human behavior are inherently constrained by language, researcher subjectivity, participant subjectivity, empirical reach, funding, and ethical standards, among other factors. Measuring the complexity and multiplicity of factors that affect behavior requires methods which allow for open exploration, namely self-report and observation. While self-report has its disadvantages, it remains one of the best ways to access personal knowledge. Other methods to obtain knowledge about abstract concepts such as personal values or identity are limited. Self-reporting reflects who they say they are or what they say they do as a form of "public speech," not what they actually do or who they actually are.[10] Since a researcher is responsible to represent accurately what a participant says, I strove to ensure that my interpretations remained true to the participant's intentions. I have left the graduates' comments untouched even in cases of gendered language. Lastly, using research literature written almost exclusively in the English language also limits this study.

DEFINITIONS

For clarity, several terms are defined for how they are employed in this project.

Culture

Culture is here defined as a "historically transmitted pattern of meanings embodied in symbols, a system of inherited conceptions expressed in symbolic forms by means of which [people] communicate, perpetuate, and develop their knowledge about and attitudes toward life."[11] Stella Ting-Toomey describes culture similarly as a "frame of reference that consists of patterns and traditions . . . shared to varying degrees by interacting mem-

10. Bender et al., *Religion*, 298.
11. Geertz, *Interpretation of Cultures*, 89.

bers of a community."[12] Cultures, then, are patterns of meaning historically constructed and changed over time.[13] Although cultures are neither distinct entities nor entirely internally consistent, a critical threshold of cultural items (whether shared or disputed) exists sufficiently to loosely differentiate human groups at a given point in time.[14] From a postmodern point of view, culture is understood as a "ground of contest in relation" in which power (and who possesses it) is fundamental in the construction of knowledge and cultural identity.[15]

Religion

Scholars have defined religion in terms of substance and function, although its boundaries are debated.[16] Similarly, religion is here defined as discourses or practices "characterized by an orientation to speak of matters transcendent (e.g., beyond the limited spaces of this world) and eternal (e.g., beyond the limits of time)," that speak "with an authority equally transcendent and eternal."[17] For this study, one's religion and faith, as personally adopted orientations, are used interchangeably.

Migration

Human migration, for the purposes of this project, refers to the international and voluntary movement of citizens from their various countries of origin to the United States to pursue academic study.

Identity

Identity has been conceptualized in various ways, but is viewed most often in terms of content and/or process.[18] While acknowledging the variant uses of the term, I define identity as "the confluence of the person's self-chosen or ascribed commitments, personal characteristics and beliefs about herself;

12. Ting-Toomey, *Communicating across Cultures*, 10.

13. Tanner, *Theories of Culture*, 25–58.

14. Tihanyi et al., "Effect of Cultural Distance," 271. See also Hanciles, *Beyond Christendom*, 141; Tanner, *Theories of Culture*, 57.

15. Phan, "Experience of Migration," 188–89.

16. McGuire, *Religion*, 8–14.

17. Braun, "Religion," 10.

18. Vignoles et al., "Introduction," 1–13.

roles and positions in relation to significant others; and her membership in social groups and categories (including both her status with the group and the group's status within the larger context); as well as her identification with treasured material possessions and her sense of where she belongs in geographical space."[19] Further, the term "negotiating identity(ies)" is a dynamic interaction between persons about the "meanings attached to symbols [e.g., labels, positions, practices] and how those involved are located in regard to these symbols."[20] "Identity salience" denotes the importance of a particular identity to the individual. Contextual factors influence its variability.

Religious Identity

MEASUREMENT

For scholars, two measurements of religious identity have remained prominent: affiliation and/or identification. In measuring one's religious group affiliation, denominational categories are often used. The subjective approach involves self-identification and often includes four criteria: belief in biblical literalism, belief in an afterlife, frequency of prayer, and frequency of church attendance.[21] I considered both denomination and self-identification in this study, and I categorized participants as evangelical Christians by both measures (see Appendix 3, questions 35–36).[22]

EVANGELICAL

What is an evangelical? The Greek word *euangélion* means "the good news" or "the gospel," that is, of Jesus Christ. Historically, it stems from the Christian religious revivals of North America and England during the 1700s and early 1800s.[23] Although the term evangelical is employed in more than one way, it often refers to a set of particular beliefs.[24] David Bebbington's classic definition of evangelicalism identifies four chief priorities: activism, biblicism, conversionism, and crucicentrism (that followers live out the gospel, revere the Bible, leave former ways of living, and keep central Christ's

---

19. Ibid., 4.
20. Christofferson, *Negotiating Identity*, 267.
21. Alwin et al., "Measuring Religious Identities," 539–40.
22. Ibid., 530, 548, 561.
23. "Defining Evangelicalism."
24. "Defining the Term."

sacrificial death, respectively).[25] More recently, Patrick Mitchel named three characteristics that are central to understanding the evangelical identity. The first is the nature of its transdenominational shared identity. The second is how strongly persons of this identity are motivated by religion, and the third is its contextual adaptability.[26] Clearly, any religious identity is influenced by its time period. A definition of evangelicalism, however, that is based on a set of criteria despite cultural variation seems possible.[27] I employ the term evangelical in the traditional sense as suggested by Bebbington. Religious identity is sociologically assessed in three primary ways: beliefs, self-ascription, and group affiliation.[28] The latter two are appraised in this study.

Ethnic and National Identity

Ethnic identity is socially constructed and categorized in terms of race and culture (see table 1).

Table 1. Ethnic Identity Interpretations[29]

	Embodied Expressions	Relational Expressions
Ethnicity as Culture	Customs/Symbols	Kin/Friendship Networks
Ethnicity as Race	Racial Appearance	Racialized Situations

The term ethnic identity includes both racial and cultural expressions relating to a shared history, language, location, mores, patterns, and values. Although its meaning can remain stable within a time period, it can also be reformulated over time.[30] Ethnic groups, then, are "any substantial aggregation of persons who are perceived by themselves and/or others to share a unique set of cultural and historical commonalities."[31] Note, however, that "groups" are not clear-cut entities of people, but societal perspectives.[32]

---

25. Bebbington, *Evangelicalism*, 2–3. A more recent discussion is Stanley, *Global Diffusion*.

26. Mitchel, "Evangelicals and Irish Identity," 207–9.

27. Morris, "Evangelical." See also, Balmer, *Encyclopedia of Evangelicalism*, 236.

28. Williams, "God's Global Professionals," 11–12.

29. Park, "Ethnic and Religious Identities," 13, 61.

30. Ibid., 16.

31. Zelinsky, *Enigma of Ethnicity*, 43.

32. Brubaker, *Ethnicity*, 79.

Self-understanding in terms of one's citizenship is a construct that can be measured. National identity reflects "the self-understanding of individual[s] and groups framed in terms of their membership in a broader collectivity coterminous with the territorial, social, and legal boundaries of an actual or potential nation-state."[33]

Religious Minority Identity

The term religious minority identity is defined as identification in a religious minority group within a country's total religious makeup. All of the interviewees identified themselves as members of a religious minority. Christian participants from Asian countries, for example, claimed a religious minority identity (see table 2). This terminology does not, however, necessarily indicate a certain level of religious persecution.

Table 2. Estimate of Percentage of Christian Population by Country (2010)[34]

	Percentage of Population that is Christian
India	2.6
Hong Kong	11.9
Singapore	18.2

The participants from Europe were not strictly members of a religious minority in the overall Christian membership of the country (see table 3). However, this general classification does not highlight the sharp dissension among Catholics, Protestants, and Orthodox as opposing memberships in these countries. If membership is broken down among these Christian traditions, Protestant membership can be seen as more of a minority identity. In Poland and Italy, for example, Protestants are outsized by Catholics while in Romania, Protestants are greatly outweighed by Orthodox.

33. Bonikowski, "Research on American Nationalism," 9.
34. *Global Religious Landscape*, 74–76.

Table 3. Percentage Christian Population by Country and Tradition (2010)[35]

	Percentage of Total Christian Population in Country	Percentage of Protestants of Total Christian Population	Percentage of Catholics of Total Christian Population	Percentage of Orthodox of Total Christian Population
Albania	18.0	<1.7	56.9	41.4
Hungary	82.7	26.2	73.2	0.24
Italy	85.1	1.6	97.5	0.23
Poland	94.3	0.44	97.8	1.4
Romania	99.5	6.3	5.7	87.7
Spain	78.6	1.3	95.7	2.5

Table 3 does not distinguish between mainline denominations and minority groups within Protestantism such as evangelicals (see table 4). In summary, those who were interviewed possessed a religious minority identity within their local and regional contexts.[36] This minority status, as well as the lesser degree of political and cultural representation that accompanies it, signifies less social power.

Table 4. Percentage Estimate of Evangelical Population by Country (2010)[37]

Percentage of Evangelicals by Country	
Albania	0.5
Hong Kong	6.1
Hungary	2.8
India	2.2
Italy	1.1
Poland	0.3
Romania	5.4
Singapore	7.8
Spain	1.0

35. Ibid., 72–73, 80–81. The negligible percentage of other Christian groups is not included; columns, therefore, do not total 100 percent.

36. Globally, they are not a religious minority, as members of all Christian traditions combined totaled 2.18 billion in 2010. *Global Christianity*, 12.

37. Mandryk and Johnstone, *Operation World*, 94, 253, 401, 408, 482, 690, 701, 744, 765.

SIGNIFICANCE OF RESEARCH

Despite the existence of extensive research on identity processes across the social sciences, few scholars have considered the identity configuration of return migrants. By the same token, few studies have considered the evangelical identities of those outside of North America, apart from Latin America and Africa where Christians constitute a greater majority of the population. By considering members of the religious evangelical minorities in parts of Asia and Europe, this study offers the experience of international migrants in their identity change and maintenance amidst multiple cultural and national transitions.

The objectives of the research are to 1) explore the role religion plays in the daily lives of educated migrants (who function as an ethnic minority in their host society and as a religious minority in their home society), 2) investigate evangelical Christian narratives occurring outside of North America, 3) inform discourse on educational migration, religious identity, and diaspora studies, and 4) determine which sources of influence (e.g., religion, citizenship, family, ethnic identity, economic status) hold strength in migrant cultural negotiation, coping, and migration outcomes, and 5) identify key practices for university offices and service organizations to employ in aiding the cultural transitions of migrants. This investigation of the relation of faith to identity in migration provides new insights into how Christian migrants cope with and introduce positive social change into both their host and home communities.

2

Precedent Literature

THE STUDY OF IDENTITY has generated a host of theories within multiple disciplines.[1] While psychological literature has tended to focus on individual agency, sociology has emphasized the social construction of identity.[2] Despite extensive research on identity processes across the social sciences, few have considered the theological configuration of identity in conversation with the social sciences. This project, therefore, engages theology, psychology, and sociology in an interdisciplinary discussion of the concept. To set the stage for subsequent chapters, this chapter reviews the theoretical frame for this research as well as recent literature on religious identity in migration studies, Christian identity, the theology of identity, and the theology of migration.

IDENTITY

Identity has been defined in this study as the totality of a person's self-conception and includes one's beliefs about oneself, one's roles, and one's group memberships. Individuals do not have identities, as people do not possess ethnicity or culture as entities. Rather, identities are formed by what people are socialized to do.[3] Identity-making, therefore, is an ongoing and

---

1. For an overview of sociological and social psychological theories, see Owens and Samblanet, "Self and Self-Concept."

2. Lawler, *Identity*, 3.

3. Jenkins, *Rethinking Ethnicity*, 15.

adaptive "process of identification."[4] Identities are derived not only from a person's self-conceptions, but are also derived from the perceptions and declarations of others that have been imposed on that individual. In this way, identity is both produced by and pushed on to the individual by social structures and operates as a "force," as people both accommodate and alter social structures based on their views of themselves.[5]

Identity can be examined at three levels: personal, social, and collective.[6] *Personal identities* relate to one's individual perception of oneself (and what one means by the use of an identity term) even though this perception is certainly impacted by one's social location. *Social identities* reflect one's individual identity based on group membership. *Collective identities* involve how collectives forge a broader group identity. Identities in this study relate to the social identity and personal identity levels, and the terms personal and individual are used interchangeably.

Identity involves both differentiation from others (who I am not) and sameness with others (who I am).[7] Because defining boundaries between oneself and others can lapse into essentializing categorization, a narrative view of identity compensates for this by including the "destabilizing dimensions of time, space, and relationality."[8] Indeed, human existence takes narrative form, and identity is the purposeful, storied configuration of multiple aspects of one's life.[9] Identities are relatively fixed and yet fluid schemas of self-understanding that intersect and overlap; they are influenced by individuals, groups, the larger collective society, and their situational context.

IDENTITY NEGOTIATION AND NARRATIVE IDENTITY

The theoretical works that inform this project employ both identity negotiation theory and the use of narrative among several disciplines. By the 1980s, a range of academic disciplines had begun to employ the concept of narrative for variant uses.[10] A discussion of narrative will appear in this project only in so far as it is useful to describe identity.

4. Susin, "A Critique," 79.

5. Park, "Ethnic and Religious Identities," 21.

6. Owens, "Self and Identity," 210–26.

7. Lawler, *Identity*, 3–6.

8. Somers, "Narrative Constitution," 605–6.

9. McAdams, "Redemptive Self," 99; Polkinghorne, *Narrative Knowing*, 150–55; Salih, *Gender in Transnationalism*, 126, 137.

10. See summary in Hauerwas and Jones, *Why Narrative?*, 2.

Identity Negotiation Theory

Theories of identity negotiation have been separately set forth by Stella Ting-Toomey in the field of communication studies and by William Swann in the field of social psychology. In the late fifties and sixties, North American sociologists increasingly discussed the negotiation of identity based on the work of Erving Goffman among others.[11]

Ting-Toomey articulated the process of identity negotiation as early as 1986.[12] In her discussion of identity negotiation theory, Ting-Toomey describes it as a confluence derived from multiple disciplines: social identity theory (social psychology), symbolic interactionism (sociology), and relational dialectics (communication studies).[13] According to Ting-Toomey, it is through symbolic communication with others that individual conceptions of the self and of others are formed. Culture serves as the "prime regulator" in forming this reflective view of oneself, which is comprised of both self-conceptions derived from group membership (social identities) and self-conceptions derived from individual comparisons (personal identities). These reflective views of one's self, formed by symbolic communication with others, in turn form one's identities.[14] She applies her theory with its ten assumptions to explain the intercultural communication process and, more recently, in relation to bicultural identity.[15] Identity negotiation theory assumes that, in any social interaction, people desire for their self-images to be positively assessed by others. If they are validated, inclusion is felt; if they are ostracized, they experience exclusion. The theory also assumes that individuals in all cultures possess the need for security, trust, inclusion, connec-

---

11. Goffman, *Presentation of Self.*

12. Ting-Toomey, "Interpersonal Ties," 114, 123; Ting-Toomey, "Communicative Resourcefulness."

13. In symbolic interactionism (a term coined by Herbert Blumer to represent Mead's work), persons act based on their interpretations, and meanings and self-perceptions are created and changed through social interaction. Symbolic interactionist identity theories such as Stryker's identity theory as well as the work of McCall and Simmons, Burke, and Turner, focus more on the personal identity level and emphasize the agency and stability of the self across situations. Separate identity theories, which focus more on the social identity level, emphasize the role of social factors affecting individual perception, as in Tajfel and Turner's social identity theory. Owens and Samblanet, "Self and Self-Concept," 482, 485, 488; Turner, *Contemporary Sociological Theory,* 331–55.

14. Ting-Toomey, *Communicating across Cultures,* 27–28. She lists eight identity domains of two types (primary and situational), differentiates ethnic, cultural, and personal identities as separate domains, and omits religious identity altogether (29–39). See also "Identity Negotiation Theory."

15. Toomey et al., "Bicultural Identity Negotiation."

tion, and stability. These needs are more often met in culturally familiar or culturally similar environments and are less often met in unfamiliar or dissimilar situations. Positive identity negotiation occurs when these needs are met, or at least when the individual's most salient domains are affirmed.[16]

Separately but simultaneously, Swann offered the term identity negotiation in 1987 to signify the processes whereby people arrange interpersonal interactions ("interpersonal principles") and fulfill their individual self-views ("intrapsychic mechanisms").[17] In Swann's view, the primary interpersonal principles of identity negotiation are clarity, cooperation, continuity, and compatibility. The main intrapsychic mechanisms people use to maintain "identity continuity and regularity" include selective attention, discounting, biased interpretation, using anxiety as information, biased recall, a striving for thematic coherence, and compartmentalization. Each individual as a social partner enters an interaction with personal identities and goals. One's process of identity negotiation produces a person's situated identity (an individual's self-concept within that given period) and a partner's situated appraisal (a partner's impression of the person) for a set of negotiation outcomes and resulting identity and relationship goals.[18]

Swann's identity negotiation theory joins the self-verification theory of social psychology and the symbolic interactionism theory of sociology.[19] His theory emphasizes the role of the self and asserts that individuals negotiate identities that remain relatively stable to match their "chronic self-views." These identities then guide one's actions, although identity change can still occur under catalytic conditions. As an interactionist theory of personality, the significance of this particular identity negotiation theory is its emphasis on both the personal attributes and the structural variables that influence social behavior.[20]

16. For a complete list of assumptions, Ting-Toomey, *Communicating across Cultures*, 40–41.

17. Swann and Bosson, "Identity Negotiation," 449, 457; Swann, "Identity Negotiation."

18. Swann and Bosson, "Identity Negotiation," 451–63. Two opposing occurrences are sorted in identity negotiation: self-verification and behavior confirmation. *Self-verification* is when one individual, the target, encourages the other party, the perceiver, to act in ways that are consistent with the target's self-conceptions. *Behavior confirmation* is when the perceiver sways the target to act according to the perceiver's views. Swann, "Identity Negotiation," 1038–39.

19. According to self-verification theory, persons prefer others to see them as they perceive themselves and seek "self-verifying evaluations" to achieve coherence. Swann, "Self-Verification Theory."

20. Swann and Bosson, "Identity Negotiation," 448, 466.

The development of Ting-Toomey's and Swann's simultaneous theories has not heretofore been discussed in identity literature. Both of these independently developed theories recognize the role of socio-cultural and personal variables on the construction of individual identity and also agree that individuals fundamentally desire to be seen and received as who they personally understand themselves to be. Swann, however, seems to differ from Ting-Toomey's assertion that people strive only for positive feedback.[21] For Swann, identity negotiation is rooted in social interaction, but, as Ting-Toomey seems to allow, I expand its definition to include the internal thought processes of negotiation and self-evaluation that occur within an individual separately from a social encounter.[22] While these two theories overlap significantly and either would be suitable for use, Ting-Toomey's theory of identity negotiation, with its discussion of individual identity in the context of multiple cultures and its special attention to the formation of cultural and ethnic identities, is preferred for the purposes of this study.[23]

Narrative Identity

Theorists from multiple disciplines have expounded on the use of narrative in self-conception. In depicting personal identity, for example, one's self-conception is described as a story. Psychologists Jenny Pak and Dan McAdams have extensively researched this idea of a *narrative identity*, the ongoing, developing self-story one tells to oneself.[24] McAdams claims that individuals create meaning and identity through storytelling. His life-story model is comprised of several components: *images* that are created in childhood, *story themes* in adolescence and young adulthood, and *imagoes*, or main characters, in adulthood.[25] Regarding the self as both the storyteller and the stories, he highlights that these stories are integrative and narrated in social relationships. He also explains that they are evolving cultural texts and that some are better stories than others.[26]

Margaret Somers, a sociologist and social theorist, affirms that human experience is narrative in form. She argues against theoretical categories of agency and identity in favor of exploring identity in terms of its

21. See her core assumption 10 and Swann's comment in Swann, "Identity Negotiation," 1045; Ting-Toomey, "Identity Negotiation Theory," 218.

22. Swann and Bosson, "Identity Negotiation," 465.

23. Ting-Toomey, "Identity Negotiation Theory."

24. See chapter 4. McAdams, "Narrative Identity," 99–101.

25. McAdams, *The Person*, 409–13, 424–25.

26. McAdams, "Personal Narratives," 243–48.

socio-historical constitution and also discusses the process of identity formation as narrative identity. Because "narrative is an *ontological condition
of social life*," stories guide individuals to act based on their location in these
narratives and in order to integrate with them.[27] She explains:

> Narrativity demands that we discern the meaning of any single
> event only in temporal and spatial relationship to other events.
> Indeed, the chief characteristic of narrative is that it renders
> understanding only by *connecting* (however unstably) *parts*
> to a constructed *configuration* or a *social network* of relations
> (however incoherent or unrealizable) composed of symbolic,
> institutional, and material practices.[28]

In relating its application to the social sciences, Somers unfolds four
features of narrativity. Narrativity includes a relationality of parts, causal
emplotment, selective appropriation, and, finally, temporality, sequence
and place. Rather than creating meaning by categorizing an event, persons
produce meaning by connecting parts of their existence along a temporal
continuum, without a specific chronology. The emplotment of connected
events (into an "intelligible plot"), no matter their order, lend them meaning. Individuals, using selective appropriation, choose from an array of
possible events to construct their narratives. Causal emplotment is the attempted explanation of "why a narrative has the story line it does" without
resorting to categorization. Locating events in a plot contextualizes them in
a specific time and historical relation.[29]

These four features lead to several dimensions of narrativity according to Somers. *Ontological narratives* are the stories individuals employ to
frame their self-view, their social location, and their explanation of who
they are.[30] These stories of relationality sustained over time become culturally institutionalized *public narratives*. *Metanarratives* constitute the "epic
dramas" of human history such as feudalism, industrialization, Marxism, or
capitalism but lack *conceptual narrativity*, the "concepts and explanations"
that individuals create through social forces.[31]

Other sociologists confirm the importance of narrative in understanding human behavior.[32] Jerry Park, for example, shows how public narra-

27. Somers, "Narrative Constitution," 614, original emphasis.

28. Ibid., 616, original emphasis.

29. Ibid., 616–17.

30. Ammerman, "Religious Identities," 213–14. Ammerman's term is
"autobiographical narratives."

31. Somers, "Narrative Constitution," 618–20.

32. For a description of narrative in relation to identity, see Lawler, *Identity*, 10–22.

tives help to explain the variation of salience and the interaction between individual ethnic and religious identities among young Asian Americans. The meanings attributed to these identities differ and show fluidity, but still demonstrate fixity by ranging around a set of common themes traced from predominant cultural narratives. Individuals demonstrate agency by picking from various "plotlines" of public and metanarratives to coherently fit the perception of their own identities. Differences in identity salience relate to the number and kind of narratives available. Individuals draw from both racial and religious public narratives and the American "freedom of choice" narrative to construct their personal ethnic and religious identities.[33] The "dialectical dynamics of personal agency and structural constraint" display their interplay and mutual alteration over time.[34]

Roman Williams discusses narrative in relation to the identity negotiation of international students in the United States. During their time abroad, the religious narratives of the host cultural context shaped, even transformed, their identities. Williams examines their identity emplotment into the narrative of U.S. evangelicalism and the idea of "calling"—a religiously motivated vocational pursuit—as a tool used to organize the self and, in turn, to provide social resources and action plans by which they lived. Narrative formation was the process by which these students "internalized an evangelical identity."[35] This idea of a personal, vocational calling structured their perceptions of their lifetime continuum (past, present, and future) as they fashioned their personal stories from the larger American evangelical public narrative and Christian metanarrative.[36]

Theologians as well, as mentioned previously, have related narrative to theology in a variety of ways. Stanley Hauerwas, while distancing himself from narrative theology in general, confirms the usefulness of narrative in depicting personal identity and Christian formation.[37] Thus, by engaging narrative work from across these disciplines combined with the theorization of identity negotiation, I will articulate a theological discussion of the construction of identity in migration.

For narrative in relation to personhood, see Smith, *Moral, Believing Animals*, 63–88.

33. Park, "Ethnic and Religious Identities," 114, 148–50, 158–61.

34. Ibid., 80.

35. Williams, "God's Global Professionals," 13, 45, 59, 69.

36. Ibid., vi, 38, 41–45.

37. Hauerwas, *Christian Existence*, 26; Hauerwas, *Performing the Faith*, 136–49; Hauerwas and Jones, *Why Narrative?*, 5.

MIGRATION, EDUCATION, AND RELIGIOUS IDENTITY

One out of every thirty-five people experiences international migration during one's lifetime. Almost 232 million migrants, or 3.2 percent of the world's population, currently live outside of their country of birth or citizenship. Of those, almost 60 percent live in industrialized nations. Europe hosts the greatest number of migrants with Asia a close second, followed by North America (72 million, 71 million, and 53 million, respectively). In contrast to the age distribution among the general population, adults (ages 20–64) comprise almost three-fourths of the migrant population.[38] The varieties of temporary and permanent migrant classes in the twenty-first century reflect a change from previous centuries and include permanent residents, laborers of low and high skill, refugee and asylum seekers, students, citizens of the European Union, and the undocumented.[39] Levitt and Jaworsky confirm a wealth of unexplored territory for research among international migrants.[40]

Individuals with higher levels of education tend to migrate more, and, as the level of education of the migrant increases, so does the level of migration.[41] For identity and migration research, international students offer a pertinent population for study. In the U.S. alone, over 866,000 foreign students enrolled in U.S. higher educational institutions during the 2013–2014 academic year, constituting 4 percent of total enrollment.[42] In spite of this significant migrant population, fewer studies have focused on those who migrate for educational purposes, and those that do have been largely limited to studies of acculturation in the host country. This project, by contrast, investigates the identity processes for educated migrants during both their period of study abroad and upon their return to their country of origin and explores how their religious identity is related to their cultural adjustment and interacted with their ethnic and national identities. A call for further research in the sociology of religion includes four areas which this research specifically addresses: beliefs, bodies (that is, how religion is embodied and lived), elites, and cross-national comparisons.[43] This project encompasses these areas in its study of the religious identity of temporary migrants seeking graduate education in the United States.

38. Population Division, "International Migration."
39. Beath, "Migration," 159.
40. Levitt and Jaworsky, "Transnational Migration Studies."
41. Beath, "Migration," 172.
42. Chow and Bhandari, "Open Doors 2014".
43. Smith, "Future Directions," 1564–68.

Along with migration, religious faith is connected to the formation of individual and corporate human identity.[44] What, then, is religious identity? One's religious identity writes a "spiritual biography," a "narrative of how one person's own spirit, living in the world, intersects with the divine Spirit more deeply afoot in that same world."[45] One's religious identity has been shown to stabilize most often prior to the advent of adulthood, and religious involvement remains relatively stable through one's adult life.[46]

Religious identity is also colored by a person's historical culture. Any given culture holds distinctive elements, mores, and scripts that serve as a filter through which humanity engages with life and different customs.[47] One's environmental context influences how one embraces or rejects a particular religion. Moreover, religious experience is inevitably forged by this larger backdrop or landscape of regional and national contexts.[48] Robert Schreiter points to three amoebic entities that shape human existence and, in particular, affect religious life: ethnicity, nationality, and globality. These contexts occur at three levels—local, regional, and global—and influence one's definition of belonging, relationships, and identity.[49] How, then, is religious identity affected when combined with international migration? At this crucial intersection of faith, education, and migration, one's religious identity is continuously formed, fractured, and fortified.

Identity has been discussed in relation to a multitude of topics, including ethnicity, nationalism, religion, and migration. Much of the literature on migration has detailed the identity (religious, ethnic, political, or otherwise) of various ethnic groups.[50] Within diaspora studies, researchers have examined migrant faith congregations, most notably in Europe and in the United Kingdom, but also on a global scale.[51] Additionally, a growing body of research focuses on the plight of undocumented migrants crossing into new territory as a result of poverty, war, or trafficking.[52] More recently, scholars have offered studies of transnationalism and the changing definition of

44. Fisher and Luyster, *Living Religions*, 10–17.

45. McKenna, "No Generic Spirituality," 211.

46. David Voas, "Are We as Religious as our Parents?" (Lecture, Department of Theology and Religious Studies, King's College London, London, October 14, 2010).

47. Howell and Williams Paris, *Introducing Cultural Anthropology*. Their preferred term for culture is a "conversation" instead of a lens or filter.

48. Phan, *Ethnicity*, 1.

49. Schreiter, "Ethnicity and Nationality," 9–25.

50. For example, Tsolidis, *Migration*.

51. See Haar, *Strangers and Sojourners*; Wild-Wood, *Migration and Christian Identity*.

52. Groody, *Border of Death*.

home.[53] These areas of research, however, offer no acute consideration of religious affiliation or identity for specifically educated migrants during their times of transition or upon their return.

Much has been accomplished in the study of identity, belonging, culture, and religion of immigrants who reside in the United States, and ethnographies have been dedicated to the study of their conversions.[54] Psychologists, for instance, have investigated the impact of culture, gender, and ethnicity on identity development.[55] Sociologists have considered the religious identities of highly skilled immigrants and students living in the U.S.[56] Other research, such as Christofferson's look at how the Hakka Chinese in Taiwan negotiate their Christian identities, examines the significance of religious identity in regard to other social identities such as ethnicity, class, and gender.[57]

Perhaps the research that most closely relates to the present project is the work of Roman Williams. Williams investigated evangelical international students in the United States upon their return to Asia and found that these educated migrants described a sense of spiritual "calling," relating religion to their occupation as a significant facet of their personal identities.[58] His research does not, however, investigate their religious belonging compared to ethnic identification or citizenship, either during their studies abroad or upon their return. On the whole, research is still needed in the area of internationals who migrate for educational purposes, their negotiations of multiple identities, and their patterns of return migration. This book focuses on the identity negotiation of predominantly non-North American evangelical migrants and explores how religious identity relates to cultural adjustment and interacts with ethnic and national identities. This project, therefore, will add a new and important voice to current conversations in sociology, theology, and migration studies.

CHRISTIAN IDENTITY AND THEOLOGY OF IDENTITY

How, then, do faith, identity, and culture intersect, particularly for the migrant Christian? If one's beliefs determine the way one lives, then theology is

53. Al-Ali and Koser, *New Approaches*; Vertovec, *Transnationalism*.

54. Chen, *Getting Saved*; Yang, *Chinese Christians*.

55. Berry, "Psychology of Immigration"; Phinney, "Three-Stage Model"; Pak, *Korean American Women*.

56. Ecklund, *Korean American Evangelicals*; Park, "Ethnic and Religious Identities."

57. Christofferson, *Negotiating Identity*.

58. Williams, "God's Global Professionals," 6–9.

a manner of life. Each person lives out their beliefs on a daily basis, and both faith and identity are influenced by cultural socialization. How do Christian adherents, who possess both a national citizenship and an avowed supernatural citizenship, navigate their cultural, religious, and migrant identities within local and global contexts? How do they see themselves, their purpose, and their roles in their local communities? How does their sense of a corporate religious mission define their individual identities? How, finally, do they negotiate their multiple identities?

Extensive research has been undertaken in the fields of sociology, psychology, anthropology, philosophy, and theology in regard to the nature of personhood, identity, and the self for a myriad of applications. For Christianity in particular, studies of early Christian identity in the Greco-Roman world have been compiled by researchers such as Judith Lieu.[59] More recently, Medi Ann Volpe considers Christian identity as discipleship in faith and practice as "a way of being in God and the world" and engages Gregory of Nyssa with contemporary constructions of Christian identity by other theologians.[60]

During the last fifty years, the subject of the evangelical identity in the U.S. has undergone considerable study. Various contextual studies on evangelicals have been undertaken, such as David Smilde's ethnographic work in Venezuela and Patrick Mitchel's study of Northern Irish evangelicals.[61] What is remarkable, however, is how little has been presented on evangelical identity in cross-cultural comparison.[62] For example, the World Evangelical Alliance, formulated in 1846 and formalized in 1951, is a coalition of churches and international organizations in 129 countries and is "the world's largest association of evangelical Christians serving a constituency of more than 600 million people."[63] The present research seeks to fill this gap by providing a cross-cultural investigation of non-North American evangelicals.

While scholars have researched the influence of Christianity on specific ethnic group identities, they have done so from a sociological or anthropological rather than a theological standpoint.[64] A few have explored themes of identity and migration as part of a biblical exposition of specific

---

59. Lieu, *Christian Identity*.

60. Volpe, *Christian Identity*, 2.

61. Mitchel, *Evangelicalism and National Identity*; Smilde, *Reason to Believe*.

62. Stanley takes an important direction. Stanley, *Global Diffusion*.

63. "History."

64. Hiebert Meneses, *Love and Revolutions*; Russell, *Conversion*.

passages in the Old and New Testaments.[65] What is lacking, however, is a theological analysis of religious identity in the context of international migration.

Few authors have written on the theology of identity and fewer have addressed a culturally specific theology of identity, as Kwame Bediako has done for the Ghanaian African context.[66] Miroslav Volf has, to date, articulated the most thorough theology of identity.[67] This paper adds to a theological discussion of Christian identity by considering its negotiation in the context of international migration.

THEOLOGY OF MIGRATION

The study of migration has been not only a subject of interest for the social sciences, but also a prominent theme in Christian theology. Indeed, the migratory nature of the Christian has been aptly termed the "pilgrim principle" by the missiological historian Andrew Walls.[68] The subject of the foreigner (Latin, *peregrinus, peregrini* (pl.), meaning "one from abroad") also forms the basis for a theology of migration. Gioacchino Campese thoroughly traces a review of the theology of migration from the first congress of the World Council of Churches on migration in 1961 through the first decade of the twenty-first century.[69] Campese offers a rationale for the recent consideration of migration among theologians, an historical overview of its theological development, a look at current migration themes, and ends with his own assessment, which focuses on Latino/a American and Asian American contextual theologies in the U.S. He organizes the theological literature on migration around nine themes: the pluralism of the theologies of migration and their methodologies, how migration illustrates God and the individual Christian, how it connects to ecclesiology, catholicity, hospitality, interreligious dialogue, and, finally, how it has been studied in relation to women and the undocumented.[70] In fact, 48 percent of international migrants in the

65. Gorospe, *Narrative and Identity*; Velloso da Silva, "Politics of Scripture."

66. Bediako, *Theology and Identity*.

67. Volf, *Exclusion and Embrace*.

68. Walls, *Missionary Movement*, 8–9.

69. Campese, "Irruption of Migrants."

70. Campese omits Koyama's stranger-focused theology. Koyama, "Extend Hospitality." Also, Keifert, *Welcoming the Stranger*.

world are female.[71] Campese notes that a "feminization of migration" has occurred, but that this has only happened in the last fifteen years.[72]

Campese offers two comments that are pertinent to a theological reflection on migration. Firstly, he disagrees that trinitarian theology has "led to the systematic theological reflection on migration" but, at the same time, suggests that a more thorough contemplation of how the study of human mobility sheds light on the trinitarian relationship is due.[73] Secondly, while he argues that migration is a *locus theologicus* (a place "where God reveals Godself"), in addition to the historical loci of the biblical text, church tradition, and more recently, context, he cautions that one should not posit that claim without a delineation of its conceptual history.[74] In his summation, Campese characterizes the theological work on migration as complex, interdisciplinary, highly contextual, pluralistic, and rooted in the Christian tradition.[75] This study seeks to build upon his review.

William T. Cavanaugh reflects on three models of mobility (migrant, tourist, and pilgrim) from the medieval age to the globalized present as well as the identities each model constructs.[76] Cavanaugh challenges the concept of a borderless world and ponders the monk—a model of stability—in his role of hospitality. While not a theological treatise, his work demonstrates that any consideration of migration must include and evaluate which kinds of stability and mobility are most worthy of the church's support.

In addition to Campese, several scholars have made substantial contributions to theologies of migration. Fabio Baggio, for example, first offered a theology of migration in Asia and has collaborated more recently on studies of the ethics of migration.[77] Daniel Groody has written extensively on a theological perspective of migration and deftly captures the alienation and spiritual conversions of these migrants.[78] A contextual theology of encounter that builds on the work of Father Pawlicki undergirds his research. Groody further describes three levels of a theology of migration: the pastoral, the spiritual, and the theological.[79] At the pastoral level, a theological

---

71. Population Division, "International Migration."

72. Campese, "Irruption of Migrants," 25–26.

73. Ibid., 31, see footnote 103.

74. Ibid., 6, 20, 29, 31, see footnote 102.

75. Ibid., 30.

76. Cavanaugh, "Migrant, Tourist, Pilgrim, Monk," 340–56.

77. Baggio and Brazal, *Faith on the Move*; Baggio and Zanfrini, *Migration Management and Ethics*.

78. Groody, *Border of Death*, 42–43, 61–69, 80–81.

79. Groody, "Spirituality of Migrants," 140–41.

discussion considers the outward journeys of migrants and the ways church ministries care for them. The spiritual level addresses the inner journeys of migrants as they encounter God in their sojourns and how their experiences can serve as a resource for the church. The theological level engages migration as a metaphor for human existence, which takes a journey away from God and subsequently returns to God through Jesus Christ.

Some scholars have argued for a theology of migration as a result of their research on migrant minorities, such as migrant domestic workers in Lebanon or Filipino/a domestic workers in Hong Kong.[80] Gemma Tulud Cruz in particular has yielded much fruit on this front. Her earlier work reviews migration for its theological implications, and she advocates that migration upsets strict boundaries (of center and margin, local and global, etc.) and shifts human identities.[81] Borders serve as "meeting points," and an intercultural theology must engage religious and cultural pluralism as well as the stranger.[82] Cruz's most recent work reflects theologically on the human and religious dimensions of migration.[83] She not only inspects the inequities of global migration—particularly for the most disadvantaged, such as unskilled laborers and women—but also details its benefits, especially in relation to human betterment. Cruz examines the ethics of migration policies in light of several themes of Catholic social teaching, discussing how migrant religious experiences benefit the host community, how migration reshapes the family and the church, how inculturation aids in church revitalization and evangelization, and what migrant spirituality can offer Christian spirituality.

Kristin Heyer integrates a Christian theology in her discussion of immigration by articulating a Christian anthropology that advocates transnational human rights. Heyer analyzes current policies, social sin, and global solidarity and frames immigration in terms of family for an immigration ethic of "civic kinship."[84] In her reflection on belonging, hospitality, and diaspora, Emma Wild-Wood adds a helpful balance to this discussion when she describes how migration showcases the distinct and common identity shared in Christ.[85]

Other scholars take a thematic approach in articulating a biblical theology of migration, in the vein of Gustavo Gutiérrez's preference for the

---

80. Cruz, *Intercultural Theology*; Hamd, "Migrant Domestic Workers."

81. Cruz, "Between Identity and Security."

82. Ibid., 371.

83. Cruz, *Theology of Migration*.

84. Heyer, *Kinship across Borders*.

85. Wild-Wood, "Common Witness."

"least of these."[86] From a Catholic perspective, William O'Neill's work iterates an ethics of migration that draws from Old and New Testament texts to discuss themes of love, justice, and hospitality.[87] An evangelical theologian, Daniel Carroll engages the contemporary immigration debate in the United States and encourages a biblical review of migration, law, and hospitality.[88] Luis N. Rivera-Pagán discusses xenophilia and xenophobia throughout the Bible.[89] Finally, after calling for different reading strategies and discussing a selection of unique biblical passages, Jean-Pierre Ruiz argues on behalf of migrants and for public policy immigration reform.[90]

The first installment of a three-part volume, *Contemporary Issues of Migration and Theology,* avows that it offers a "multifocal" theology rather than a "doctrinal system" of migration.[91] The edited volume addresses migration themes that are similar to those mentioned by Campese, such as hospitality, scriptural engagement, ecclesiology, interreligious dialogue, intercultural theology, and its theological view of migrants as "actors."[92] Several new subjects, however, are considered: space and place, urbanization, and graduate theological education. Another work, *Home and Away,* uses postal codes to ground theology as local and discusses similar themes of place, hospitality, diaspora, displacement, and migration in a polyvocal discussion of the imperative of contextualizing theology locally while maintaining a wider vision of locality in its global context.[93] While theologies of migration have historically focused on Christianity, recent works have expanded this discussion to include the Abrahamic faiths.[94] Literature remains focused on the foregoing themes and various issues such as the relation of migration to Christian mission.[95]

---

86. Matt 25:40; Gutiérrez, "Promised Land."

87. O'Neill, "No Longer Strangers," 227–33.

88. Carroll R., *Christians at the Border.* Another evangelical treatment is Soerens and Hwang, *Welcoming the Stranger.*

89. Rivera-Pagán, "Xenophilia."

90. Ruiz, *Reading.*

91. Padilla and Phan, *Contemporary Issues of Migration,* 5.

92. Ibid., 4.

93. Burns and Pearson, *Home and Away.*

94. Padilla and Phan, *Theology of Migration.*

95. Bevans and Ross, *Mission*; Nguyen and Prior, *God's People.*

CONCLUDING REMARKS

This work combines knowledge of previous fields of literature—narrative and identity theories, migration and identity studies, and the theologies of identity and migration—and builds on them in a study of international evangelical migrants to construct an initial theology of Christian identity in migration. This concludes Part I with an introduction and background of the study.

Theology, that field of study that challenges the two predominant presuppositions of secularism—naturalism and humanism, has been described succinctly as the vast "investigation of God" and the relationship God maintains with humanity and nature.[96] Three interlocutors, psychologist Jenny Hyun Chung Pak and theologians Miroslav Volf and Stanley Hauerwas, will be engaged in a larger discussion of the Judeo-Christian understanding of the nature of self and identity.

Part II offers a critical delineation of the views of these scholars on self and identity. Miroslav Volf's extensive theological writing offers a European perspective on reconciliation and identity, violence and memory, and interreligious dialogue and peace building. Jenny Hyun Chung Pak brings a female, Asian, and psychological perspective to the areas of acculturation, gender studies, and identity development. Stanley Hauerwas addresses a myriad of topics such as the self, identity, and missions from a North American perspective. All three scholars represent a different migration experience: Hauerwas, the U.S.-born American; Pak, who immigrated to the United States from South Korea at ten years of age; and Volf, who first entered the United States as an international graduate student.[97]

96. Hiebert Meneses, "No Other Foundation," 533.
97. Pak, *Korean American Women*, 2; Volf, *Captive*, 179–80.

II

Approaches toward Self and Identity

3

Theological Contribution
of Miroslav Volf

MIROSLAV VOLF, FOUNDING DIRECTOR of the Yale Center for Faith and Culture and Henry B. Wright Professor of Systematic Theology, is known for his theological considerations of identity, forgiveness, and memory.[1] The impetus for his work came in part from the violent cultural conflicts he observed during the nineties, such as the bloody "cleansings" of the Balkans.[2] He began to contemplate this question: How might one circumvent the evil human animosity brings? How does the acknowledgement of one's distinct race or creed not lead to prejudice and violence? In his exploration of identity, Volf describes how individuals and groups can maintain their particularity and coexist peacefully. As a Croatian deeply connected to the Balkan Wars, a child of bicultural parentage, a son whose father was imprisoned by the communist regime, as the accused and interrogated himself, and now as a leader in interreligious peace negotiation, Miroslav Volf speaks from his intimate experience with identity conflict and reconciliation.[3]

From a young age, Volf lived among various ethnic and religious groups. As a member of an evangelical minority in a predominantly Catholic Croatia that was controlled by an atheist communist government, he identified early in his life with outsiders. As the son of a Pentecostal pastor in

1. Having penned or edited over fifteen books and seventy articles, Volf has written on an array of subjects which has been lauded by those outside of theology.

2. Volf, *Exclusion and Embrace*, 17–18.

3. Gundry-Volf and Volf, *Spacious Heart*, 35–36; Volf, *Exclusion and Embrace*, 16; Volf, *End of Memory*, 3–18; Volf et al., *Common Word*.

Novi Sad, former Yugoslavia, Volf's religious upbringing took place amidst Catholic, Muslim, and Orthodox populations.[4] Over the years his ecclesiological experience has ranged from free churches to mainstream Protestantism.[5] His career in theological education spans over three decades, and Volf's writings reflect the study of a spectrum of theologians including Peter Kuzmič, Martin Luther, Jürgen Moltmann, John Zizoulas, Joseph Ratzinger (Pope Benedict XVI), and Nicholas of Cusa.[6]

In a consideration of Volf's work, the nature of the self will be described, along with the dependence, the allegiance, and the key constituents of the self (namely, its communality in setting and personhood). Next, the formation of identity will be discussed, including its dualism and its concepts of exclusion, judgment, and boundaries. This section will discuss a trinitarian model for the construction of self and identity. Finally, the implications for the formation of a cultural identity for the Christian will be given in relation to cultural distance and belonging. For those who have received the gospel, what now is their identity in Christ?

NATURE OF THE SELF

Volf's central terms should be briefly defined for the purposes of this study. His use of the term *self* refers to the "human being in totality." A *person,* for Volf, is a self bestowed with humanhood only because of one's relation to God for God's constitution of that self. Because God relates to that self, that self becomes human and one's *being* is maintained.[7] *Identity,* then, is the "instinctive will to be oneself."[8] Volf writes, "Personality, or one's identity, is what the self makes of itself in interactions (passive or active) with God, multiple environments (human, nonhuman, personal and systemic), and itself." Individuals can hold multiple identities as they relate to their personal, historical, and social contexts. At times, Volf may refer to the term self as tantamount to identity, but only in the general, "nontechnical sense."[9] Whatever the nature of the self is, it intimately forms its own sense of identity.

4. "Meet Miroslav Volf."

5. Volf, *After Our Likeness,* ix.; Volf, *Allah,* 11. Sarot, "Trinity and Church," 43.

6. Volf, *Exclusion and Embrace,* dedication page; Volf, *After Our Likeness*; Volf, *Free of Charge.*

7. Volf, *After Our Likeness,* 204–13.

8. Volf, *Exclusion and Embrace,* 90.

9. Miroslav Volf, personal email communication with author, April 13, 2011.

Dependence of the Self

The self is vulnerable, susceptible to predation, and possesses limited resources.[10] Pauline writings attest that the self does not have, apart from what
it has been given (Acts 17:25; 1 Cor 4:7; Eph 2:10). Volf affirms the claim
that God gives humans everything they have, and the self lives on a "given
breath" from the everlasting and infinite triune God.[11] One's personhood is
intricately tied to the giving nature of God. Even Karl Marx, as Volf cleverly
points out, acknowledged who the self is, if not independent:

> A being only counts itself as independent . . . as long as it owes
> its existence to itself. A man who lives by grace of another con-
> siders himself a dependent being. But I live completely by grace
> of another when I owe him not only the maintenance of my life
> but when he has also created my life.[12]

Karl Marx understood the dual claims on the nature of the self so
perceptively that he insisted on the inverse affirmation of the existence of
an independent self and, by its corollary, a denial of the reality of God. To
acknowledge the existence of a transcendent creator God is to acknowledge
the dependence of self on another. As such, the essence of self exists according to a particular design, fashioned by its author. Since the self was
designed for both dependence and freedom by God, it cannot be both free
and independent from God. This claim to self-contained independence
contradicts the *bona fide* nature of the self. Volf argues, "If God were to
stop giving, we would stop existing."[13] The self, in claiming independence,
commits a sort of plagiarism, claiming for oneself what is another's. Independence, operating outside of a finite system, is God's alone.[14] The self
must admit its own dependent nature and its need for the other. How does
the self manage this? The Christian theological perspective claims the self
obtains its life in alterity, from the resources of another external authority:
the one eternal God as revealed in Christ by God's Spirit.

In relating to the human other, the self is dependent on another to
love out of God's love rather than self-love. Volf reclassifies Martin Luther's
"human love" as "distorted love" and argues that it precedes a self that is de-
centered and re-centered in Christ. This love possesses for self-gain. Divine
love, conversely, is not earned or frugally given; it lavishly offers, seeks no

10. Volf, *Free of Charge*, 110.

11. Ibid., 34–35, 115–16, 149.

12. Marx, *Selected Writings*, 94.

13. Volf, *Free of Charge*, 37.

14. Ibid., 34–36.

benefit, owes no debt, and gives without expectation. The self is contingent on the divine other to love similarly.[15]

Self and Its Center

The leading postmodern view holds that the self has no center. In his departure from Richard Rorty, Volf argues, "though the self may lack an 'objective' and 'immovable' center, *the self is never without a center*; it is always in the production of its own center."[16] While Volf may believe in a centered self, he is sympathetic to the postmodern view of the fragmented self.[17] He focuses, however, on the nature of the self's center in its tumultuous and thrashing construction. The self strives in its process of reconfiguring identification and attempts whatever coherence it can manage. Again, the self is not centerless in its construction; the self has been "wrongly centered." Volf's views align with the apostle Paul's, who viewed the self as improperly self-centric and needing to be de-centered (Rom 6:6; Gal 2:20; 6:14).[18] Figuratively speaking, the self enthrones itself to reign over all that surrounds it. This centering of self refers to one's innate tendency to position oneself as the chief authority, the nexus from which decisions of the will are made in self-reliance.[19] Paul's terminology for this internal self-rule, which is resistant to divine will, is the "flesh" (Gal 2:19–20; 3:3; 5:17).[20] Jerome (347–420 CE) describes that the soul strives between the flesh and God's Spirit, choosing to follow but "unable to maintain its choice indefinitely" before it succumbs again to the sway of the flesh.[21]

The self engages in this intense and vehement struggle, laboring in a process of rejection, repression, identification, projection, deception, subjugation, and domination in its construction.[22] This cycle of ever-twisting

---

15. Ibid., 38–43.

16 Original emphasis. *Exclusion and Embrace*, 69. Rorty's centerless self has no reference to weave in alternating beliefs and desires.

17. Volf, *End of Memory*, 98, 198, 202.

18. Volf, *Exclusion and Embrace*, 69–71.

19. TeSelle, "Exploring," 118–20.

20. Bock, *Bible Knowledge Word Study*, 384. Paul's use of flesh [*sarx*] varies. It can refer at minimum to the physical body or human life, but most often, when used by Paul, refers to a human independence that orients itself set apart from God.

21. Hieronymus and Cain, *St. Jerome*, 224–25.

22. Volf, *Exclusion and Embrace*, 69–70. Martin Luther (1483–1546) did not think the self capable of guiding itself to freedom. Luther, *Freedom*, 28. To the objection that a will unable to act without grace is not free or is unable to be saved, see Luther's response in Luther et al., *Bondage of the Will*, 104–7, 313–14.

alteration leads to its identity production. Why, then, must the self be de-centered? The self is constrained by the power of evil, Volf answers. He ex-plains that "a particular evil not only inhabits us so that we do what we hate (Rom 7:15), it has colonized us to such a thoroughgoing extent that there seems to be no moral space left within the self in which it could occur to us to hate what we want because it is evil."[23] The self, in its search for identity, struggles to center itself, thereby displacing God, showcasing its egocen-trism, and displaying its propensity for exclusion.

De-centering Self for Christological Re-centering

Although the self is difficult to describe in analogical terms, both the mod-ern and the postmodern identities place the self as its central authority. Despite the fact that it is inescapably affected by outside forces, the self at-tempts to determine its ongoing experience and identity. Volf, on the other hand, describes the discovery of one's identity as a de-centering of the self and its new "re-centering" in Christ:

> By being "crucified with Christ" the self has received a new cen-ter—the Christ who lives in it and with whom it lives. Notice that the new center of the self is not a timeless "essence" hid-den . . . an essence that waits only to be discovered, unearthed, set free. Neither is the center an inner narrative . . . whose in-tegrity must be guarded from editorial intrusions by rival "vo-cabularies" and competing "stories" . . . the center is Jesus Christ crucified and resurrected who has become part and parcel of the very structure of the self.[24]

This de-centering and re-centering is not an obliteration of one's in-dividual identity but rather a re-creation of the original self with the same essence but a new allegiance. The self, from an ontological perspective, sub-mits to the gospel message of Christ's crucifixion and resurrection through a personal attestation of faith and baptism. The self, then, is identified in and "structured" by the crucifixion and resurrection of Jesus Christ (Rom

23. Volf, *Exclusion and Embrace*, 89–90. See Gal 5:16–17. Due to his strong belief that the self is disabled by sin, Luther challenged the superiority of human reason long before modernity's ideals were overthrown in the twentieth century. Volf echoes here Luther's contention that the old man, the flesh, is so hostile to the Spirit of God that the self is rendered powerless to overcome without God's intervention. Luther et al., *Bond-age of the Will*, 313. Also, Lull and Russell, *Martin Luther's Writings*, 19–20. Gabrielson articulates the opposing forces of the flesh and Spirit vying for the self's allegiance well. See Gabrielson, "Paul's Non-Violent Gospel," 132–35.

24. Volf, *Exclusion and Embrace*, 70.

6:4–6).[25] Jeremy Gabrielson elaborates on this metaphor of co-crucifixion when he discusses Paul's conversion and his violent past.[26] A certain dissatisfaction with one's self must exist for an individual to pursue this kind of change, a metaphysical re-centering, as Paul lowered his standing from a chief Jewish leader who was eradicating a religious uprising to a slave and servant of Christ (Gal 1:10; Phil 3:3–10; 1 Tim 1:15–16).

This newly shaped self is a paradox. Those who re-center themselves in Christ live out their own existence and yet, in a real sense, live out Christ's life (Gal 2:19–20). The character of Christ is expressed through the individual nature and person of the self as the representative image of God. This transformation enables the self to separate itself from others and from outside forces that do not conform to the goodness of God. The palingenesis of self leads to a new center that is open to others, considerate of judgment, opposed to exclusion, but—above all—stabilized in the "self-giving love" of Christ.[27]

This re-centering, however, does not create religious marionettes. Gabrielson emphasizes that what God offers through Christ's resurrection and God's Spirit must still be received and enacted by its undertaker.[28] As Volf writes, "God is in the 'space' of I. . . . It is I who wants, thinks, and does, and at the same time it is Christ who acts in and through me."[29] This new indwelling creates a strange realization in the Christian self since it neither makes the self divine in essence nor does it maintain the old sense of self-will. This shared space in Christ liberates the self from an exclusive self-focus, and, what is more, it constrains the self to a new focus—to seek and to serve God and neighbor.[30]

For those who would reject this notion of indwelling, Volf discusses the paradox of self-love. He claims that the self cannot find fulfillment in seeking its own gain or in self-indulgence. "The self turned in upon itself loses itself in the emptiness of its own meaninglessness. And the emptier the

---

25. Ibid., 70–71, 92. Whereas the self has enthroned itself as center, in the sense of authority, it strives for some semblance of management (order, for modern philosophy, or chaos, for postmodern). The center of the converted self has been displaced and finds a new center in Jesus Christ.

26. Gabrielson, "Paul's Non-Violent Gospel," 121, 125. According to Gabrielson, Paul's violence changed from perpetration on others to self-absorption of violence upon himself in non-retaliation (123). It is not that violence disappears in the present age, but that a co-crucified self changes its method of participation.

27. Volf, *Exclusion and Embrace*, 70–71.

28. Gabrielson, "Paul's Non-Violent Gospel," 125–26.

29. Volf, *Free of Charge*, 51.

30. Ibid., 62, 65–67, 85.

self is, the more obsessed with the self we become; and the more obsessed with the self we are, the emptier the self becomes."[31] This cycle of obsession and emptiness continues unless and until the self is repositioned in Christ.

In the Christian model of creation (premised by the moral categories of evil and good and a Creator God who fashioned the self), the self acknowledges an external source of existence. The Christian then moves from self-centeredness to self-fulfillment in God. This re-centering of the self does not reduce the self to pawn, but rather elevates it to participate with the triune God in relationship.[32]

The Social Self

Individuals find themselves within social settings that are initially beyond their own determination. These settings then condition the self from birth to reflect its given social background with a distinct set of customs, expectations, and beliefs. The self is created both reflexively by the situation into which a person is born or raised and intentionally by a person's choices. One's identity is first shaped by birth history and family and later formed by one's conscious choice to identify with one particular person or group.[33]

This complicated relationship between self and society sets the stage for, or situates, the individual's "tribal" self. According to Volf, the particularity of each culture provides such "a matrix for the emergence of the self," and he highlights three characteristics of these "tribal identities": complexity, strength, and permanence. The *complexities* of a given culture or tribe cannot be reduced to one core form. As people are shaped by the influence of the individual other, so too are tribal identities affected by interaction with neighboring societies. Secondly, tribal identities exhibit *strength* in the way they hold the self to its identity once it is adopted, especially during times of conflict and polarization between groups. Finally, the "psychosocial functions" that particular groups fulfill demand their *permanence*. The self can possess multiple and sometimes conflicting group identities (as well as

---

31. Volf, *Against the Tide*, 10.

32. Volf, *Free of Charge*, 51–52. For a discussion of this reciprocal encounter with party distinctions left intact (given in the Incarnation, the Trinity, and individual life in Christ), see Williams, "Assimilation and Otherness," 264–65.

33. Taylor, "Politics of Recognition," 32–34. This voluntary selection in identity formation is one reason why psychologists Erikson and McAdams consider children as possessing selves but not identities until adolescence, at which they volitionally choose with whom to identify. McAdams, "Redemptive Self," 99–101.

values and roles) from which the "fragmented" self must choose one over another.[34]

In addition to the ways the self is defined by its social context, Volf believes it is also defined by its relationships. To *be* is to always be in some relation to another. Volf agrees with Charles Taylor that the self is dialogically negotiated and formed by its interaction with others.[35] According to Taylor, prior to the close of the eighteenth century, society's stricter hierarchy meant that one's identity was determined by one's place in that order.[36] As social hierarchies relaxed, this understanding of self changed, and identity became self-discovered, forged from within one's own being. Even so, Taylor stresses that one's sense of being is still socially derived. Identity remains dialogical, defined by the individual but directed by the voices the individual hears. Self-definition is born from the languages others have spoken to that individual. Taylor and Volf do not consider this social influence to be wholly negative, for some benefits are available to the self only in relationship with others.

Volf further argues that the self is never without the other, even from genesis. It does not begin as a separate entity and then incorporate the other; the self is created by virtue of the individual *and* the other. To cut off the other—who is a "structuring element of the self" and whose presence feeds an inclination in the self *for* the other—is to sever a fundamental part of one's self.[37] For Léopold Sédar Senghor (1906–2001), a Senegalese poet and the first postcolonial president of Senegal, his consideration of the concept of *négritude* illustrates this idea. It expresses an identity inclusive of the other, a self created by an "encounter with the other." A self does not exist apart from a self with the other.[38] *Négritude* praises and includes the diversity of the other as constitutive of self. So too, *métissage* (literally, "being mixed-race") represents a self-openness to draw in difference intentionally, resulting in a "modulation" of the self rather than a strict rejection of the

---

34. Volf, *Exclusion and Embrace*, 19. Volf builds on Michael Walzer's discussion of cultures as tribes.

35. Ibid., 65–66, 91.

36. Taylor, "Politics of Recognition," 26–34.

37. This injunction is reminiscent of how the parts of the body of Christ should interrelate (Rom 12:3–6 and 1 Cor 12).

38. Williams, "Assimilation and Otherness," 250. While *négritude* connotes a Parisian literary movement of black writers from French colonies and has been associated with racial pride, Senghor saw its definition as more encompassing.

other. To be *métis* is to proactively take some aspect of the other into one's identity.[39] Space created for the other in the self, in fact, begets space.[40]

Visions of superiority result from a self that views itself in an isolated manner, when in fact identity is forged in relation to the other. In the case of masculine and feminine gender identities, for example, these identities are chiefly rooted in the biology of "sexed bodies" but are also shaped by cultural and familial factors. The identity of man comes from the fact that he is not woman, but also because he is not without woman, and vice versa. Gender identity, due to the nature of social images that reflect each other yet are interrelated, cannot be reduced to a strict dichotomy: that whatever one gender is, the other is not.[41] This relationship parallels how the identity of the self includes the other but is not the other.[42]

Volf maintains that the "irreducible duality" of gender avoids the danger of *synthesizing* gender differences ('both-the-one-and-the-other") as well as the danger of *erasing* those differences ('neither-one-nor-the-other"). This duality corresponds to the complexity of the identity of the self as both the self and the other as two irreducible entities that share space and join together in alterity. Both the alterity and the internality of the two (female/male, other/self) in both explanations of gender and the self must be preserved and lead to an interdependent, mutual construction of identities.[43]

FORMATION OF IDENTITY

In his contribution to the theology of identity, Volf distinguishes several features of identity formation. He describes its dual nature and its non-exclusionary judgment, which includes the necessity of boundary-marking without exclusion. Volf draws from the model of trinitarian relations and

---

39. Ibid., 251–56. While Williams rightly points out that Volf writes often from the perspective of the victim, this is not problematic per se, even if incomplete (268–69). Much work in identity theory remains to distinguish how the self should interact with the other when parties differ: as in victim to penitent, previous aggressor; victim to non-penitent, previous aggressor; victim to present aggressor; unforgiving victim to penitent, previous aggressor; unforgiving victim to non-penitent, previous aggressor; and unforgiving victim to present aggressor. The categories are rarely clear-cut. Volf cites the pernicious trouble when both parties identity as victims, or worse, as innocents. Volf, *Exclusion and Embrace*, 79–85.

40. Ibid., 141.

41. Volf argues that the biological dichotomy of sexed bodies cannot be applied to the identities of genders, which are socialized and defined in a reflection of its alternate pair.

42. Ibid., 184–87.

43. Ibid., 187.

applies similar principles to the configuration of self and identity. This configuration articulates that the self is comprised of both the self and the other and includes a caution that one's identity involves both distance from and the embrace of the other.

Duality of Identity Formation

Volf, above all, observes the complexity of identity formation. He proposes that identity is not necessarily repressive by being "self-identical," isolated, or inaccessible. Volf's understanding of identity does not reduce it to repression, as can happen when identity is only understood as separation from another.[44] He instead considers identity from within the self as neither exclusive nor all-inclusive but rather emphasizes identity from the commonality and unity of humanity—from personhood. He points to the Judeo-Christian account of creation, where identity was analogously formed by a process of "separating" and "binding." Volf writes:

> The account of creation as "separating-and-binding" rather than simply "separating" suggests that "identity" includes connection, difference, heterogeneity. The human self is formed not through a simple rejection of the other—through a binary logic of opposition and negation—but through a complex process of "taking in" *and* "keeping out." We are who we are not because we are separate from the others who are next to us, but because we are *both* separate *and* connected, *both* distinct *and* related. . . . Identity is a result of the distinction from the other *and* the internationalization of the relationship to the other.[45]

In Volf's estimation, therefore, difference forms identity, and the recognition of one's distinctiveness precedes one's choice to join the other or to maintain distance. Volf's theology of identity emphasizes both the self's inclusion of the other and its differentiation from the other within the self rather than limiting the discussion to any one element of difference. The self both delineates and draws in. Identity is formed from a designation of

---

44. Ibid., 65–66. Volf diverges from the feminist thinkers he names, such as Luce Irigaray and Judith Butler, who, according to Volf, discuss identity as what can only but separate (repress) what is "nonidentical" in relationship or within the self. Judith Butler challenges the conception of binary male-female categories altogether as subjectivity in Cheah et al., "Future of Sexual Difference," 27–28. According to Volf, identity should not be limited to being understood only as exclusive and advocates that a legitimate form of separation does exist.

45. Volf, *Exclusion and Embrace*, 66, original emphasis.

who I am not and what I share in common with the other. The identity of self requires both *differentiation*, which delineates difference, as well as an *embrace*, which dwells with difference.[46] Léopold Senghor shows a similar strain of duality in his writing. He promotes a self and an identity that critically evaluates the other and takes into oneself from the other what can be accepted and rejects what it cannot accept. The self reaches outside of one's defined parameters to its *opposition* (in the sense of difference, without negative connotation) for a rearrangement of the self.[47]

Non-Exclusionary Judgment

The self creates its own identity in an environment of ambiguity, uncertainty, and threat.[48] This process marks another type of duality that presents itself in identity formation: the challenge of the self to maintain its identity without trespassing on the space of the other to be different. The strength of will required to protect the integrity of one's identity can easily overcompensate to exclude the other. To address this need for balance, Volf offers an identity of *non-exclusionary judgment*.[49]

Necessity of Boundaries

Personal and group identities exist by virtue of boundaries. Difference, which is a good, comes from one's distinction from another unique individual. Volf holds that, even though they can be misused for evil, differentiation and boundary-drawing is necessary in the formation of identity. In his work *Exclusion and Embrace*, Volf rejects Michel Foucault's postmodern emphasis on "radical indeterminacy" and *all*-inclusion. While he agrees with Foucault that exclusion is an ill and inclusion advantageous, he argues that inclusion without the existence of boundaries is detrimental. He believes that, in a rally to destroy exclusion by the removing of any and all

---

46. Ibid., 65–68.

47. Williams, "Assimilation and Otherness," 256–57, 265. While Senghor's use of boundaries seems similar to that of Volf's, Williams describes how they differ in their definition of assimilation. Volf treats assimilation in its more commonly held sense (where particular identity is lost), whereas Senghor considers assimilation a voluntary act to accept something of the dominant group. Senghor's notion is superior, according to Williams, because it is volitional and cannot be rejected by the other party. It proactively takes in the good of another (256, 268–69).

48. Volf, *Exclusion and Embrace*, 90–91, 96.

49. Ibid., 91–92.

boundaries, new boundaries of exclusion are unintentionally formed. He further argues that in Foucault's new chaotic "nonorder," society's inability to identify and refuse evils founds a new impotence to protect its victims. Inclusion, for Volf, cannot be fully realized without the drawing of boundaries. Volf does acknowledge Foucault's point that the practice of inclusion with boundaries invariably allows some boundaries to function as oppressive structures.[50] Still, Volf maintains an "intelligent struggle against exclusion demands categories and normative criteria that enable us to distinguish between repressive identities and practices that should be subverted and non-repressive ones that should be affirmed."[51] For society to address its own ills, a choosing and denying (separating and binding, respectively) of differentiation must take place.

Boundaries create limitations that enable order, and without order, the self cannot be fully known. In his distinction between differentiation, exclusion, and judgment, Volf considers exclusion an evil but endorses the action of judgment to distinguish wrongful exclusion from differentiation, which is a beneficial, constructive act. Drawing distinctions is not "inherently problematic or necessarily the basis of hostility" but rather allows individuals to recognize themselves and regard each other *en face à face*.[52] Differentiation offers the self the resistance it needs to avoid passive resignation and simply become the other in undifferentiated pattern. This resistance, however, should not be misused by actively renouncing the other. With the employment of negotiable boundaries, resistance can be self-protective without being other-militant.[53]

Exclusionary Threats

A differentiated identity can, however, succumb to an exclusionary tendency. Though boundaries are a primary ingredient in differentiation, they still allow migration and should not be confused as exclusionary. "Barriers," on the other hand, prevent connection with the other and are exclusionary. In the connecting and distinguishing process within the self, harmful exclusion can occur in two ways. It can destroy a connection between the self and

50. Ibid., 62–64. According to Volf, Foucault downplays the use of boundaries with his "radical indeterminacy of negative freedom," which assumes that a total lack of boundaries is actually able to free the self from oppressive social power structures. On the contrary, a lack of discretion opens the self up to oppression in new and different ways, equally as dangerous (63).

51. Ibid., 63–64.

52. Williams, "Assimilation and Otherness," 259.

53. Volf, *Exclusion and Embrace*, 67–68.

the other (by pushing the other out in a forceful expulsion or distancing), or it can destroy a separation between the self and the other where the other's unique qualities are subsumed or extinguished, as can happen in the process of assimilation or domination. The former works against binding; the latter frustrates appropriate separating.[54]

Trinitarian Model for Identity of Self

The doctrine of the Trinity models a description for identity that is dynamic, interrelated, and includes the other without the expense of self. God's triune nature demonstrates sociality without the denial of unique persons. Volf makes the distinction that the Trinity is not a "dissolved" set of relations where the identity of each is defined *only* in relation to the other. While it does reflect three persons in one being, the Trinity is not composed of three separate individuals.[55] The triune God interacts within itself without losing distinction or equality and depicts how the created self and the other might interrelate on a created level. Volf's principle of "personal interiority" describes how the trinitarian persons are "internal" to each other without negating each other. This perichoretic "mutual indwelling" also illustrates how humans may have Christ dwelling within their core by God's Spirit without ceasing to be themselves. Human personhood demonstrates the mysterious interplay within a created being that can experience both constitution (passive, in creation and recreation) and communion (participative, with God and human).[56]

These patterns of "self-giving" and "mutual indwelling" in the self frame Volf's concept of individual human identity. Self-giving does not require an emptying of personal value, a passive resignation to domination, or a loss of one's particularity.[57] On the contrary, self-giving stems from a healthy individuated self who can distinguish how to give sacrificially (in action) to another without sacrificing one's self (in essence). Self-giving and furthermore, self-denial, do not preclude self-existence or self-affirmation.[58] The

54. Ibid.

55. Ibid., 128.

56. Volf, *After Our Likeness*, 184, 186–88.

57. Volf, *Exclusion and Embrace*, 179, 188–89. Moltmann calls the intra-relation of the Trinity a "reciprocal self-surrender to one another" (Moltmann, *Spirit of Life*, 137).

58. Divine self-giving reflects the nature of God which humans may emulate. Self-denial relates to the human self alone which has been distorted by virtue of birth and personal choice (original and volitional sin). God has nothing impure to deny, and, therefore, gives. What must be crucified in human self-denial is all that which is not pure (thus not of God), and this self-emptying, in fact, fills (Gal 2:20).

self remains both distinct from and constrained to the other. It can be crucified—cut away from all that is not purely its essence—while maintaining its
truest essence of self, as demonstrated by the aforementioned re-centering
process. The dynamic of human self-giving requires some kind of loss, even
a loss of who one thought one was, but this loss frees the individual to discover who one was actually created to be (John 10:10; 12:25; Eph 2:10).

Identity Formation of Self

A healthy self must both draw boundary lines and invite others in beyond
them, and Volf uses the analogy of an embrace to describe this process of
proactively seeking and receiving the other. For Volf, the self reaches its
arms outward in initiation, pauses for the other to participate, embraces
the other, and reopens its arms. In Volf's theology, the movement is dual.
An individual creates space to allow the other entrance; the other extends
itself into this created space that the first fashioned. Christ exemplified this
figurative and literal act of embrace on the cross when he emptied himself
to include the other (sinful humanity). Moreover, the act of an embrace pic-
tures the dynamic identity of the self, which remains differentiated from the
other while being changed by the other, a *pas de deux* where each maintains
its distinctiveness but joins the other to share combined space. The union
of the embrace does not require permanent absorption or the dissolution
of either's identities. The identities of self and the other are maintained and
exist both together and apart in their alterity. This act illustrates both a mutually defined independence and submission to interrelate, that is signified
first by embracing and then releasing, allowing flexible identity alteration
and identity preservation. A "taking in" and a "letting go" in the process of
identity formation mirrors the initial divine act of creation in "separating"
and "binding."[59]

In the differentiating process, the self must avoid two extremes. The
self is vulnerable to making judgments of exclusion, rejecting the other. The
self's internal organization that necessitates a dissimilar identity (distinguishing self and other) can be susceptible to over-asserting its separateness
"at the expense of the other." Secondly, one can allow inadequate boundaries
with insufficient differentiation between the two. Negotiating an identity
that is both healthy (an individuation of self) and whole (encompassing the
other) poses a formidable challenge.[60]

---

59. Volf, *Exclusion and Embrace*, 140–44.
60. Ibid., 91–92.

This ongoing movement of embrace with the other, joining and releasing to join again, results in a continual reshaping of identities. In this way, identities between selves have the potential to become complementary, where one "mutually conditions" the other. This relationship also paves a path for reconciliation between selves when their identities (at the individual or group level) transgress boundaries and cause injury. Identities must be constituted in a particular way in order for severed relations to be redeemed.[61] The other's reception to one reaching toward the other, however, is limited by two factors. Firstly, the other may express disinterest in being included. Secondly, the other may fear violence and feel that exclusion is warranted to avoid it. One's identity is constituted by its relation to others and is reconstituted when those relations change—whether by choice, circumstances, or betrayal. Progress in the relationship between the self and the other involves a patient process of invitation, forgiveness, and reconciliation.[62]

When the self deserts those to whom it relates, however, the self frays the thread that binds itself together. Volf distinguishes between "acts of separation"—which are necessary for individuation and a healthy self—and "acts of exclusion" by which the self abandons a relationship "without which it would not be what it is, and cuts itself off from responsibilities to others and makes itself their enemy."[63] When those who have severed relations later seek restitution, they must re-negotiate their constitutions to accommodate what injuries have transpired and introduce a new pattern of interaction. Since identities are neither static nor do they live outside of the other, in the case of reconciliation, identities do not remain what they once were. Relationships must be re-configured. This reshaping, while it does not abandon the rules of order, allows enough elasticity to pursue the overarching priority—relational peace.[64]

Formation of Cultural Identity

What does this identity of the redeemed self signify in its cultural context of interactions? Volf posits that the self recreated by God has the ability to allow others entry into its person. This change also introduces new parameters to create both distance from and a connection to one's cultural milieu. Volf proposes that each person should maintain both a sense of

61. Ibid., 156.
62. Ibid., 144–47.
63. Ibid., 158.
64. Ibid., 157–67.

distance from and a sense of belonging to their cultural identity. A destructive cultural identity, on the other hand, requires every other to conform to its image without allowing for difference. As Volf writes, "If belonging without distance destroys, distance without belonging isolates. . . . Difference from a culture must never degenerate into a simple flight from that culture."[65] Keith Ferdinando confirms this sense of cultural alienation and cultural affinity when he concurs that an inevitable dual tension will exist for the Christian self. He maintains that complete cultural acceptance is inappropriate after conversion, yet allows that it is positive for certain cultural aspects to remain grounded in one's identity. Cultural identity, therefore, is conformed to, but not erased by, one's Christian identity; it is reconfigured (Rom 12:1–2).[66]

In appropriating the bounds of the self's cultural belonging and cultural departure, one's religious and cultural identities coexist but do not merge. The latter is subordinate to the former in terms of allegiance, if not expression.[67] Patrick Mitchel offers the example of contemporary Irish evangelicals who consider cultural and political interests subject to the law of Christ. Given the embattled history of Protestants and Catholics in Ireland, these evangelicals feel no compelling need to forgo their cultural Irish identity to adopt a religious one—Protestant. While their central identity lies in their relationship to Christ, their evangelical identity retains its historical core of doctrine but eschews the distinct cultural expressions of Protestantism and unionism from that region.[68]

What are the appropriate bounds of cultural proximity and distance? Maintaining one's cultural distance does not and should not necessarily remove one from one's cultural context. Firstly, the distance created by an individual's loyalty to a religious identity that outweighs a cultural identity, frees one from the limitations of that given culture. This internal differentiation allows the self to identify with its culture while still maintaining distance from a particular cultural practice.[69] One can say, for example, that "I" can share those cultural practices, or "I" can choose to not share them. I share those cultural tendencies, but these are not my only cultural tendencies. Secondly, this cultural distance, according to Volf, "creates space in us

65. Gundry-Volf and Volf, *Spacious Heart*, 42–43.

66. Ferdinando, "Christian Identity," 135–36.

67. Volf, *Exclusion and Embrace*, 37, 50–51.

68. Mitchel, "Evangelicals and Irish Identity," 222–23. Employing Volf's themes of cultural distance and belonging, Mitchel distances the evangelical identity from Protestant unionism in Northern Ireland. See *Evangelicalism and National Identity*.

69. Volf, *Exclusion and Embrace*, 49–51.

to receive the other."[70] Without this distance, space (room for generosity, goodwill, mutuality, understanding, and forgiveness) will not be afforded to the other. Thirdly, this cultural distance in the recreated self allows "a judgment against evil in every culture."[71] For Volf, those who claim no place for judgment have no recourse to name injustice. The cultural distance, then, for one who adopts the Judeo-Christian worldview is both an aperture and a closure. The distance both opens space for the self to be inclusive of the other and precludes space in judgment of the other.

ASSESSMENT OF VOLF

Volf's theology of identity offers immediate and profound application to daily life. He sets forth the concepts of identity, differentiation, and embrace in a comprehendible guide to human conduct. He frames his discussion of identity in a fresh way—using terms of differentiation and openness, of non-uniformity and association. While earlier identity theories have originated from a singular difference as definitive and resulted in a multitude of single-focused theories with limited applicability, Volf transcends that limitation by treating difference as a collective and basing it on what is common to all—shared humanity.[72] This approach encompasses a wider audience than simply describing identity from the standpoint of each difference. He builds from a positive stance, from commonality.

Despite his focus on commonality, the fact that Volf discusses identity within a theological framework might itself invite a charge of limited application. Volf offers little motivation to pursue reconciliation with the other to those who do not embrace the Christian faith and identity.[73] While Volf does not directly address this objection, he does seem to indicate that God is working by divine purpose despite the unbelief among humanity. He hints that God's Spirit is active outside of the church and works on the behalf of even those who do not acknowledge God, but he does not describe what this idea entails.[74] Volf has discussed the theme of commonality more often from within interreligious dialogue. One of his most recent works, *Allah*, ventures to bridge the alienation between Christianity and Islam by drawing the conclusion that both world religions worship the same God.[75]

70. Ibid., 51.

71. Ibid., 52.

72. Pak, *Korean American Women*, 15–17.

73. Brown, "Review of *Exclusion and Embrace*," 921–22.

74. Volf, *Exclusion and Embrace*, 92. Shortt, *God's Advocates*, 228.

75. Volf, *Allah*.

Volf makes a remarkable contribution to the theological discussion of identity by relating key doctrines of the Christian faith—creation, the passion of Christ, and the Trinity—to the concept. He shows how the proper identification process for the self reflects and is guided by, for example, the divine process of separating and binding in creation. Volf also draws from the divine example on the cross to illustrate how one self can love the other.[76] The passion of God in Christ condescended the divine self toward the distant other in order to judge, free, and reconcile with humanity. This event consummately manifested identification and enabled the reunification between persons: between God and human and between human and human. Christ's divine example—of extending the self to include the other—sets a pattern for the self to emulate. The willed action to give and to adjust one's identity to permit the other entrance is necessary to facilitate individual and group reconciliation.[77] Those who have been re-centered and identified in Christ can follow in "self-donation" with those small and supreme acts of identification.[78] Volf's emphasis on the self-donation of the crucifixion neglects, perhaps, a focus on Christ's resurrection. It was not only Christ's payment that secured human salvation, but his resurrection that demonstrated God's satisfaction with humanity. Christians' ability to share what they have flows from what they have been given in Christ—the completed work of salvation He wrought in his death, burial, and resurrection. Volf aptly portrays, however, what the communion of the Trinity models for human interaction and expresses the trinitarian relationship for the configuration of self and identity without trivializing the Godhead, multiplying the Godhead, or deifying humanity.

76. Anna Williams refuses to place the locus of divine reconciliation in the crucifixion. Arguing against violence as the foundation, she places it in the resurrection. Williams, "Assimilation and Otherness," 268–70. The crucifixion, however, was a violent satisfaction to make reconciliation possible (Lev 17:11; Isa 53:10; Heb 9:22; 10:29).

77. Volf, *Exclusion and Embrace*, 25, 29.

78. Williams disdains Volf's emphasis on self-donation for two reasons: 1) the possible lack of reception and 2) the potential for condescension. Retreating from kenotic emptying, she prefers the assimilation of Senghor, that giving is done only by voluntarily taking upon oneself something from the other, rather than a giving of oneself to the other. Williams, "Assimilation and Otherness," 269. On the contrary, both actions (giving out and taking in) are paramount. The ever present danger of patronization in self-donation is apparent. That is why self-awareness and location within a community for the giver are required. Self-donation should not be excised. Human existence entails occasions where the one who has gives to the one who has not, hopefully in the right spirit of motivation (Luke 3:11; 10:25–37; John 15:13; Heb 13:16). Consider Christ's crucifixion; humanity was unable to take into itself any good from the other to be redeemed. Volf is right to promote self-donation as a means of love. Further, he is sympathetic to the predicament of non-reciprocity. See Volf, *Exclusion and Embrace*, 24–26.

Volf seems to forgo further discussion about the origin of identity. One's identity includes self and other, as he argues, but it is not primarily created by the self to include the self and the other. Since he does not speak at length as to the origin of identity as outside of oneself, Volf does not adequately emphasize its theological origin. He would readily agree that God creates the individual for community and to be a self-in-relation, and while he discusses the self as a creation and personhood as bestowed by God, he does not develop a theology of (or at least does not elaborate on the theology of) the God-given origin of identity and its implications. Volf does well to appropriate trinitarian relations as analogous for the social self; however, a further discussion of the creation of one's identity as an ecclesial self, formed by spiritual baptism into Christ Jesus (Rom 6:3–4) and ecclesiological baptism into the church by God's Spirit (Acts 1:4–5; 1 Cor 12:13), is paramount.[79]

Volf's construction of the self evidences a European-American Western perspective and neglects an Eastern conceptualization of the self where the individual enmeshes more fully within a group collective. The historical East-West dichotomy may adjust with the onset of globalization, but a discussion of how the perception of the self differs on a cultural basis should be considered. Within cultures where social hierarchies remain more fully intact (such as Korea or China), one's position within these societies very much determines one's identity. How, then, would an approach from this cultural understanding of the self reflect a description of self? Volf writes mostly of the self as self and distant other, whereas in a traditional Eastern context the self is wholly part of the other and reflects the other. The challenge in an Eastern cultural context may lie in differentiating the self from being wholly other. Further, how does an understanding of self and identity differ by religious definition or between predominant Eastern religions such as the Judeo-Christian concept of self and the Buddhist concept of no-self? The Confucian concept of *ren* (benevolence, cultivation of humanness) offers helpful insights from a historical Eastern perspective on the self that have long been embedded within Asian cultural understanding. The Eastern discussion of self and identity could be expanded for comparison to traditional Western opinions, but Volf, despite his involvement in inter-religious dialogue, seems not to touch on this topic for any length. On the surface, Volf's description of the self seems reminiscent of Confucius's. This similarity invites a proper comparison and contrast between the two

79. Shortt, *God's Advocates*, 217–18. Volf discusses the nature of personhood and the ecclesial self as part in relation to the whole community but does not greatly expound on the nature of and ecclesiological impact on personal identity.

thinkers, even as their understanding of personhood differs.[80] A study that incorporates a historical Eastern understanding of the self and the other, as well as of propriety and *shu* (reciprocity), with Volf's work on identity and reconciliation would prove most valuable.

In summary, since an undifferentiated inclusion of all things holds little advantage over a rejection of all things, Volf strikes the proper balance in his construction of the self when he avoids both all-inclusion and exclusion. Volf claims the permission—indeed, the moral right—to draw boundaries. His formulation of a theology of identity yields powerful insights into the nature of the self and identity formation that are applicable to contemporary issues of cultural and ethnic divisions, international migration, and seeking the common good for all.

80. Rosenlee, *Confucianism and Women*, 35, 42. See his distinction, Volf, *Captive*, 113. Volf goes importantly beyond Confucian teaching on the nature of benevolence and personhood. Volf describes a Christian self-giving love which expects nothing in return; Confucian thought seems to indicate that benevolence is performed with a hopeful and obligated reciprocation of good will. Secondly, Volf assigns personhood ontologically as given initially by God when a person is created. Confucius teaches that humanity is an ethic, a virtue, which must be strived to be attained. This seems to be a performance-based understanding to achieve personhood.

4

Psychological Contribution of Jenny Pak

JENNY HYUN CHUNG PAK, a licensed psychologist and Associate Professor of Psychology at Fuller Theological Seminary, was the first to employ narrative analysis in articulating the identity formation of Korean American women in their acculturation to the United States.[1] A Korean immigrant, Pak has contributed both cultural and psychological research to the field of ethnic studies, particularly to the conceptual development of identity. As a ten-year-old, Pak was thrust into a new environment—linguistically, ethnically, and culturally—when her family moved from South Korea to California. Through her personal struggles as an outsider (she endured a sense of male preferential treatment in her Asian upbringing and felt ostracized by her Anglo peers during adolescence), she identifies with the acculturation difficulties of her counseling clients.[2] She has added considerably to the practice of narrative analysis, the study of cultural dynamics in self-development, and the fields of Asian and gender studies.

Pak's pertinence to the present study lies in her investigation of the Korean American immigrant female identity within the U.S. and the way these women understand their own self-development in the cultural change process.[3] Pak favors a narrative approach to address the diversity and conflict that is bound up in the identities of ethnic minorities.[4] The historical conceptualization of ethnic identity and acculturation will be briefly sum-

---

1. Pak, *Korean American Women*, 26.

2. Ibid., 1–2.

3. Ibid., 4.

4. Pak, "Acculturation and Identity," 7–8.

marized, followed by an overview of acculturation models. Since Pak prefers the methodology of narrative analysis for the study of identity development and the acculturation process, a narrative understanding of self and identity will be given. Cultural images, historical settings, and main character roles will be addressed as they relate to the identity configuration of minority groups and to immigrant women in particular. Pak's research on the female identities of Korean American women will be described, and distinct elements that significantly impacted the identity development of these women in their migration experiences will be examined. Finally, an overview of Pak's continuing approach in her psychological studies of minority groups will be appraised and a critical evaluation offered.

ETHNIC IDENTITY

As Kathryn Tanner has noted, historians generally agree that the abstract term culture was not conceptualized until the early twentieth century when anthropologists began to use the term more broadly in their studies of various people groups.[5] Scholars, at least in the United States, began referring to these cultural groups (which are now more commonly referred to as ethnic minorities) as different rather than inferior only by the sixties, a shift that was perhaps related to the advent of civil rights legislation as well as the immigration flux during that decade. The subsequent two decades expanded the attention given to minority subcultures and highlighted the need to acknowledge specific cultures, although this practice was soon accompanied by allegations of stereotyping.[6] With Erik Erikson's groundbreaking identity development theory in the sixties and W. E. Cross's four-stage paradigm a decade later, racial identity theories flourished in the seventies.[7] Racial identity theories first focused on African Americans, patterned the way for ethnic minority theories, and have expanded to include nearly every vantage point of difference (gender, disability, sexuality, age), creating as many separate identity models as distinctions.

Scholars have over the decades defined three forms of cultural identity—racial, minority, and ethnic—differently in their individual conception and their interrelation. The differentiations made between ethnic identity and acculturation add to the confusion as well. With conceptual differences, disparate research findings ensue. Some use the concept of race to highlight societal power structures but reject race as a biological concept. Others

5. Tanner, *Theories of Culture*, 3, 21, 24.

6. Pak, *Korean American Women*, 5–7.

7. Ibid., 10–12.

reject the idea that ethnic groups are homogenous (the homogeneity myth) in favor of the term tribes to highlight intragroup differences within ethnicities.[8] Ruba Salih argues against the "racist reification" of ethnic identity and challenges the current use of certain terms—ethnic groups, hybridity, and diaspora—as misconceptions of migrant identity.[9] She argues that ethnicity does not determine identity, but rather that identity constantly shifts and renegotiates in response to one's experiences and location.[10]

Ethnic identity in terms of both race and culture has been discussed externally (as related to biological characteristics) and internally (as related to one's cultural beliefs and conventions).[11] This inconsistency has led to mixed findings in psychological research. Pak argues that the concept of race should be distinguished from culture and suggests that those in ethnicity studies should delineate which concept they are investigating.[12] In her research, Pak most often associates race with biological classification and ethnicity with a particular cultural entity that is defined by specific practices, language, and societal obstacles.[13]

Most twentieth-century models fail to describe identity in multifaceted terms. Since they tend to focus on one aspect of identity rather than a compilation of factors that work in dynamic tandem, Pak considers these models largely inadequate. The dynamism of ethnic identity is charged in part by varying social contexts, and she believes that acculturation is better suited for the study of individual differences.[14] Similarly, while Salih cautions against classifying individuals by ethnic belonging, she affirms the dynamism of identity and the fact that location shifts do affect identity boundaries.[15] What is more, in recent years ethnic identification and acculturation have been increasingly identified as two distinct processes.[16]

8. Ibid., 10–14.

9. Salih, *Gender in Transnationalism*, 120.

10. Ibid., 118–20.

11. Pak, *Korean American Women*, 12–14.

12. Jenny Pak, personal email communication with author, June 30, 2011.

13. Wolff et al., "Understanding Why Fathers," 146.

14. Pak, *Korean American Women*, 15–17. Pak cites the Minority Identity Development (MID) five-stage model, created by Atkinson et al. (1983), which incorporates more populations by grouping together a variety of individual differences into a larger set, as does the Racial/Cultural Identity Development (R/CID) by Sue and Sue (1990). In subsuming these populations, however, the model may obfuscate their comparative histories. These minority groups have not all been equally attacked historically and combining them may mute the differing severities of their oppression, or at least confound them (7–13).

15. Salih, *Gender in Transnationalism*, 120–21.

16. Pak, *Korean American Women*, 15.

While much research has been conducted on ethnic identity in terms of group membership and cultural affiliation, Pak stresses that the *process* of acculturation requires further study. Pak, rather than classifying the process into stages or steps, elucidates both the complexity and the narrative structure of ethnic identity.[17]

I argue that a description of identity formation benefits from both a categorical bird's-eye view (if it allows for unpredicted variability) as well as individual assessment (if conclusions are not over-generalized). While Phinney does propose a three-stage formation of ethnic identity, no comparable description has been formulated for religious identity, particularly one that includes ethnicity, race, gender, and culture.[18]

ACCULTURATION

While assimilation refers to how an individual identifies with new cultural traits, Pak considers acculturation to be more complex since it also encompasses the process by which one continues to identify with elements of one's heritage of origin. Pak prefers to link the process of ethnic identification solely to social identity (an aspect of the self that is identified with group membership) and keep it separate from the acculturation process, which reflects how individuals differ by the cultural traits they adopt.[19] Traditional acculturation models have not successfully addressed this aspect of human variability. Pak, who favors a narrative approach to describe self and identity, summarizes the five historical models of acculturation to illustrate their weaknesses. She faults the three oldest models (assimilation, bipolar, and multidimensional) as simplistic and linear. She disagrees with how the *assimilation model* presupposes an individual will prefer a majority culture in a "unidirectional" manner. She also dissents from the *bipolar model* since it describes a continuum between two cultures where the individual moves between the two in a "bidirectional" manner but only in one direction at the expense of the other. She finds that while the *multidimensional model* adds versatility to the process of cultural adaption, the model still remains on a linear spectrum. Sue and Sue, who introduced the *transcultural model* in 1971, suggest a third entity as a blend of previous cultures, although they do not fully explain how disparate cultures can be adequately incorporated.[20] Pak finds the *orthogonal model*, however, which was suggested

17. Ibid., 17, 19.
18. Phinney, "Three-Stage Model."
19. Pak, *Korean American Women*, 15, 18–19.
20. Ibid., 19–23.

by Oetting and Beauvais in 1991, to be so "flexible and situational" as to be unable to establish an individual unity of self-cohesion. Moreover, in their summation of the four types of cultural identifications (acculturated, bicultural, traditional, and marginal) between old and new cultures, they forfeit an actual description of the acculturation process in favor of a delineation of the resulting cultural identity.[21]

Pak's philosophical assumption seems to be that the concept of a unified self does exist and varies by person and culture. Whereas Oetting and Beauvais allow for any and all possible identification, Pak cautions against this conclusion. She instead cites the research of Noels, who found that dual-culture individuals still emotionally identify with one group in a given scenario but also noticed that this identification could alternate between groups depending on the circumstances. Most scholars do not question a person's identification with multiple cultures on a macro level, but Pak questions if individuals are able to identify with more than one cultural ideal of different groups that perhaps conflict in value *at the same time*.[22] This question of simultaneous cultural belonging offers a significant area for further research.

All of the previous identity models, Pak submits, are inadequate to describe the identification of the self and its cultural adaptation from multiple dimensions or contexts. All of the contexts in which an individual finds oneself—familial setting, traumatic episodes, personality, demographic characteristics, and routes of migration—must be considered. These variants make the creation of generalized models or comparison between and within group ethnicities difficult. She critiques previous models for their oversimplification, their incoherence, their overemphasis on acculturation outcomes, their insufficient descriptions of the process, and, chiefly, for their inability to analyze the acculturation process from a coincident collection of life factors. In light of these inadequacies, further study of how identities form and change is warranted.[23]

Pak reasons that an efficacious model of acculturation should reflect a "coherent sense of self" as well as elucidate the dynamism of the process. She advocates a different methodology—a narrative approach—to study self-construction at the individual level.[24] In her view, this approach better

21. Ibid., 23–24.
22. Ibid., 24.
23. Pak, "Acculturation and Identity," 5–7.
24. Pak, *Korean American Women*, 22–26.

captures the actual process of acculturation and the development of identity and meaning.[25]

A NARRATIVE UNDERSTANDING
OF SELF AND IDENTITY

Humanity is particularly compelled to create meaning, and narrative describes this process well.[26] An essential aspect of making meaning is the articulation of identity.[27] Other scholars have confirmed that narrative helps to frame individual self-reflection and to portray the multiculturalism of individual lives.[28]

Psychologist Dan McAdams emphasizes the life story as a model for self and identity.[29] He posits that each person functions as a storyteller who writes an internal "personal myth" that connects one's life events along a linear timeline and plotline. McAdams holds that identity formation is a lifelong task that is reformulated as one's story unfolds. In early childhood, a life story's "narrative tone" is set by images that will generate life story themes during the school-age years. As teenagers, individuals begin to realize their own story identity and to form a personal ideology, a collection of beliefs they hold to be true and use to guide their life plot. McAdams identifies two motivational themes, agency and communion, that he considers central to the human experience. Self-agency is the yen for autonomy; communion is the desire for relational intimacy.[30] As individuals age, adults create main characters (imagoes) as they formulate social commitments and seek identity integration. McAdams names six essential qualities of a developed and strong life story: coherence, openness, credibility, differentiation, reconciliation, and generative integration.[31] Society participates in identity development through the use of images that promote what is perceived to be the good to be achieved, and cultural differences exist in part due to differing social imagery.[32]

To frame her study of minority identities, Pak borrows heavily from McAdams's narrative theory. In her approach to immigrant Korean women

25. Ibid., 60.

26. Ricoeur, *Figuring the Sacred*, 308–10.

27. Polkinghorne, *Narrative Knowing*, 150–55.

28. McAdams, "Narrative Identity"; Riessman, *Narrative Methods*.

29. Pak, *Korean American Women*, 28.

30. McAdams, *The Person*, 409–13.

31. Ibid., 424–25.

32. McAdams, *Stories*, 60.

and her continuing ethnic research, Pak offers a psychological perspective in her narrative description of identity.

Identity in Narrative Explanation: The Korean Female

In her description of the Korean female narrative, Pak employs the life-story model to consider two predominant Korean social images—family and religion. These culturally indoctrinating icons have powerfully influenced the conception of self and identity for Korean women.[33] A discussion of these images will be preceded by an overview of Korean history to establish their social setting.

Historical Background of Korea

The history of Korea can be categorized into three periods: its prehistory until the Confucian state was established in 1392, its five hundred years under China's influence, and its twentieth-century history.[34] In the land now formally known as Korea, Tan'gun, according to myth, founded the Choson Dynasty circa 2333 BCE. Centuries later, Emperor Wu of China (Han Dynasty) defeated the Choson Dynasty in 108 or 109 BCE. This event commenced a long history of occupation by its surrounding neighbors. The three kingdoms of Shilla (originally Saro) in the south, Paekche, and Koguryo in the north remained from 57 BCE to 668 CE. Each of the kingdoms officially adopted Buddhism, beginning with Koguryo in 372 CE and ending with Shilla in 528. In the seventh century, Chinese tribes (e.g., Sui, Tang) invaded Korea until the three kingdoms were bloodily unified into the Korea of Shilla in 668. The first Confucian school was established in Korea in 682.[35] Features of the Shilla kingdom included the "bone-rank" system (a class system based on blood lineage), an educational system that was limited to nobility, the introduction of Confucian bureaucracy, and the widespread practice of slavery. During this time, growing dissension allowed a rebel leader, Wang Kon, to overthrow Shilla and establish Koryo, a kingdom characterized by Wang Kon's diplomatic reign and slavery reform. The Koryo Period (918–1392) saw multiple invasions by the Khitans, Jurchens, and Mongols and ultimate Mongol domination until King Kongmin

---

33. Pak, "Acculturation and Identity," 12.

34. Breen, *Koreans*, 75.

35. Nahm, *Historical Dictionary*, xxi–xxvi.

assumed the throne in 1365 as a result of General Song-gye Yi's successful military tactics.[36]

General Yi succeeded the throne as King Taejo and established Han-yang (Seoul) as the new capital, commencing the Yi (Choson) Dynasty (1392–1910). His government adopted Confucianism as its official religion in 1394 (demoting Buddhism) and introduced the elaborate Chinese bureaucratic and civil service examination system.[37] This development gave rise to a rigid five-class system with slaves (nobi) accounting for one-third of the population.[38] Korea suffered still more invasions by the Japanese and the Manchu in the sixteenth and seventeenth centuries followed by two hundred years of relative peace. By 1871 Korea had developed an isolationist policy to avoid domination by imperialistic powers (such as Russia, France, and the United States), a stance that earned it the name "The Hermit Kingdom." Korea, however, was eventually forced to open trade with Japan and fell prey to its occupation (1910–1945). Notably for this study, during this time of annexation Japan attempted to erase the national identity of the Korean people by requiring subjects to take Japanese surnames, suppressing nationalistic movements for Korean independence, and conscripting Korean males to fight in World War II.[39] While Korea was liberated after Japan's defeat in WWII, it then fell under a new kind of domination. Korea was subjected to a three-year occupation by the Allied Powers and a division of its country into north and south, with the Soviet Union and the United States presiding over the two regions. Although the Allied Powers (which also included China and Britain) originally agreed that Korea would become "free and independent" (and at several points the occasion could have materialized), the plan for an independent Korea was ultimately stymied, lastly when the Soviet Union rejected the U.N.'s call to elect a new Korean government.[40] North Korea's political ideology became communist, and South Korea's became free-market democratic. Just five years later in 1950, North Korea, using Soviet artillery, invaded South Korea and began the Korean Conflict. After the two sides signed an armistice in 1953, South Korea (the Republic of Korea) has flourished economically while North Korea (the Democratic People's Republic of Korea) has suffered political

36. Breen, Koreans, 79–85; Walker, East Asia, 263.
37. Nahm, Historical Dictionary, 9–10.
38. Breen, Koreans, 86–87.
39. Nahm, Historical Dictionary, 48–49.
40. Ibid., 15–21.

repression and economic hardship due in part to its dictatorial government, the Soviet Union's collapse in 1990, and the floods and famine of 1995.[41]

Images: Family and Religion

The image of family is principal in Korean culture, and its structure has been heavily influenced by Confucian thought for societal order that was introduced during Korea's Chinese occupation.[42] The term Confucianism was originally introduced by the Jesuits in China in the latter part of the 1700s.[43] The legendary Confucius, or Kong Qiu (551–479 BCE), however, whose teachings were recorded by his followers in the *Analects*, or *Lunyu*, lived centuries before. He stressed the importance of education and self-discipline and the primary concepts of *ren* and *li*, among other principles.[44] *Ren* (benevolence, cultivation of humanness) signifies the virtue that, if accomplished, indicates the achievement of personhood and is illustrated most clearly by a respectful devotion to one's parents, elder relations, and superiors.[45] Confucius emphasized that honoring societal positions maintained both national security and social harmony. *Li* (ritual, propriety) refers to the rules of proper human conduct and functions as the primary means of

41. Buzo, *Making of Modern Korea*, 175–76. While North Korea's dictators have been Kim Il-Sung and his son, Kim Jong-Il, South Korea has had its run of authoritarian presidents, namely Rhee Syngman (1948–1960), Park Chung-Hee (1961–79), and Chun Doo-Hwan (1981–88), with the latter two achieving power via military coup.

42. Pak, "Acculturation and Identity," 12.

43. Rosenlee argues that the term *Confucianism* was not introduced to represent the historical figure, but the concept of *Ru*, the symbol of Chinese high culture as recorded by official literati, predating Confucius and ultimately forming the Chinese (Han) group identity (17). Her five-point summary of the historical and cultural meaning of *Ru* is particularly revealing (34). Rosenlee, *Confucianism and Women*, 17–43.

44. These five virtues are *ren*, *li*, *yi* (rightness, appropriateness), *zhi* (wisdom), and *xin* (trustworthiness). *Shu* (reciprocity) is an indispensable Confucian concept but will not be elaborated here. Ibid., 32, 74. Confucius did not directly name the five relations (father-son, ruler-subject, husband-wife, old-young/elder brother-younger brother, and friend-friend), although he primarily discussed the father-son and ruler-subject relations. See Lei, "Forgiveness," 29–31.

45. *Ren* (仁) is the virtue that must be achieved in order to evidence one's humanness. In other words, the Confucian concept of personhood, one's humanity, was achieved only by demonstrating this ethic of *ren*. *Ren* classically was a description for a pleasing quality or talent and, after Confucius, came to signify a moral ethic. The Confucian concept of person, *ren* (人) is a gender neutral ethical category. See Rosenlee, *Confucianism and Women*, 35–42. While the term has been translated with a variety of nuances, Confucius used *ren* most clearly to denote the virtue of humanity. See also Rainey, *Confucius and Confucianism*, 34–35.

attaining *ren*.[46] Further, *li* reflects a "shared social grammar" that indicates which behavioral scripts should be followed in a given social context.[47] To this day, Korean family expectations and social propriety continue to reflect the teachings of this Chinese philosopher.[48]

Pak confirms Ai Ra Kim's estimation that the Korean ideals of *namjon yobi* (male precedence, literally, "men should be respected; women should be lowered") and *hyonmo yangch'o* (sage mother, compliant wife) that predominate Korean thinking descend from Confucian hierarchism.[49] Pak considers the tenets of Confucianism to be sexist and attributes much of the inferior self-identity of Korean women to these views.[50] As she describes:

> Just as heaven (*yang*) dominates earth (*yin*), male superiority and precedence over female was viewed as cosmologically sanctioned. . . . Thus, the view that the law of nature accorded the woman in a subordinate, dependent position to a man was commonly accepted, and she was expected to follow the Rule of Three Obedience or *samjong chidok* (obedience to father, obedience to husband, and obedience to son) throughout her lifetime.[51]

This attitude from the Yi (Choson) Dynasty (1392–1910) has endured over the centuries to create a collective identity for Korean women of "self-in-the-family," a family constituted by and centered around a male figure. Without personal individualization, the identity of Korean females became largely familial and nonexistent (or, at a minimum, stigmatized) if it was not located within a context that included a male (father, husband, or son). Since her family's well-being reflected her identity and worth, societal stature for a Korean woman became role-oriented and others-driven.[52] According to

46. Lei, "Forgiveness," 24.

47. Rosenlee, *Confucianism and Women*, 41.

48. Choi-Kim, "Continuing Gender Issues," 1.

49. Kim, *Women Struggling*, 6; Pak, "Acculturation and Identity," 12–13.

50. While many feminists have made a similar claim to Pak's, not all equate Confucius with sexism. Rosenlee questions if Confucian thought is intrinsically sexist. She distinguishes Confucian ideals of "self-cultivation and proper relations" from cultural Chinese sexism, cautioning that too hasty a judgment leads to prematurely preferring Western philosophy as hierarchically superior and short-circuiting the other causes behind gender oppression. She finds that distinguishing cultural Confucianism from Confucian theoretical ideals, such as *ren*, yields value. See Rosenlee, *Confucianism and Women*, 15–17, 119, 149. Confucius's ascribed pejorative comments regarding women may indicate otherwise (as cited in the *Analects* 17:25). See also Lei, "Forgiveness," 31.

51. Pak, "Acculturation and Identity," 12–13.

52. Park, "Practices," 159–60.

Pak, familism, whereby family supersedes individual desire, has been "the national ethnic" in Korea since the mid-1600s.[53]

Religion is the second key social image that has been shaped by Confucian philosophy and, in turn, shapes Korean female identity. Confucianism appoints men to all roles in its practice, such as ancestor worship rituals. When Confucianism became the official state religion in 1394, this shift removed women from any positions of public service. Shamanism, the indigenous other Korean religion, became women's household religion. They began to believe that it was their responsibility to appease the *kosa* (house gods) within the home and saw themselves as directly responsible for the boon or bane of the family. The family priestess (*mudang*), despite her lack of power in society and her confinement bounded by Confucian male superiority, became intricately tied to the Korean female understanding of herself as a "woman warrior." Her identity became synonymous with self-denial as a means to secure familial fortune.[54]

Setting

A person's historical past structures one's identity. A person's ideology, when mapped in a particular social context, creates a setting upon which the self is defined.[55] According to Pak, Korean women have largely maintained the Confucian rules of family order and an identity of social isolation and subservience. While Korea functioned as a contained dynasty until it entered the global trade industry in 1876, after this shift, women were viewed as more of a social asset in the embrace of *Kaehwa Undong*, the Modernization Movement of Korea. With Korea's openness to foreign visitors, Pak notes the efficacy of American Christian missionary efforts for Korean women. With the missionary establishment of schools, orphanages, and hospitals, females were afforded access to education, care, and health services. According to Pak, the ideology of Christianity encouraged public participation of women in leadership roles. Japan's colonization (1920–1945) and the immigration of men increased women's labor opportunities in Korea. These advances, however, had little impact in extinguishing deeply-held ideological views of women as inferior, and these women were consistently underpaid and underpromoted. The year 1965 marked the next wave of Korean immigration to the United States since the first at the turn of the twentieth century. Pak reiterates that, despite their migration to more socially progressive

53. Pak, "Acculturation and Identity," 13.

54. Ibid., 13–15.

55. McAdams, *Stories*, 84.

environments, many Koreans still hold traditional Confucian views. Many first-generation immigrant wives work, but these jobs often contribute to a family-run small business. Their work at home and on the job is fused, accomplished from a tireless devotion to the family collective rather than for any individual pursuits. These traditional roles persist, even for Korean Christians who have immigrated and created a new cultural center for the Korean community in the United States.[56]

Imagoes: Main Characters

Individuals manage to collate the various aspects and roles of daily life by creating main characters, imagoes, in their personal plot. Especially in later stages of life, they pursue the primary goal of an integrated singular identity that provides them with internal meaning and unity. McAdams warns that an individual cannot fulfill all roles simultaneously, but, by employing the narrative concept of main characters, disparate roles can be woven into a single story. He asserts that individuals often have two prominent dual characters that demonstrate motivational agency and motivational communion.[57]

Pak confirms this challenge of dual identities for Korean American women who seek to unite their discordant roles and values. Women in general struggle to balance their public and private lives, and first-generation immigrant Korean women in particular experience an internal conflict between the strong family priestess and the "other-oriented, selfless self." Pak anticipates that, due to the modeling behavior of their mothers, this pattern of conflicting imagoes (main characters) will continue for 1.5 and second generation Korean American women. In fact, given their exposure to salient cultural cues of Western individualism, these young women are likely to experience a more rigid dichotomy between their professional and personal lives as well as more difficulty in harmonizing a meaningful identity and a cohesive self. A unification and reconciliation of social roles should occur for an individuated self to mature into a purposeful identity.[58]

The identity formation of Korean American women requires them to navigate at least three areas: social systems, lifestyles, and philosophies. These women are often torn between their previous kinship-based society and their new individualistic American system. In terms of lifestyle, they must place themselves on the spectrum between the traditional *hyonmo*

56. Pak, *Korean American Women*, 15–21.
57. McAdams, *The Person*, 412–13.
58. Pak, "Acculturation and Identity," 21–26.

yangch'o and the contemporary female who is educated and employed. Finally, they face the competing ideologies of Confucianism and Christianity.[59] Young Song describes four stages that Korean American women may encounter in their development of a feminist self-consciousness which I have termed: acceptance, query, solidarity, and action. Initially, the woman fulfills her traditional social roles, although she may do so with a sense of powerlessness and discontentment (perhaps even denial). Secondly, dissonant events may result in a new awareness and an internal examination of her assumptions, purposes, and positions. If her self-examination results in dissatisfaction, she may enter a third stage characterized by anger and a desire to seek solidarity with likeminded others in pursuing cultural change. The final stage involves role disorientation and confusion but ultimately is one of active response as she makes choices in the process of self-determination and self-solidification.[60] These stages may be particularly illustrative of female migrants as they negotiate identity in a new social context.

Collective Case Study: Korean American Women

Pak considers Korean American females in her psychological narrative analysis of immigrant identity. She interviewed women who were Korean, foreign-born, and between the ages of 25 to 40. These immigrants to the U.S. also identified as living in a dual-culture context and professed a Christian affiliation. Apart from their shared higher level of education, their individual stories differed. While the fact that this group was highly educated might draw criticism of the study for not reflecting a larger population, Pak's goal is not to mirror the population in the manner of quantitative sampling but instead to elicit deeper descriptions of individual experiences and understanding that quantitative study cannot obtain. Also, in the Korean community a higher level of education is more common than in other ethnic groups.[61]

Despite Pak's critique that systematic stages confine individual variability, her narrative analysis follows chronological periods. She collapses the women's stories into five stages of early childhood, late childhood, adolescence, college years, and young adulthood.[62] Utilizing McAdams's theory, she highlights themes that emerged from the collected data to plot development with "narrative smoothing" to tell a coherent story. To ad-

59. Park, "Practices," 133.
60. Song, "Woman-Centered Perspective," 4–7.
61. Pak, *Korean American Women*, 45–48.
62. Ibid., 16–17, 59–61.

dress any concerns regarding researcher bias, she reassures her audience that "narrative configuration does not suggest the researcher can impose any order on the data, but must be guided by the principle that the final story must both fit the data as well as provide a meaningful explanation."[63] Pak discusses several aspects of her subjects' identity development, beginning with their early years. She then considers their gender socialization, the type of city in which they were raised, the ambition of their fathers and the impact of paternal *han*, their maternal examples, and their notion and application of choice.[64]

Childhood and Culture of Location

These Korean American women reported that they endured a harsh transition when they immigrated to a new land as children. While it is difficult to determine how aware they were of their family's economic struggles and its effects on them, each did recall her family's collective response to those years of poverty: a firm sense of resolve to establish security and success. With strong parental pressure for educational achievement, each girl internalized this drive for survival and excellence despite any opposition. Each of these women faced a second cultural transition. Their parents' occupational success was typically accompanied by a move to a safer neighborhood in the white middle-class suburbs. As a result of these relocations, issues of assimilation, minority status, popularity, academic performance, personal confidence, and peer and parental approval appeared as major factors in their identity development during their adolescent years.[65]

Socializing Gender in Childhood

These women reported both birth order and gender bias as central to their personal narrative. According to the conventions of Confucian filial piety, the eldest sibling serves as the patron/ess who assumes responsibility for one's family as the parents begin to decline. Since the socialization of Korean children directed their identities to match this cultural ideal, their self-described identities differed based on their birth order. Hanna, without the responsibility of being the firstborn, defined her aspirations in terms of more individual standards and felt free to pursue a more American ideal of

---

63. Ibid., 58.
64. Ibid., 203–22.
65. Ibid., 202–8.

femininity. Ruth and Esther, both firstborn daughters, defined their goals in terms of their birth family collective. Despite the fact that they bore the same responsibilities as an eldest son, Ruth and Esther did not inherit a son's rights and privileges. Being a son made the difference. When they compared themselves to their male siblings, Ruth and Hanna reported a stifling of expression and lack of permission from their parents. Esther, who had no brother, felt gender pressure only when in Korea, not from her family. All three women reported a lack of female social privilege but noted that the parental demand for academic performance and success was gender equivalent.[66]

Paternal Han

Pak's narrative analysis also shows the effects of paternal ambition on her participants. Each of their fathers had lived in Korea during Japan's occupation, World War II, and the Korean Conflict. These men faced the meagre economic prospects of the Korean Reconstruction (1946–1960) as well as the *han* (unrealized hopes and thwarted dreams) that arose from this social climate; each left their homeland for opportunities abroad. Pak summarizes *han* as "a complicated concept born out of a long history of collective experiences of oppression."[67] These Korean males met resistance as first-generation immigrants to the U.S., struggled with a new language and culture, and experienced marginalization in their occupations. Their frustrations influenced their daughters, and in response, their daughters dutifully pursued similar aims for professional success while delaying or altogether denying their personal desires for marriage and children.[68]

Maternal Support

The influence of the participants' Korean mothers on their identity development was not pronounced. The daughters did not name their mothers

---

66. Ibid., 204–6.

67. Ibid., 212. Others, however, differ in the emphasized referent of *han*. *Han* connotes a deep angst, even depression, among primarily women over male oppression in a patriarchal society. Women in Confucian Korea were given very few rights and little access to education or literacy. In short, females had no voice in society but were meant to endure sacrificially. Kang argues that if *han* is only understood as minjung (social and economic deprivation), it neglects the *han* of women in sexual discrimination. Kang, "Han."

68. Pak, *Korean American Women*, 210–13.

as influential figures in their personal lives but described them as strong "silent figures" in the home. In contrast, their fathers trained these women for public interaction and instructed them in "warrior" skills. Their mothers pursued all domestic matters with less verbalization, enforcing the example of the "selfless self." Despite the shadow of her mother, each of the women identified herself as imitating this supportive role as she married and had her own children.[69]

Individual versus Collective Choice

Scholars have designated certain cultural continuums that reflect the range of cultural practices in societies. Geert Hofstede, for example, identifies five dimensions, one of which is individualism-collectivism.[70] Pak finds that individual freedom of choice recurs as a prominent theme in these 1.5 and second generation narratives, despite her interviewees' collective-oriented upbringing. These women articulated that they wanted to have a choice to maintain traditional Korean values; in other words, they desired the freedom to choose, even though that choice was often to promote or to preserve the collective family good. Grace Choi-Kim, in her research on second generation Korean American Christian women, found their religious identities were more prominently based on Christianity and directed by a personal relationship with God and a sense of "identity in Christ" rather than by traditional Korean ideology.[71] While Confucianism consigns the female by duty, these immigrant children reproduced that behavior of their own accord. These Korean American women possessed a greater sense of individuality but often chose to sacrifice intentionally for the collective honor. As they negotiated the conflicting demands of multiple roles, they continually refined their identities.[72]

In summary, Pak uses narrative discourse to illustrate how Confucian ideology has profoundly tailored these women's self-definitions. In addition to this historical force, family and religion operate as central socializing images in the Korean community and continue to apply pressure in identity development. Pak's analysis does not align with previous ethnic identity models' assertions that minorities favor the dominant culture and distance themselves from their culture of origin. Pak's research shows that these women did not feel contempt toward their culture of origin and did

69. Ibid., 213–15.
70. Hofstede, "National Culture Dimensions."
71. Choi-Kim, "Continuing Gender Issues," 5–6, 11.
72. Pak, *Korean American Women*, 215–17.

not prefer the majority culture at any point in their development.[73] While her research focuses on the individual acculturation of Korean American women in the United States, Pak validates previous findings that when an ethnic minority faces structural oppression from a dominant culture, the group does not assimilate as a whole. Rather, the oppression seems to further solidify their established patterns of group and family allegiance for social support.[74] This discovery pertains to the study at hand since a religious minority may also demonstrate a strong, within-group collectivism for community cohesion (e.g., church family) when it is located in a majority culture that is antagonistic to their beliefs and practices.

Pak's Continuing Narrative Approach

During her years of research, Pak has extensively studied ethnic minorities, including Korean, Hispanic, African American, and Vietnamese populations. As a psychologist and an immigrant, she has used her professional and personal experiences to serve these immigrant populations. When she realized that her quantitative research was incapable of capturing internal aspects of human behavior, she began to pursue narrative analysis for identity research. Her scholarly interest in the integration of psychology and theology to study the self and identity development has continued to gain momentum.[75]

Pak has made significant contributions to ethnic and cultural psychology. Some of her early work highlights the existence of important yet overlooked cultural differences among counseling professionals which, if not taken into proper account, could be misconstrued. Pak draws from Hsu's theory of differing cultural self-constructions to investigate how the Western "independent" self and the non-Western "interdependent" self may elicit varied individual responses. The independent self has been socialized to be more casual, to reveal itself more readily, and to be willing to engage in conflict as it establishes boundaries between itself and the other. The non-Western interdependent self sees the other as constitutive of self, is more reserved, and minimizes conflict with others.[76] While previous literature examines only the Caucasian pattern of response, Pak et al. have found that Caucasian and Asian counseling supervisees differed in their degrees

73. Ibid., 209.

74. Ibid., 221–22.

75. Jenny Pak, interview by author, recorded by phone, Dallas, TX, November 11, 2011.

76. Pak, "Cultural Differences," 4–5.

of self-disclosure and working alliance formation. As a result, inaccurate assessments in the supervision process of counseling trainees could be made without paying adequate attention to differing ethnic expressions.[77]

During her doctoral training in psychology, Pak transitioned to a narrative analytical method of inquiry. Since that time, she has largely relied on the qualitative method of narrative analysis to explore the underdeveloped study of minority group identities, roles, and beliefs. She believes this method to be capable of producing vital information about the self and identity that quantitative methods cannot draw out. As Pak has demonstrated, the way people narrate the events of their lives yields valuable data for discovering nuances of self-understanding and experienced difficulties. This complex data can be used for analysis and the consequent creation of clinical services to properly address these challenges and needs. Pak has made significant inroads in this field; in one instance she served as the senior researcher for a study to ascertain why fathers adopted medical caretaking responsibilities for their gravely ill children.[78] Ethnicity and socioeconomic status emerged as important factors in this phenomenon, particularly for immigrant men. Pak's findings were used to formulate an appropriate awareness of and to help hospitals and clinicians better serve this particular population.

Pak's most common methodology is the collective case study that details each life story for individual analysis and cross-comparison.[79] An individual's life continuum orders data chronologically and emphasizes singular events as they are recognized and labeled by the participant. Pak has most often drawn her informational data from the categories of cultural background, childhood, recent family history, employment history, and aspects specific to the individual study. From these, she draws sub-domains and recognizes particular themes. These themes are identified with the use of a multiple case study with two facets.[80] The first, a within-case analysis, sorts each interview separately as a unique explanatory set of data for the participant's behavior. The second compiles a cross-case analysis of all the interview data into tables of coded information whereby patterns can be distinguished across individual cases for summary and implications.

This kind of narrative approach to self and identity allows for each individual's unique life history to be considered while permitting aspects of their experiences to be compared among a group. In this way, the study of an individual is not wholly reduced to numerical, quantifiable data. For

77. Ibid., 6–20.

78. Wolff et al., "Understanding Why Fathers," 144–46, 155.

79. Pak, *Korean American Women*, 44–45, 50.

80. Wolff et al., "Understanding Why Fathers," 146–52.

example, when Pak researched college students that had transferred from a two-year community college to a four-year university (most of whom were members of an ethnic minority and all of whom were of a lower socioeconomic status), she surveyed significant life experiences before and after a point on their life timeline. When she analyzed their experiences (such as parental influences, negative school events, persons of positive impact, and turning points) prior to, during, and after their pursuit of higher education, she discovered several themes shared among the participants. She found that while each had a particular path and a personality that was conducive to educational success, all shared in common the existence of a "transfer agent," an individual who was integral to their school transfer process being completed. This study highlighted the role of significant agents and the relationality required for an institutional structural process to be completed.[81]

Pak's narrative approach, whether in counseling or research, allows her to treat an individual holistically by considering the entire client's or participant's life narrative in addition to formative individual events. Narrative analysis seems particularly suited for the individual construction of personal meaning and therefore the study of identity. It allows for the complexity of human experience without quantitative reductionism. Pak has appropriated it astutely in her research on identity development among minority populations.[82]

Pak uses a psychological approach to the division of self in her work with minority and bicultural individuals who struggle between social contexts. Since the self maintains both social and individual interactions between I and the other, the self's competing motivations and values appear prominently at both the individual and social level. The examination of competing values often leads to a "diametrically opposed" choice. Individuals choose within themselves which value (or role or identity) they will demonstrate socially even when they do not hold to this value personally. Whereas Erikson names identity development to be the central task of one's adolescence, Pak views it as an ongoing process for the bicultural person. Pak counters the quantitative psychological analysis of self and identity and argues that if identity is only considered at the external behavioral level, the complexity of internal divisions and conflicts will be overlooked.

In her research on acculturation and identity, Pak integrates her psychological and theological training. Since disparate cultural worldviews of appropriate self-orientation cultivate and reinforce differing behavioral patterns, values, and thought processes, a culture's differing emphasis on more

---

81. Pak et al., "Life Histories," 3.
82. Kim and Pak, "Journeys."

individualistic or collectivistic traits shapes a person. For Pak, however, in the Christian development of self and identity, both an I-consciousness and a we-consciousness must be present and function properly for psychological health and spiritual wholeness. She values the relationships that the self has with the divine One as well as with human others.[83] A healthy self relates both individually and collectively: vertically to God in an "individual-centered choice and response" and horizontally to others in a "relationship-centered interdependence."[84] Pak's notion of the values conflict within the bicultural self parallels both Volf's and Hauerwas's discussions of the spiritual self's internal division.

For Pak, the self possesses an internal organization that makes existence meaningful. Citing 1 Corinthians 14:33, she extrapolates that God's orderly character would apply to God's design in creation including the formation of self. Ultimately, Pak considers both the nature of God's character as well as the striving of the self for narrative unity to be evidence for the final coherence of self.[85]

ASSESSMENT OF PAK

Despite its less frequent use within the field of psychology, Jenny Pak employs narrative analysis in her practice and research. She has added considerably to the study of identity development within minority groups, particularly Korean American immigrant women. Her research has also highlighted the indispensability of history and culture in comprehending someone's psychological development and self-understanding. In following Dan McAdams's life story method, she has elucidated how important narrative patterns, particular to a given context in which the individual is located, affect these individuals, such as how strictly the images of family and religion effect the psyches and daily behaviors of Korean women. What her approach may lose in breadth (her Korean American sample rested on only three women due to time and resource constraints), it gains in depth by using rich descriptions of individual analysis.

In discussing Korean culture, Pak engages thoroughly the issues of family and religion and only briefly with setting. She could have in addition drawn on general themes from Korea's political history in her investigation such as oppression, slavery, and its ruler-subject mentality. Much of

83. Yangarber-Hicks et al., "Invitation," 346.

84. Ibid., 345–46.

85. Jenny Pak, interview by author, recorded by phone, Dallas, TX, November 11, 2011.

Korea's historical narrative involves a series of invasions and occupations by neighboring forces, namely, China, Mongolia, Japan, and, more briefly, Russia and the United States. It is worthwhile to consider the questions of whether these occupations have affected the cultural self-understanding of Koreans and if Korea has had ample opportunity to form a national identity and to practice self-rule to own itself. In addition to outside perpetrators, Korea has experienced slavery from within during the Shilla period and the Yi (Choson) Dynasty. From the nobility/commoner class divisions of the Shilla period to the five castes of Yi, the Korean population has endured centuries where individual worth was defined by social rank. Furthermore, when Confucianism was officially adopted by Yi in 1394, a ruler-subject understanding of community relations was reinforced and Korea as a national family was divided. How has this sense of hierarchy impacted the self-understanding of subsequent generations? Considering the importance Koreans have placed on family and blood heritage, how has this division affected their sense of national and ethnic identity?[86] These political dynamics have important ramifications in describing individual narratives, self-conception, and identity. The effects of Korean *han*—given the years of invasions, annexations, and slavery as well as class, gender, and national divisions—on the Korean psyche could be discussed in much greater detail.

In addition, the principles of Confucianism are more dynamic than merely a set of gender rules.[87] Pak seems not to address this complexity for any length and does not highlight Confucian concepts, such as the ideal of self-cultivation, that may have some meritorious application. For example, the understanding of the self as both a relational self and part of a collective mentality is often missing from Western conceptions. Pak seems to disregard Confucius for the negative ramifications of his writings and does not investigate which of his ideas might be commended. Pak short-circuits a discussion of Confucianism without considering, for instance, how his ideas redress individualistic thinking. If Confucius is to be taken as wholly misogynous and his relational hierarchy blamed for creating a culturally sexist framework, then different cultural scripts of particular contexts should be elaborated.

Given that she guides the data by thematic organization, Pak's narrative method seems susceptible to considerable bias. Themes could deteriorate into stereotypes that have been assumed by the researcher and could affect research outcomes. Pak, however, does acknowledge this propensity and

86. Breen, *Koreans*, 49–53.
87. Rosenlee, *Confucianism and Women*, 15–16.

comments at great length regarding her established precautions.[88] Could there be a more systematic approach or other techniques she could introduce to further safeguard against this potential for bias? She readily clarifies that this type of research is best for exploratory study rather than for a systematic study of hypothesized variables.[89] Remarkably, her narrative research allows for the uniqueness of individual cases to be expressed, which in turn can reveal new areas for quantitative study.[90] Still, without a quantitative study at the exploration stage, researcher bias likely cannot be altogether avoided. Pak's methodology might be strengthened by integrating the use of quantitative and qualitative methods; including surveys or selecting interviews randomly would allow for a more complete description.

In the study of immigrant identity, it seems important to introduce the conceptual understanding of self and personhood that has been dictated by their culture. Pak does not, however, consider the Confucian concept of self or the Buddhist concept of the no-self and their historical influence on Korean immigrants. These two ideological influences remain a vital area for discussion. Furthermore, Pak does not fully address the Western conceptualization of self in relation to immigrant identity. Her Korean female participants were thrust into a new cultural setting with two typologies of self that remain prominent in the U.S.: a notion of self that lingers in the collective cultural consciousness of Americans (the Western modern self) and a second notion that has surfaced during the last fifty years (the Western postmodern self). While the modern, rational self may have been philosophically crucified, it remains in the cultural and institutional frameworks of the United States, along with its belief that an individual can achieve success if determined, educated, and empowered. This understanding of a self-sufficient self promotes an optimism in the self's ability to methodically strive, succeed, and create its own story. The postmodern self, particularly as expressed in literature, art, and music as well as by the entertainment industry and the academy, posits the futility of the self and the death of an autonomous, rational self. It believes that knowledge is unknowable, meaning is ungraspable, assertion is a will to power, and the splintered self is largely powerless to structural forces. This pessimistic rendering of the self rejects being bound by any story. These two cursory overviews of the self are by no means wholly dichotomous but convey a polarity of orientation. A discussion of these shifting American notions of self in relation to the identity development of immigrant populations is pertinent. What notion

88. Pak, *Korean American Women*, 54–55.
89. Wolff et al., "Understanding Why Fathers," 146.
90. Ibid., 155.

of self do immigrants adhere to in their attempts to navigate their new cultural environment? Do they align themselves with the traditionally defined modern self and, if so, how does this alignment inform the postmodern understanding of the self? Pak argues that individuals do strive for a sense of internal cohesion which is brought out best by narrative research analysis.

As Pak has added greatly to the body of psychological research, academic and therapeutic psychology would be further helped by its use of narrative analysis in research and therapy. Pak's individual contributions on contemporary issues of migration, ethnic identity, and acculturation should be lauded.

5

Theo-Ethical Contribution of Stanley Hauerwas

Stanley Martin Hauerwas, Gilbert T. Rowe Professor Emeritus of Divinity and Law at Duke Divinity School, has written on a wide range of topics that defy systematic ordering and in particular discusses theological ethics and "theological politics" in his writings. Hauerwas's work considers Christology, ecclesiology, and eschatology and is perhaps most influenced by John Howard Yoder (1927–1997), a twentieth-century Mennonite theologian.[1] He also has engaged, however, the writings of Aristotle, Aquinas, Barth, Reinhold and H. Richard Niebuhr, Wittgenstein, and Alasdair MacIntyre, among numerous others.[2]

Hauerwas's theology was indelibly shaped by his story. He grew up in a white, blue-collar family in East Texas, was raised in a Methodist church, and discovered Anabaptist theology during his years with John Howard Yoder at the University of Notre Dame. He has experienced life as an outsider multiple times in his life: as a philosopher and writer within his working-class family, as a Protestant at the University of Notre Dame, as a pacifist in the United States, as the husband of a mentally ill wife when the topic was socially taboo, as a boisterous Texan in the polite South, and as a Christian theologian within the academy.[3] Although Hauerwas has written prolifically on a magnitude of topics such as story, community, character, and the

1. Sider, "Friendship, Alienation, Love," 61.

2. Hauerwas, *Christian Existence*, viii; Cartwright, "Hauerwas's Essays," 658, 660, 664.

3. Hauerwas, *Hannah's Child*, 180–81.

disabled, he primarily emphasizes the philosophy and theology of ethics and calls his fellow Christians to live in the manner of a minority.

Hauerwas has also written extensively on the individual self, the corporate identity of the church, and the national identity of the United States. He engages history, anthropology, politics, and the Bible regarding the nature of the self and its implications for a theology of identity. This chapter will summarize his description of the nature of the self and will explicate his theological principles for the Christian identity, which focus on its migrant, alien, minority, and narrative character. Lastly, an assessment of his views will be presented.

NATURE OF SELF

Stanley Hauerwas has gained recognition for his thorough critique of philosophical liberalism and how its ideals, such as the independent rationality of the mind, promote a false sense of self. Hauerwas frames selfhood as "character," giving it a form of agency.[4] While a discussion of self-agency and free will are beyond the scope of this study, two aspects of Hauerwas's definition of the self will be relayed here as they relate to a theology of identity. The first is his affirmation of a story-formed self; the second is his denial of the self's autonomy.

A Story-Formed Self

Hauerwas describes the nature of the self as narrative. He asserts that to be a self is to possess a story, and that it is within a story that the self is morally formed.[5] For Hauerwas, the self is fashioned so elementally by the stories into which it is born—family of origin, socioeconomic status, region, nation—that it has no power to form autonomously. Narrative localizes each self and grounds it to a particular time and social context. This process sets boundaries that aid the self in distinguishing its own narrative from those of others.[6] The nature of narrative creates a recognizable weave that links the past, present, and future events of the self in a continuous fashion and instructs the self how to move forward. The narrative, precisely into which the self was placed, is one's own tutor. The particularity of the story that shaped the self not only informs the way one considers the particularity of

---

4. Bauerschmidt, "Aquinas," 26, 28.

5. Hauerwas, *Community of Character*, 66, 149.

6. Hauerwas, *Christian Existence*, 34, 36.

another's story, but also trains the self in how to engage with these other stories. A freedom of self comes not only from acknowledging which stories have formed it, but also by employing them to move forward.[7]

A narrative provides a landscape for the self to become an integrated whole, but the narrative-forming self must be substantial and truthful enough to correspond its actions with its identity in order to form a consistent self. In doing so, the self should not exile parts of its past in an attempt to obliterate the memory of an action that is inconsistent with a desired identity. A worthy narrative, for Hauerwas, informs the self; if the narrative is deceived or shallow, so too is the self. When a narrative does not permit the self to face its own actions, good and ill, the self remains fractured. Using his own heritage as an example, Hauerwas describes how his identity, as a white Texan, provides a plot that shapes his life but also constrains it, since this story tends to avoid the acknowledgement of racial injustice. To the extent that it fails to enable an individual or group to accept its history entirely, a narrative is insufficient to functionally change its members. To own ourselves, we must live within a narrative of honesty that is free from internally inflicted fear. If a particular narrative is unable to fully disclose aspects of reality, the self is deprived of skills to extricate itself from self-deception, and this deception disables freedom.[8] The self is not free in any initial, detached status; however, those, who are formed by a truthful narrative, experience a freedom in realizing that the "limits and possibilities of those stories [they] have not chosen" own them.[9] Hauerwas exposes the fallacious supremacy of the self and heralds a reframed way of thinking about it; namely, the self is inexplicable apart from the narrative in which it is located. Indeed, its own history orients the self.[10]

How, then, does a narrative self relate to a theology of Christian identity in migration? The sojourner is born into a particular time and place, and one's self is formed by the continuing stories that, in turn, form character. The migrant develops an ongoing narrative that fuses multiple identities into a composite self. While migratory experiences add variety, one's narrative unifies the self. The storied examples within the Bible inform the migrant's present existence, and the migrant Christian's identification with that particular person in history, Jesus Christ (and his unfolding narrative from creation to redemption to the earth's consummation), shapes their self-understanding. The experience of migration highlights these narrative

7. Ibid., 29, 31.
8. Ibid., 29–31, 37–41.
9. Ibid., 29.
10. Cartwright, "Hauerwas's Essays," 651.

truths: their lives are a pilgrimage,[11] they have not been abandoned by God, and their present experiences do not reflect their full reality.

Myth of the Autonomous Self

For Hauerwas, human existence is contingent, and freedom is not possible when it is divorced from context and unshackled by constitutive ties. Self-determination does not occur separately from one's lived narrative; one's cultural setting in a particular time and place in history unavoidably affects the individual self. The unattached autonomous self is a myth, and those who claim that the freedom of selfhood has an inverse relationship with narrative (that freedom increases as one's attachment to one's story decreases) are misled.[12] In fact, the self (as an individual) relates to a whole (one's historical narrative), and the dignity of the self is grounded in its participation in that larger story.[13] Even the attempt to loosen all ties—from a given tradition that constrains the self socially, familially, and culturally—is bounded by a given context. As Hauerwas argues:

> What it means to a person, to be free, and/or autonomous, is to be capable of creating or "choosing" our "identity." Thus, we do not think of ourselves as inheriting a family tradition or a group identity with which we must learn to live. Rather, our particular story is that we have no history and thus we can pick and choose among the many options offered by our culture.[14]

The people for whom freedom is a rejection of all cultural limitations wrongly assume that they can and should wholly extricate themselves from the stories that have shaped them.[15] Hauerwas challenges the philosophical remnants of the Enlightenment that uphold the ideal of a person "without convictions" as free from "ideological perversions." The highest value in current Western society and the United States in particular seems to be a freedom that is equated with a detached self-sufficiency, one that eschews all bonds in order to be free. The fact that Westerners and Americans consider their personal lives to be private matters is but one distilling effect of a societal framework that has grown out of political liberalism.[16] Freedom,

11. I use the term pilgrimage loosely to refer to a personal or spiritual journey.

12. Hauerwas, *Community of Character*, 12.

13. Ibid., 11, 13.

14. Hauerwas, *Christian Existence*, 27.

15. Ibid., 27–29.

16. Hauerwas, *Community of Character*, 171, 181.

however, is not autonomous. The self is not freed when it has no story, nor when it escapes a particular story. Hauerwas not only contends that the self is fractured, but also that recent ideologies do not remedy this situation. Neither modernity, with its optimistic but fallacious belief in an unattached self that is capable of independent reason, nor postmodernity, with its illusive contention that people should not be bound by historical ties, sufficiently explain or redress the divided self.[17]

Ellen Charry aligns with Hauerwas in her discussion of the modern self.[18] Her historical summary of modernity's "secular emancipation narrative" traces the autonomous self back to its emancipation from all external repressive structures as proposed by Descartes (philosophically), Rousseau (educationally), Marx (politically), Nietzsche (religiously), and Freud (psychologically and sexually). In the present day, the autonomous self has been emancipated from any internal restraint and from meaning altogether by Derrida, Foucault, and others. This philosophical mutiny has extended to all reaches of society. In the name of "inclusivity and freedom," any and all structures are considered to be repressive. The hyperindividualistic self, however, cannot sustain its course, and this unchecked sense of liberation leaves the self with a curious and anarchic power to dominate, which is the antithesis of freedom.[19] Charry, along with Hauerwas, understands the self needs more than autonomy, more than a "hermeneutic of release," to flourish.[20] The redress for modernity's crisis will only come from a rejection of modernity's secular mindset. Emancipation comes not from one's attempted liberation from God, but, as the patristic fathers claimed, in one's emancipation from the ignoble part of the self that lies in opposition to God's love and purpose. Unbridled emancipation is not freedom.[21]

Furthermore, if the self is the sole engineer of its destiny and may do whatever it wills on its own, it must create a story without assistance from others. To concede that one has received aid from others confesses *dependence*, and the self must navigate its own way through life.[22] Charry

---

17. Hauerwas, *A Better Hope*, 37, 40–41.

18. Charry, "Crisis of Modernity," 89–112. Charry argues the secularization (of the concept of the self) is the culprit for the ills of society more than Christian doctrine, the latter being Moltmann's suggestion in her estimation (91). She claims the greater devastation to society and nature has been the secular declaration that the self has no need of God (91–96).

19. Ibid., 98.

20. Ibid., 96.

21. Ibid., 93.

22. Hauerwas, *A Better Hope*, 176.

identifies the highest value for the secular modern self in one word: self-trust.[23] In a world consumed by the struggle for power, this stance leaves the self to its own devices and limited resources, which is to say its own isolated vulnerability. Hauerwas believes this account of humanity is inadequate and eschews a self that is not located within a historical community that helps it to decipher life. Freedom of self is not born from discarding or disregarding the past, but rather by naming and integrating one's history into one's present existence. To live honestly in the present, the self must acknowledge its dependence on others and its inextricable connection to its past.[24] For a self that believes itself autonomous, socialization is anathema. In reality, since all are inescapably socialized by virtue of living in a given context, the self relies not only on God but on others. Again, Charry reinforces Hauerwas when she argues that self-sufficiency and self-construction are betrayed by the social construction of the self, which always requires a dependence on outside parties.[25]

Hauerwas's deconstruction of autonomy contributes to a theology of self and identity in migration in two ways. First of all, from a sociological perspective, cultures differ in their promotion or renunciation of this sense of autonomy and the degree to which it is embedded in the social infrastructure of their societies. Individuals learn their culture's version of autonomy contextually and adapt accordingly. Migration into another culture, then, can present a shift in the level of autonomy individuals are expected to possess. An appreciation of a particular society's historical view of autonomy can assist individuals in their adjustment to new communities. By the same token, an understanding of identity differentiations between what is considered to be public and private and what is considered to be communal and individual can guide a variety of interactions, whether they are business, religious, political, academic, or personal in nature. Secondly, from a theological perspective, self-autonomy is antithetical to Christian faith and practice. The Christian self acknowledges a dependence on a divine God and understands the purpose of a socially constructed self. The Christian self develops precisely through a process of socialization that includes the innervation of God's Spirit and the influence of groups such as one's family and church. Rather than reveling in unattachment, Christians are called to be deeply tied to each other, to be bound by faith even more than by nation. This sense of belonging can profoundly affect the migration experience of the Christian, for as a member of one global church,

23. Charry, "Crisis of Modernity," 99.
24. Hauerwas, *Community of Character*, 171, 181.
25. Charry, "Crisis of Modernity," 97, 99–103.

the migrant has relatives around the world.[26] As will be further explained below, Hauerwas's theology of self and identity is especially pertinent to the wayfarer's experience.

A Dependent Self

All of existence is contingent upon something outside itself, and human existence is no exception.[27] The self is dependent upon both the divine community by which it dwells and the human community in which it dwells.

Divine Dependence

In the Christian narrative, God imparts history to humans, and they in turn acknowledge God's existence in order to comprehend this history. Since the Creator enacts a project that humanity neither designed nor can anticipate, the self is dependent by nature and receives life as a gift. To exist, then, is to be at risk and, in fact, helpless.[28] The self was not crafted to function alone; it was made to relate to its Originator and to others. To operate truthfully, the self needs the other to both affirm the veracity of a situation as well as to challenge the self's delusion. Hauerwas discusses the dependency of the self in light of two populations: the elderly and the disabled. For a time the young can feign control, independence, and strength, but inescapably, aging takes its toll. This stark reality informs persons of their limited power and finitude.[29] The gradual but dramatic decline to death discloses the true nature of the self. Secondly, Hauerwas examines the lives of the disabled to claim that ontological dependency is a reality for all human existence. The disabled refute the claim that contingency is a choice. They instead exemplify what it is to *be* human—that is, reliant—rather than rational or self-determined.[30]

Just as the self has no hand in its own existence, it has little power to dictate or arrange its own circumstances. Notwithstanding its capacity to affect others, the self is limited in its ability to manage life.[31] When the self recognizes this dependency, it becomes free to learn to live as a creature. The

---

26. Hauerwas, *Peaceable Kingdom*, 150.

27. Hauerwas, *Performing the Faith*, 120–21, 129.

28. Hauerwas, *Community of Character*, 11.

29. Hauerwas, *A Better Hope*, 151, 177, 184.

30. Reinders, "Virtue of Writing," 57–59.

31. Hauerwas and Vanier, *Living Gently*, 92–93.

discipline of learning its own contingency teaches the self not to confuse itself with divinity and, in an embrace of its created status, how to discern what forms of mortal worship are not idolatrous.[32]

Communal Dependence

The idea of a self that is detached from a sense of familial, social, and historical rootedness, individually derived, and autonomously rational, has fuelled the current Kantian notion of an isolated self since the Enlightenment (1600–1700s).[33] Hauerwas's theology of self, by contrast, has been described as "person-in-community," meaning that a person's existence fundamentally includes community.[34] A Christian's identity includes both attachment to and input from the church community within local and global contexts. The individual Christian does not exist apart from the church but is formed by the church, which is the God-given collective to cultivate christological virtue and to moderate self-deception (Jer 49:16).[35] Moreover, this alien community is not primarily purposed for kinship or to bolster the individual ego; the purpose of community is to help individuals faithfully follow The Way—the person of Christ Jesus—and to reflect the coming kingdom (John 14:6).[36]

Hauerwas describes identity formation along the same lines as ethical formation. He stresses the communal formation of Christians and how they are trained to see and live the truth of Christian convictions together. Just as procedural ethics are not innately discovered and must be acquired, so is the Christian identity not self-derived but rather taught and learned. Christians initially do not know who they are; God's Spirit, the Bible, church tradition, and the Christian community instruct them. The ecclesial self is incomprehensible outside of a historical narrative tradition. One's individual Christian identity must be learned and formed in the community of other Christians, in a mentoring dynamic similar to Christ's pattern of discipleship. Secondly, individuals forget who they are. The church, as God's alien community in the world, teaches the nature of an individual's true identity in Christ and reminds when this truth is forgotten.[37]

---

32. Lash, "Immense Darkness," 278.
33. Hauerwas and Willimon, *Resident Aliens*, 79, 100–101.
34. Richardson, "What's Going On?," 240.
35. Hauerwas and Willimon, *Resident Aliens*, 77–78, 81, 85, 123, 131, 136.
36. Cartwright, "Hauerwas's Essays," 670.
37. Hauerwas and Willimon, *Resident Aliens*, 79, 91, 100–102, 109.

The renovation of the self comes not from its own ability, but from God's Spirit as it works through a person's congregational community.[38] Since people are members of multiple communities that are defined by region, profession, and citizenship, Christians are not members of only a sacred community. The church, however, guides the self to form its Christian character through the sacraments and discipleship in shared communal participation.[39] Hauerwas holds that there can be no "individualistic conceptions of virtue"; they are communally derived.[40] He emphasizes the church as God's essential tool for the individual transformation of lives. The communal witness of the church testifies to how one should live—truthfully, obediently, and habitually, grounded in the knowledge of Christ's story from the biblical text, steeped in the historical church tradition, and guided by God's Spirit in the present day.[41] Greer ties Hauerwas to Augustine in their shared assessment that 1) the formation of Christian character comes through one's community and through the teaching of its narrative, and 2) the truth of the scriptural story necessarily leads to demonstrations of truth.[42]

Transformation of Self by Conversion

Hauerwas asserts that the self is fractured and unsettled, incapable of independent integration. Because of this division, it is unable to be moral and requires a turn to a new manner of living truthfully (Rom 3:21–25). How, then, is the self reformed? God's Spirit enacts this change within an apprenticeship of a particular community: the church.[43]

Hauerwas summarizes:

> The New Testament assertion that the purpose [is] to change lives, to be *re-formed* in light of the stunning assertions of the gospel. . . . This we can know, not through accommodation, but through conversion. . . . Everyone does not already believe that he or she is a sinner. We must be taught that we sin.[44]

38. Charry, "Crisis of Modernity," 109.
39. Hauerwas, *Christian Existence*, 15.
40. Ibid., 76–77.
41. Ibid., 10–11.
42. Greer, "Sighing," 28–31.
43. Hauerwas, *Community of Character*, 128–31.
44. Hauerwas and Willimon, *Resident Aliens*, 28, emphasis added.

Hauerwas understands that theology can be extended to personal identity, and the self cannot realize its identity without conversion. The self must first acknowledge itself as broken and inclined toward evil (Jer 17:9; Rom 3:10–12). Only after acknowledging the role of justice may the self seek deliverance, redemption, and change. The Christian identity is born out of this drastic change. The self undergoes a conversion; the former self dies in order for a genuine self to be regenerated. This new self is baptized and raised to life in the identity of Christ and as a part of one entity, the church.

Rather than defining salvation as a moment when self-understanding is reborn, Hauerwas and Willimon declare that it is "a baptism into a community" after one is captivated by the powerfully true story of God's Word, Israel, and the church.[45] The self transforms as it learns and imitates Christ's story within a church community over the course of time.[46] This protracted process puts away the former self through discipleship, apprenticeship, and a new manner of living within the church (Col 3:1–17). The self does not forget what it once was but understands its new narrative and lives out this new truth.[47] Freedom unto conversion is progressive. In this present existence, the self more closely approximates a righteous nature by discerning and embracing which desires are life-giving and shunning those that bring death.[48] Greer suggests that the life of a Christian reflects a migration from diffusion to cohesion in its journey toward embracing God.[49]

When one applies Hauerwas's discussion on the nature and origin of ethics to the subject of identity, it becomes clear that one's Christian identity originates from witnessing God. For Christians, God can be seen most clearly in Jesus's human form (Heb 1:3). Identity, that which distinguishes the self, is determined and interpreted by the individual against the character

---

45. Ibid., 59, 91. Self-formation—sanctification—is ongoing, as opposed to justification, the point at which a believer's sins are forgiven and one is declared righteous by God (Heb 10:14, ESV). Salvation is a legal pronouncement of moral justification enacted by God and received through faith by the believer. Hauerwas seems to place salvation in the sociality of the church. Hauerwas echoes Yoder in that salvation is the "creation of a social body." Sider, "Friendship, Alienation, Love," 64. "Justification is only another way of talking about sanctification, since it requires our transformation by initiation into the new community made possible by Jesus's death and resurrection." For Hauerwas, they form an unbroken cord in the continuity of the Christian self. Hauerwas, *Peaceable Kingdom*, 94.

46. Hauerwas, *Community of Character*, 128, 131.

47. Hauerwas, *A Better Hope*, 151.

48. Burrell, "Can We Be Free?," 48–49.

49. Greer, "Sighing," 15, 25–27.

and nature of the Divine Source.[50] God's incarnation and behavior on the cross, according to Hauerwas, crucially defines the self and what it means to be human "in Jesus." Jesus, in that act of self-extension, bridged relations between individuals and showed that the boundaries of self, according to human understanding, were misplaced. Secondly, the Bible informs the self of its identity as well as its character, not because their textual form is narrative, but because they describe the nature of God. Thirdly, the church informs the self. The church, through its practice of community, teaches the individual to know, to recover, and to remember itself in alignment with God's story.[51] Christian witnesses can only be shaped through baptism into the church and by becoming part of the community God redeemed through Christ.[52]

TRANSFORMATION OF CHRISTIAN IDENTITY

In addition to the myth of autonomy, the dependency of the self, and the reality of story for self-construal, the Christian self is transformed, and its identity takes on new theological implications. Hauerwas outlines several of these implications in a non-uniform fashion when he explains that this new identity positions the self as migrant, alien, and as a minority power in the Christian narrative. Hauerwas maintains that humanity was "created for happiness," a state that comes from amity with God. To approach this state of happiness, however, requires an utter transformation of self.[53]

Identity of a Transformed Self

As the self and identity can interchangeably characterize one's orientation and lifestyle, Hauerwas does not significantly differentiate between the two. Instead, Hauerwas introduces thematic components of Christian life, which include the migrant, alien, and minority nature of Christian identity.

---

50. Hauerwas and Willimon, *Resident Aliens*, 90, 121–22.

51. Hauerwas, *Community of Character*, 49, 55, 91.

52. Hauerwas, *A Better Hope*, 125–28. Some actualities can only be realized post-transformation, Hauerwas, *Grain of the Universe*, 50–61.

53. Hauerwas and Vanier, *Living Gently*, 95–96.

Christian Identity as Migrant

A physical sojourn is a purposeful movement toward an attainable goal or achievement.[54] The Christian identity likewise involves a purposeful migration: a journey to God. Hauerwas highlights the Christian identity of migration in two respects, the first of which is migration within the self by the daily practice of Christian virtues. The self's form, its character, increasingly conforms by this to the person of Christ.[55] The Christian self, in seeking obedience to God, migrates and is recreated by God's grace through the Holy Spirit. Hauerwas reminds us that Christ's command to follow him called his disciples to step into a journey and to *move* from their present location, not in some self-guided direction but after him.[56] Each follower of Christ, then, decides to become a migrant and to leave one's former sense of self (Matt 26:40–1; Rom 7:7–24). This alters the process of self-decision; decisions are made not by the individual alone, but in keeping with Christ's commands and in communion with other believers. This stance radically departs from the philosophies of humanism, secularism, positivism, atheism, and rationalism—all of which share a penchant for self-devotion.[57]

Secondly, the Christian is a migrant in one's self-formation and as a member of the church community. One makes up part of an alienated collective. In fact, Hauerwas questions how much Christians have become affiliated with church accommodation of the state if they do not feel a sense of exile in world affairs and political imaginations (1 Pet 1:1). The narrative of God must be continually remembered to not forget the temporality of the present. While the world pursues individual wealth and pleasure, the Christian identity contrasts sharply. As Christians, a group of strangers are transformed into one identity and one communion as the body of Christ, and together they migrate expectantly toward the Eschaton.[58]

Christian Identity as Alien

Hauerwas contends that the United States' history of political liberalism, with its false conception of the self and individual rights, has created a

54. I refer to voluntary migration rather than forced migration. However, even those moved involuntarily are not without the sovereign shadow of God's presence and purposeful maneuvering.

55. Bauerschmidt, "Aquinas," 26–27.

56. Jesus's commands to follow him are many: Matt 4:19; 8:22; 9:9; 10:38; 16:24; 19:21; Mark 1:17; 2:14; John 1:43; 10:27; 12:26; 21:19, 22.

57. Hauerwas and Willimon, *Resident Aliens*, 49–50.

58. Ibid., 17–18.

society of strangers. The church, by contrast, functions as a God-knitted community. He employs the term *resident alien* to connote the church's strangeness in and even estrangement from secular society. The term refers to someone who focuses not only on the present world, but also possesses another residence: the kingdom of God. Since the church remains distinct from secular society, the Christian identity is politically and spiritually alien, and Christians should not be daunted if they feel disjointed from societal opinion.[59] Christians may feel more at home in the United States than in other parts of the world, but this feeling will only last so long as the U.S. retains the (fading) acceptance of Christianity that is embedded within its cultural systems.

While an alien status does connote foreignness, it does not necessarily mean withdrawal from society. On the contrary, one's Christian faith can propel engagement at all levels of society (Jer 29:7). The coming eternal city of peace provides the Christian with the imagination to pursue activities of peace and blessing in the present. Rowan Greer likens Hauerwas's stance to that of Augustine when he points out that neither theologian advocates a Christian's withdrawal from society. Rather, as far as heavenly pilgrims can pursue peace in their locale, without capitulation of Christian code and conduct, they should.[60] For example, Hauerwas has helped others apply their alien Christian identities in a critique of the social and political setting of postcolonial Africa in order to point a way forward.[61]

Rasmusson's summation of how the church relates to the state may offer a parallel for the Christian self. He advocates a diaspora ecclesiology in which the church does not compartmentalize its identity. "[This diaspora ecclesiology] will not think of the church as forming a particular (or even private) identity and the nation-state or international communities as shaping more universal (and public) identities."[62] In Rasmusson's vision the church's citizens would share their lives and means with other nationals with a "relative and critical loyalty to local entities." Christians would clamor for neither the self-detached autonomy advocated by the liberal state (as impossible) nor seclusion from the state's civil context (as anathema). They would wholeheartedly invest in society and participate in it both openly and guardedly.

---

59. Ibid., 114–15.

60. Greer, "Sighing," 14–15, 33.

61. Katongole, "Hauerwasian Hooks," 136, 150–51.

62. Rasmusson, "Politics of Diaspora," 111. Religious convictions neither are necessarily private nor should be relegated by the state to be so. See Hauerwas and Vanier, *Living Gently*, 96.

The alien identity of the Christian simultaneously connotes both a distance from and identification with God. As a human, the Christian is ontologically foreign from God, but one bears God's likeness. This likeness is analogous to God's virtue because of the Christian's conversion, an event that makes God's followers appear very strange indeed to the world. Hauerwas speaks of the alien nature of Christian identity more often in relation to this identification with God that creates a foreignness in the world.[63] The Christian is an alien both in rightful difference from God and in rightful difference from the world. In identifying with those whom God does—the weak and the oppressed—the Christian is alienated from a society that praises efficiency, accumulation, and material success. In a world that competes for access to limited goods, Christians learn to imitate the virtues of God through training (Heb 5:14).[64] As Moltmann avows, "We are always inclined to perceive God, the Absolute, only in whatever is like ourselves. What is like us confirms us in our identity, what is alien to us makes us uncertain."[65] This twofold alienation does not grow out of a desire to be different for difference's sake, as it so often does in the modern cultural context.[66] The alien nature of the Christian identity evidences an increasingly Christ-like character (1 John). The believer becomes less alien to God and more alien to a world that pursues different values.

Christian Identity as Minority Power

Hauerwas considers the Christian community a political minority in relation to state power.[67] Hauerwas does not discourage Christians from taking an interest in politics. He stipulates, however, that if their political agenda is to gain power, they have mistaken their identity.[68] Hauerwas and Willimon refer to the collective church as a colony amidst a secular society, and this settlement represents one manner of living amidst pluralism.[69] They compare Christians to the Israelite migrants and note how they were alienated within polytheistic societies. In the second giving of the law, God's command is clear (Deut 6:6–8). The Israelites lived in a foreign land; maintaining their

63. Hauerwas, *Performing the Faith*, 119–20.

64. Ibid., 119, 128.

65. Moltmann, "Theology," 17.

66. Charry, "Crisis of Modernity," 100.

67. Hauerwas, *Christian Existence*, 189.

68. Hauerwas and Willimon, *Resident Aliens*, 19–43.

69. Ibid., 51–52. Colony is a movement of people (the church) and does not connote a permanent settlement made either from satisfaction or withdrawal.

true identity required them to repeatedly remind themselves who they were. Grafted onto this history, Christians belong to heaven's community. Their sojourn is not one to gain earthly power. Instead, Christians should strive to be heaven *on* earth, in the limited sense that 1) they do not seek to force the world's conversion, 2) they, although not yet fully sanctified, reflect the divine life (2 Pet 1:4). This odd community comprises a foreign people in a new countercultural "polis," the church.[70]

Christian identity belongs to those individuals who are "called out" by God to personify Christ and work within the church to advance God's coming kingdom.[71] As such, Hauerwas laments the union of church and state, which has existed from the time of Constantine's reign in 313 CE when the Edict of Milan officially endorsed Christianity.[72] He instead argues that Christianity, as a religious entity, is incompatible with the position of state rule. Christianity is a manner of belief and life and will not be a system of government until God's eschatological kingdom. Christians must remember their identity of difference; to be a Christian is to be an outsider. This identity pursues an alternative lifestyle as well as a different set of customs, morals, and beliefs.

According to Hauerwas, theologians err when they attempt to translate the Christian message into terms the modern world can digest. The accommodation of the gospel to appease modern sensibilities distorts the Christian identity, and the endeavor to make Christianity more palatable in order to obtain cultural power is misplaced. Christians who comply with the status quo (which is, for the populace, the striving for goods and services and, for the elite, the wielding of power to access them regularly) fail to live morally. Since Hauerwas stresses that the world will recognize the truth of Christianity when they see its proponents living authentically (John 17:14, 21), a political movement to culturally legitimize Christianity detours the message that Christian identity is based on being called out from the world (1 John 3:1, 13).[73] The challenge of Hauerwas's proposal—that a communally-shaped Christian identity demonstrates an alternative to the

70. Ibid., 12, 30, 38.

71. Ekklēsia (Gr.) refers to an assembly (Acts 20:28; 1 Cor 1:2; 2 Cor 1:2; 1 Thess 1:1).

72. Hauerwas and Willimon, *Resident Aliens*, 17–18. While Hauerwas laments Constantine, previous kingdoms have consented to various religions which Hauerwas does not mention. King Cyrus II (referred also to as Cyrus the Great) gave Persia's national edict for Judaism after he conquered Babylon in 539 BCE (Dan 6:25–28). The kingdom of Shilla adopted Buddhism as the official religion in 528 CE, and the Yi Dynasty adopted Confucianism in 1394 (both occurring in what is present-day Korea).

73. Ibid., 17–28.

nation-state's ideology—is its spirit of subversion.[74] Living in the manner of Christ is a radical shift in loyalty and poses a potential threat to ruling authorities. For Hauerwas, the Christian identity chooses to culturally marginalize itself. Emmanuel Katongole, in discussing Hauerwas's political claims, emphasizes that the church's political identity offers more than a message of earthly endurance and a focus on the prospect of heaven; the church is the "revolutionary future" for societal change.[75] While Hauerwas may not disagree with this, he has clarified that his primary goal for the Christian in the nation-state *is* survival.[76]

Importance of Narrative for Christian Identity

If history orients the self, then the historical Christian narrative (which is comprised of the Bible and church tradition) reorients the self. While many associate Hauerwas with narrative theology, his employment of narrative has shifted over the decades.[77] While Hauerwas does not believe that a literary genre should birth a theological system, he still finds the concept of narrative useful for two reasons. Firstly, he regards narrative to be instructive for the permanence of self formed from character.[78] One's identity is part of and contingent upon a greater narrative. The self is unified by a narrative as it acquires virtues over time.[79] The story of God, with the cross as its acme, directs self-understanding and gives purpose to being and to the development of character. Secondly, Hauerwas emphasizes the narrative structure of Christian beliefs.[80] One's knowledge of God is, in fact, narrative. A narrative construction of ethics and of identity, then, avoids reductive theological analysis and, because of its relation to character, constructs a better understanding of the knowledge and morality of God.

Hauerwas maintains that narrative aids in the self-construction of identity.[81] The self needs more than a set of rules for a coherent identity;

---

74. Katongole, "Hauerwasian Hooks," 139.

75. Ibid.

76. Hauerwas, "Stanley Hauerwas in Conversation."

77. Cartwright, "Hauerwas's Essays," 625, 651.

78. Hauerwas, *Christian Existence*, 26. Narrative is instructive for "the continuity of self we associate with character."

79. Bauerschmidt, "Aquinas," 28.

80. Hauerwas, *Performing the Faith*, 139, 145. Of chief importance is not that principles are supposedly believed, but how those beliefs are embodied and lived out, Hauerwas, *Peaceable Kingdom*, 16.

81. Hauerwas, *Community of Character*, 94–95, 144.

narrative affords the self a "moral vision," an ability to see beyond its earthly context. Because it is guided by a particular narrative, the Christian community is able to envision how life should be.[82] The stories the self assumes shape its identity, its associations, and its distances.[83] The self is formed by its particular narrative polity—the organized society in which it lives—and garners freedom from it. For the Christian self, freedom comes from belonging to a "truthful polity" that develops virtue in its members.[84]

The narrative of Jesus Christ demonstrates God's character and God's pre-eminence over the world, which shapes the identity of the church and, in a similar fashion, centrally informs the identity of the self.[85] Through belief in the person and the work of Christ, one commits to imitate the character of his life and learn how to negotiate the self and one's social existence. To admit one's powerlessness and shortcomings requires a stance of humility, and, in addition to its need for forgiveness, the Christian self acknowledges that its existence is vulnerable and is a gift.[86] In trusting Christ's declaration and example, one discovers that life is not one's own, and that discovery allows the person to possess self in a way never before realized.[87] By releasing any pre-conceived designs of what it should be, the Christian finds one's self (Mark 8:34–38; John 12:24–26).

Identity, then, is realized and altered in relation to the triune God, whose nature is relayed by the biblical narrative.[88] The self is transformed by this revelation of God's truth: humans are God's creatures who have failed but have also been redeemed. Those who can embrace this truth join the life that is in God. For Hauerwas, the depth of this narrative, which is founded in love, allows the self sufficient space to be and to live truthfully without fear or hiding (1 John 4:18).[89] Not all narrative are equally valid.[90] Hauerwas, describing the Christian narrative, writes, "The church is quite simply those converted, those made vulnerable, to God's history of forgiveness. They are those who have been given a new history, a new story, rather than the world's story."[91]

---

82. Hauerwas, "Church as God's New Language," 142, 165, 171.

83. Katongole, "Hauerwasian Hooks," 136, 142–43.

84. Hauerwas, *Community of Character*, 3.

85. Hauerwas, *Christian Existence*, 162.

86. Hauerwas, *Community of Character*, 37, 50.

87. Hauerwas, *Christian Existence*, 41, 91.

88. Hauerwas, *Community of Character*, 45, 47.

89. Hauerwas, *Christian Existence*, 102–3, 216.

90. Hauerwas, "Church as God's New Language," 170.

91. Hauerwas, *A Better Hope*, 151.

Emmanuel Katongole has drawn out another aspect of narrative from Hauerwas's work in regard to Christian identity. While Christians can create their stories within a given economic and political reality in an attempt to achieve relevance (which Katongole does not favor), Hauerwas instead provides an alternative manner of thinking in story and envisioning social reality that enables humans to flourish in a fresh, imaginative way. From stories come cultures, and these cultures possess a set of beliefs and mores that shape personal identities. The fact that stories can mold worlds means that the Christian story can uniquely influence its social context. Katongole praises Hauerwas for sparking the "Christian social imagination" within the narrative reality of Christian identity.[92] The Christian imagination and human experience, Hauerwas insists, must be narrated by church liturgy within the context of a worshipping community in order to shape Christian identity.[93]

ASSESSMENT OF HAUERWAS

Hauerwas has made an immense contribution to the theology of self and identity. In light of the present summary of his work, however, a few points of vulnerability will be identified. While Hauerwas thoroughly discusses the conceptualization of the individual self in Western modernity (1700–2000s), he forgoes a discussion of the Eastern collective self. Secondly, his argument could be criticized for neglecting the efficacy of individuality. Lastly, because he intentionally does not offer a systematic treatment of the tenets of theology he discusses, he draws criticism for the confusion he creates. These three points of weakness will now be discussed further.

Hauerwas not only forgoes a historical overview of self-understanding, but also largely neglects a discussion of the self beyond the Europe and the United States. What, for example, is an ancient Eastern pagan understanding of the self? What is the Eastern Christian understanding? Hauerwas thoroughly delineates what a European secular understanding of self has come to mean and how this change has infiltrated the North American Christian understanding of the self. His focus, however, remains limited to this Christianity rather than including the Christian self in a global context. Apart from a few individual comments, he does not consider these broader categories.

Hauerwas also risks vilifying individuality altogether. Communality is not inherently superordinate to individuality; both are meaningful and

92. Katongole, "Hauerwasian Hooks," 152.
93. Cartwright, "Hauerwas's Essays," 651.

necessary. He is right to show that individualism has become unevenly scaled in the American mind, but his efforts to critique unchecked individualism may obfuscate the importance of individual obedience to God, which is as crucial as communal obedience (Mic 6:8). Communities, like individuals, can be misled, and individuals can be instrumental in calling a community to task.[94] Secondly, individualism can breed commendable characteristics, about which Hauerwas does not expound. As offered by Musschenga, ethical values that have been promoted in individualistic societies include individual human worth, self-determination, personal responsibility, authenticity, self-analysis, self-development, uniqueness, and privacy.[95] Hauerwas seems to neglect the fact that one's identity in Christ is both individual and collective. An individual member in the corporate body of Christ does derive one's Christian identity from the community, but, just as importantly, one personally undergoes a unique and individual experience in Christ by God's Spirit.

The positive aspects of individualism should be differentiated from "selfism." Selfism, furthers "a herd mentality that has much more in common with a sort of socially encouraged communitarianism . . . to conform to a mythical, community-shared construct."[96] While the terms offer a helpful distinction, both individualism and selfism can be ill-directed. The agent's motivation—whether that agent is an individual or a community— makes the difference. If, for example, the motivation is hedonistic, societal harmony and mutual respect will not be achieved.

One does not read Hauerwas without learning that, for the Christian, virtue and identity are cultivated within the church community. Despite his extensive description of how virtue develops within the church, Hauerwas's ecclesiology, with its significant implications for the self, is ill-defined.[97] Hauerwas leaves the identity of the church underdeveloped, even nebulous, and leaves room for widely varying interpretations (which seems to be his intention). Any unqualified recreation of the church's identity can lead to erroneous conclusions about its nature. Hauerwas may have an explicit identity of the church in mind, but he leaves it rather undefined, perhaps because of his belief that the church is an "extended argument."[98] On the one hand, Hauerwas wisely leaves flexibility for ecclesiological identity to reflect

94. Examples of individuals who have named the madness of society include a host of biblical prophets, William Wilberforce, Mahatma Gandhi, Rosa Parks, and Wangari Maathai, among others.

95. Musschenga, "Personalized Identity," 26.

96. Carson, "Contrarian Reflections."

97. Richardson, "What's Going On?," 241.

98. Hauerwas, *Peaceable Kingdom*, 107.

periods of history and cultures in their diversity of expression. On the other, the body of Christ must have sufficient definition to be distinguishable from other groups. It is the distinctiveness of the church that crucially defines individual Christian identity, a question Hauerwas is applauded for raising but does not answer with doctrinal clarity.[99]

Another deficiency of Hauerwas's theology of self and identity is his weakly expressed soteriology. Hauerwas's goal has never been to relay a systematic theology, as he is fundamentally opposed to the misleading Enlightenment assumptions of "system."[100] He discusses the nature of the self and the Christian life intensely, yet, his description of the gospel message is unclear. If that is not defined, a description of what Christian identity is will remain elusive. Hauerwas does not dwell on certain questions that are central to a discussion of self and identity; namely, what is the message of the gospel? How and when, soteriologically, does this identity transformation occur? What makes one a Christian? Answers to these questions critically direct the Christian explication of the self and identity. Notwithstanding his sincere call to appropriate the biblical text in the life of its community, Hauerwas eschews a stronger doctrinal description of the gospel for Christian self-formation.[101]

As for salvation and its transformation of the self, Hauerwas stresses certain elements of the story while neglecting others. First, he accentuates practice over proposition. While he aligns himself with Aquinas's view that action is being, Hauerwas seems to promote certain kinds of behavior without first discussing what one must believe. Certainly, one is as one does, and Hauerwas illumines this truth well, especially within the context of North American cultural Christianity. This maxim, however, is not unconditional. Hauerwas, while promoting what he considers to be a Christian lifestyle, seems to downplay which beliefs drive behavior and how they do so. Actions spring from thoughts, and thoughts from actions, fashioning each other. His emphasis may be neglectful, since the biblical text encourages both action and reflection and by no means emphasizes the former over the latter.[102] Hauerwas rightfully warns that "insights" mean little if they are not translated into behavior.[103] While many will be found false at the time

99. Englehardt, "Belligerent Kingdom," 202. Hauerwas's lack of "dogmatic interpretation" is addressed in Healy, *Hauerwas*, 71.

100. Heide, *System and Story*, xiii–xxiv. See also, Hauerwas, *Approaching the End*, 4.

101. While Hauerwas resists defining what beliefs constitute what makes one a Christian, he rightly argues that Christian faith is physically expressed. Hauerwas, "Church Matters," 347–58.

102. The content of faith is essential to produce character, that is, love (2 Pet 1:5–7).

103. Hauerwas, *Performing the Faith*, 139.

of reckoning (Matt 7:21–23), the gospel message is not, however, served by neglecting its clear verbal articulation. In this regard, Hauerwas muddies the soteriological waters. Healy further critiques:

> [Practices] are "conceptually formed" by the logic of Christian belief, by the broader Christian understanding of who the triune God is and how that God acts toward us. . . . The point is that there is a conceptual component within that embodiment, so our practices involve the whole person. . . . Without due regard to the logic of belief as such, unconflated with more dominant accounts of the logic of Christian living and its truthfulness and benefits, the conceptuality of our practices can become distorted.[104]

Secondly, Hauerwas accentuates the body of Christ over the Holy Spirit, if only by virtue of his voluminous outpourings on ecclesiology without a sufficient consideration of pneumatology. Hauerwas asserts that the church is the vehicle for self-formation while inadequately emphasizing the Holy Spirit's role.

Finally, Hauerwas seems to emphasize community and nonviolence over faith and holiness.[105] Is nonviolence *the* linchpin for the expression of a Christian identity, the singular demonstration of true faith? Hauerwas's absolutism (interestingly, on this issue and not others) neglects many who have demonstrated faith in Christ despite their views on or participation in military war. He overlooks how many, who promote the use of force for self-defense or protection, practice lives of nonviolence. Nonviolence, then, is not necessarily the litmus test for who is a Christian. Faith, a very specific assertion of the content of that faith, is. Hauerwas would insist that true faith demands nonviolence, but the very process of truth he promotes—that the liturgical community over time discovers truth—leaves an opening for the legitimate practice of violence in times of war.[106]

Hauerwas is accused of supplying a theology that bolsters the present societal "discourse of negation."[107] Others confirm Hauerwas's negative political theology and construe it positively; Wannenwetsch, for example, submits that a "presence of the absence" is needed to illustrate the good that is missing.[108] Hauerwas denies that his position is one of withdrawal from

---

104. Healy, *Hauerwas*, 117–18, 120.

105. Englehardt, "Belligerent Kingdom," 208. Also, Hunter, *To Change the World*, 150–66.

106. Cartwright, "Hauerwas's Essays," 639.

107. Hunter, *To Change the World*, 166.

108. Wannenwetsch, "Representing the Absent," 168, 172, 182.

the world or that a critique of liberalism requires such a withdrawal.[109] In his discussion of the self, he does well to describe what the self is (dependent) and what it is not (autonomous). Therefore, the charge of negation in this regard may be unfounded, for, as Hauerwas argues against any particular topic, he simultaneously argues for a greater obedience to Christ.

Allowing for his criticism of systematic theology, Hauerwas's lack of specificity in his biblical theology leaves it unclear where to engage him in regard to key distinctions that, according to historical tradition, define a Christian identity. Despite his capacious writing, he has penned little on the Holy Spirit and salvation, which are central facets of the Christian narrative. Hauerwas's inclination is to theologically describe the Christian manner of living rather than defending particularities, save nonviolence.[110] Doctrine and lifestyle, however, are intimately intertwined and should be expounded in tandem.

In conclusion, Stanley Hauerwas offers an important resource for the Christian community in his assessment of the contemporary self and the nature of Christian identity. Hauerwas voices a minority opinion at times, but perhaps his stance typifies where he, as a follower of Christ, wishes to be—at the margins.

109. Hauerwas, "Christianity," 522–35; Hauerwas, "Reflection on Dependency," 195.

110. Richardson, "What's Going On?," 237.

6

A Theology of Christian Identity

TO BE A SELF is to evaluate levels of fulfillment in life. One is not wholly satisfied to breathe, to eat, to rest; one inclines to understand, to create, to remember, to strive. This pursuit of personal fulfillment drives human behavior. One pursues that with which one identifies, and one is less inclined to pursue that with which one does not identify. This simple dichotomy illustrates the compelling, inverted golden rule of self: I will do what I deem best for my self. This maxim emerges not only in individualistic cultures that emphasize personal empowerment, but also in collective cultures where individuals traditionally view themselves within a group orientation. In each context, the individual conforms to the established pattern of expectations for one's own good. The internal motivation of the self is to preserve itself, regardless of the external cultural system that surrounds it. People do engage in self-destructive behavior but are inclined generally toward self-preservation.

If the nature of the self is to seek its own good, and groups are comprised of self-serving individuals, several questions come to the fore. How do individuals and groups identify with one another? In a world of limited material resources and increasing globalization, if one hopes to coexist peacefully with others who define justice differently, how will a theology of identity make an impact? Indeed, what is a theology of identity, and what insight can it offer into how diverse persons should interrelate in a global society? What specific insights, then, could be applied to a theology of identity in migration?

The work of three interlocutors, Miroslav Volf, Jenny Pak, and Stanley Hauerwas, will enhance the following theological discussion of identity.

Whereas Volf analyzes the subject of identity at an individual level and sees it as driven by the constitution of the self as self-and-other for all contexts, Hauerwas emphasizes identity at the corporate level of the church and offers a communal Christian identity in society. Pak tenders a thorough navigation of the individual identity within dual cultural contexts from a psychological perspective. This chapter will establish the common ground among all three scholars in regard to their independent but common claims that the self is given, related, and divided. These claims will serve as benchmarks for a further discussion of a theology of identity that is specifically applied to the context of physical and spiritual migration. A discussion of theological aspects of migration, increasingly relevant in a century of rapid globalization and rising rates of transnationalism, will assist in a later articulation of a theology of Christian identity in migration (chapter 9). The identity of the converted self will be examined in terms of the nature of its departure, belonging, and displacement.

THEOLOGICAL NATURE OF SELF AND IDENTITY

A Christian theological and anthropological view of humankind distinguishes it from the rest of livingkind in nature. Whereas animist religions consider humanity to be a part of nature, Christian theology (as well as the monotheistic religions of Judaism and, in some respects, Islam) holds that human beings, since they are made in the image of God, are distinct from the created order and unlike any other natural creature. This view also presupposes that God is separate from nature. Humanity, because of its particular relation to God, is endowed with personhood and holds a unique status in the natural order.[1] While humanity and nature share the same originator and are kept alive by God's breath (Gen 1:20–29; 2:7; Acts 17:28; Col 1:17–18), personhood affords humanity distinction and, by it, special consideration. A clear theological understanding of creation gives way to a deeper sense of self and identity.

In a consideration of human identity, Christian theologians consult the Hebrew and Greek Testaments for their anthropological and spiritual descriptions of humanity.[2] The biblical hierarchy of the divine Maker and human creation that is presented in these texts offers practical implications for a theology of identity. Firstly, it implies that God has certain intentions for humanity. Secondly, it asserts that, by considering these intentions, humanity may understand its identity. Pak's Christian theological view, filtered

1. Moltmann, "Theology," 34–35, 38–40, 56.
2. Luther, *Freedom*, 49.

through her psychological lens, shares some common presuppositions with Volf and Hauerwas, and she applies these in her study of bicultural identity. Pak asserts that the contemporary understanding of human nature is limited and that certain approaches should be expanded to allow perspectives from other disciplines, such as psychology in theology and vice versa.[3]

In a treatment of the theological nature of self and identity, three aspects of the self will be discussed. Firstly, the nature of the self will be explored. Next, the relationality of the self will be considered, including a description of how its relational component yields the potential for division within the self. In its propensity for vacillation and deception, the self can be left wanting, and its identity formation can be stunted.

Self as Given

The self's genesis originates from God's spoken word; the self is formed by God's address.[4] Humans possess a self, not by their own achievement, but because they are God's creations. This "given" nature of the self indicates its dependency, and a theology of self and identity must engage this divine intention (1 Cor 4:7). How, then, should the self live?

The self lives reflectively and reveals the divine artwork of creation, not because humanity is divine in essence, but because it reflects God's handiwork.[5] The self reflects God because God is both transcendent from and near to creation. For those in Christ, God's presence resides in them, yet they remain distinct entities. God, with omniscience and omnipresence, intimately knows the self greater than it can understand itself.[6] One is not to think of this reflective capacity merely as the imitation of an imposing, impersonal God; it is God's nearness that frees humans to act. Secondly, humans are participative in this reflective capacity, not merely used.

The self must also live within a historical particularity that is set in a given time and place as well as through the framework of a particular culture and language. The fact that the self is not its own possession does not mean that it is bereft of choice or any self-direction. It does mean that the self is not self-generating outside of any system. As Hauerwas argues, no standpoint exists at which the self can position itself so as to be removed from its particular story.[7] Rather than claiming its independent disloca-

3. Yangarber-Hicks et al., "Invitation," 345–46.

4. Horton, *Christian Faith*, 391, 396.

5. McGrath, *Theology*, 60–62.

6. Volf, *Free of Charge*, 48–49.

7. Hauerwas, *Community of Character*, 148–49.

tion, the given self understands its existence as a part of a larger story. The Christian narrative claims to be a story of truth that accurately portrays a reality into which the self can enter.

Rather than possessing an autonomous constitution, people derive their selfhood and identity from God. Although they exist within a creational state, people do possess self-determination. This human state constitutes both freedom for the self as well as a considerable degree of constraint. The given self cannot do everything it desires. It is constrained to live within the finite human limits of breath, power, generation, and capacity. The self does, however, have a measure of flexibility or freedom; it is not merely a product of nature that is constrained by the passive determination of genetic or environmental stimuli. Precisely because humanity receives its personhood from God, it is distinctly able to interact with its environment in an integrative and creative manner.[8]

For the Christian, God frees the self to benevolently live for the benefit of the other (Rom 6:13; Eph 2:4–10). While freedom is often thought of in terms of release from a named constraint, freedom for the self extends beyond the ability to avoid certain alternatives; it also includes the freedom to move *toward* new alternatives. The self is not fully itself and does not live as an authentic being if not in Christ. The self cannot be itself without imitating Christ's love of the triune God. The self is an imitation of God incarnate, a mirror of Christ, and a testimony of God's presence to the world. The Christian self seeks to be who God created it to be. Conversely, the Christian self, with its newfound freedom in Christ, is constrained by that same love to live virtuously (Rom 12:1–2, 9; 2 Cor 5:14–15). Consider Burrell's depiction of the new self in his discussion of the will:

> [T]he point of our freedom [is] to return everything to the One from whom we have received everything . . . it can be accomplished . . . through discrete actions embodying an orientation to the good. The image is progressive: as infatuations are sloughed off, noble desires are consummated, and the true self emerges . . . to be assimilated to the One whose gift of being constitutes our very existence.[9]

The self's response to its givenness can be acceptance, rejection, or any variation in between. The Christian self chooses to receive God's gift of life by this response: to appropriate its actions from an identity of givenness and live out its accompanying calling. By illustration, the art of giving is best reciprocated by the art of receiving. When a legitimate gift—such as God's gift

8. Volf, *After Our Likeness*, 184–85.
9. Burrell, "Can We Be Free?," 48–49.

of the self to humanity—is given, credit is not due to the recipient's efforts; the gift is humbly accepted and acknowledged to be an act of grace that was granted with pleasure and good intent.[10] What of the self that does not wish to be given? The self can deny its given state, but God cannot deny the responsibility to it as its Creator. Those who do not acknowledge God's existence are permitted to live in this manner without forfeiting God's blessing of creation or sustenance (Matt 5:44–46). They demonstrate the freedom of the self to believe as it wills.[11] Continuing with the previous illustration, a legitimate gift can also be effectually refused.

If the self is indeed given by God, how is "being given" a gift? Firstly, the human spirit experiences a powerful good when it realizes it is *wanted*. Creation is an animated spring of joy. God's creative power is blessing; to participate as part of God's creation is to be *blessed*. To experience life, pleasure, risk, adventure, and relation is to live out of this blessing, both in reception and in reciprocal giving. To experience the dynamism of flexibility, creativity, and choice—albeit within creaturehood—is unique. God's creative plan develops progressively; the human self is not born into a regimented pattern with a creative ceiling but rather into a God-given self with an imaginative ability to grow, adapt, and become. Still, the fact that the human self is designed by a Giver not of its own choosing offends the independent self.[12] A gift, by definition, is not controlled by the recipient. Thus, the Giver, and to an extent the gift itself, maintain an independence from the self.[13] Jesus demonstrated supremely the art of receiving the givenness of self. Although very God, Jesus "did not consider equality with God something to be grasped" and accepted the human condition (Phil 2:6). Humility offers the self a passage to receive its givenness.

Self as Related

Not only is the self given by God, but it is also determined by its relationality. To exist is to relate to others. Since the self is intrinsically social rather than an isolated unit, it is set in relation from the time of its conception.[14]

10. The discussion of the classic doctrine of creation not being an imposition of power is helpful in Williams, *On Christian Theology*, 68–73.

11. Burrell argues that unless a creator exists, human freedom cannot in Burrell, "Can We Be Free?," 37–52.

12. The dilemma of givenness is similarly illustrated in children who do not have the capacity to choose to which parents they are born.

13. Hauerwas, "Reflection on Dependency," 155.

14. Horton, *Christian Faith*, 380.

Volf describes that the self and, by extension, its identity include the other in its construction.[15] As it navigates life, the self acknowledges the roles that others play, and it is from the other that the self learns who it is or who it could become. The vulnerability required to admit that the other is indispensable for the self's wholeness, however, must be learned.[16] In recent decades of scholarship, this concept of the relationality of the self has reached the foreground.

The relationship of the self with the other does not merely refer to the human other. How does the self relate to the divine Other? Humans, according to the Judeo-Christian interpretation, were created "in a particular history of a covenantal relatedness" with an intrinsic connection to God, to each other, and to their environment. Far from Descartes's idea of *res cogitans* (a contemplative thinking self that is abstracted from the world and the body) is the Christian understanding that the self is related.[17] This relatedness locates the notion of personhood in God's creative presence and incorporates the material, relational, and reflective dimensions of the self.[18] Charles Taylor terms the unattached self, independent from God and its environment in an individualistic fervor, "disengaged." In stark contrast to the unattached self, in Christian anthropology the self engages in special relationships—with God, humanity, and nature—and assumes the responsibility to maintain these relationships. Horton notes "covenantal relationality is essential to our being human."[19] The self does not exist in abstraction, but in continual relationship with others. Human self-consciousness was not meant to be a consciousness of one's separate existence, as if detached and unconnected. Self-consciousness instead means an awareness of one's relational existence and intimacy with others—God, persons, and nonhuman creation.

A person does not relate in covenant to God alone; the self has been created in covenant with others. Before the Fall, self-consciousness included an essential awareness of others; the individually focused I-consciousness

15. Volf, *Exclusion and Embrace*, 66. Hauerwas has similarly described this relation of the self to the other. Loving the part of the other that is dissimilar to the self more significantly constitutes friendship. See Reinders, "Virtue of Writing," 67.

16. Hauerwas, *Community of Character*, 5; Hauerwas and Coles, *Christianity*.

17. Horton, *Christian Faith*, 379.

18. Seigel, *Idea of the Self*, 5–6. Seigel names these three dimensions but not in relation to divine relation.

19. Horton, *Christian Faith*, 380. Horton notes the description of the self as disengaged is reflected even in Platonic thought where embodiment was thought to be a curse and "the divine and immortal soul [strives] to ascend above its imprisonment in the realm of appearances" was thought to be the ideal (378, 380).

did not exist apart from the relatedness of the we-consciousness.[20] In its present state, however, the self's sense of interdependence has been threatened.

The covenantal relatedness of the self, rather than merely its relationality, presupposes that the self is created and placed within a network of relationships. For the Christian, this network includes the foremost relationship between the individual self and God, as well as relationships between the individual self and others (the physical world, the family, the human world, and the church). Not only does the self relate to the other, but it also connects in a special way to certain others that define and determine, in large part, its existence. This relatedness directs one's self-existence. In this sense the Eastern conceptualization of relationships rather than the historically Western model more closely resembles the biblical design for the self. Eastern kinship-based societies more readily understand the related self, since individuals do not separate themselves from the group dynamic as strictly.[21] Despite the fact that Confucian thought and Christ's teachings reflect differing motivations and outcomes, the concept of the related self is present in both accounts.

This concept of the covenantal relatedness of humanity encompasses both Volf's description of the self as self-with-other and Hauerwas's self in need of community. Although Volf seems to approach the issue, neither discusses human communion directly in terms of this covenantal premise at length.[22] Perhaps the best expression of the related self can be seen in Enoch Wan's maxim, "I AM; therefore, 'i am'"(Exod 3:14; John 8:58; 10:30).[23] Because of its relationship to God, the self exists within God's existence. I AM indicates an ever-present God who ties the self's existence along a God-constructed time continuum. The self subsists by this relationship (Col 1:17).

Because humans are creaturely and interrelated, they are neither what they make themselves to be nor what they merely imagine themselves to be. Identity is not only revealed, but also reflects a being's Creator. Christian identity reflects a Christian's union with Christ. Although personal identity begins within divine creation and revelation, the self possesses the remarkable capacity to either respond to or reject its creaturely status and, therefore, shape its identity.

20. Ibid., 387.

21. Rosenlee, *Confucianism and Women*, 121.

22. Volf, *After Our Likeness*, 182–83, 206.

23. Wan, "Comparative Study." Wan prefers an ontological view of the self based on "relational realism."

Self as Divided

Unlike some contemporary accounts, Medi Ann Volpe's account of Christian identity construction acknowledges how sin can perniciously block its formation. Beyond a mere discussion of *eros*, she presses for a consideration of not only desire, but also the effect of sin on desire in the construction of subjectivity and Christian formation.[24] In fact, she asserts that "desire orients the self," but sin both darkens human understanding and turns it off-course to such a thoroughgoing extent that one becomes disoriented.[25] These "disordered desires" then allow human beings to:

> desire created things rather than the creator. Although humans
> were created in relationship with God and ought to desire God
> as a function of having been created *imago Dei*, this desire no
> longer orders the soul as it should.[26]

N. T. Wright clarifies that it is not the self's created status that is evil; rather, evil enters when the created turns away from its Creator. This rebellion against worship and rejection of God (whose essence is all that is good and holy) in favor of a lesser pleasure or a less exacting deity is the idolatry that leads humanity further astray. The reverberations of this rebellion have been and still are enormous, since they cause the entire cosmos—not merely humanity—to become disjointed.[27]

Since the self is created but also volitional, it can become disoriented and fragmented. This internal division can occur when the self attempts to resolve its dual values internally within personal conscience and by externally negotiating cultural expectations through social relationships. The self can be consistently disrupted by a sense of shame, the pursuit of validation, the act of hiding (from itself and others), and by an understanding that not all is as it should be. This disruption can result in innumerable consequences—two of which are competing motivations and a susceptibility to deception.

Values Conflict and Vacillation of Self

The first consequence of this internal fragmentation is a vacillation of competing motivations and values that reside within the self. In a given

24. Volpe, *Christian Identity*, 12, 19, 29, 36, 51, 230–33.

25. Ibid., 73–74, 156–57.

26. Ibid., 19–20.

27. Wright, *Surprised by Hope*, 95.

circumstance, the self must act by choosing from an array of options. The differences between options, values, and priorities necessitate selective judgment, particularly when their outcomes are mutually exclusive. One cannot typically achieve both outcomes equally at the same time. Moreover, as the self is inevitably shaped by its relation to the other, the differences that exist between the self and the other create friction and formation. For any given action, the self faces a choice between self-preservation and self-effacement. Some actions, of course, are inconsequential, but actions are rarely without motivation toward a meaningful outcome. The self may promote itself at the expense of the other, and yet it is capable of beneficent action toward the other at its own expense. What, therefore, determines the self's course of action?

In one sense, the self is fairly consistent in its drive for self-promotion.[28] Ultimately, however, the self lives a divided, undulating existence. It displays its internal division through its contradictory attitudes and actions; its sense of separatism conflicts with its desire for moral rectitude and social justice. It vacillates between admitting dependence and demanding independence, getting and giving, and living both covenantally and contractually.[29] It lacks the resources it needs to organize itself independently, and social situations often arise for which it is unable to discern the best response. What is more, when a choice offers two mutually exclusive and conflicting outcomes, the self must choose between self-preservation and acting for the good of another. Because it "lacks any schema" to determine its ethics and, as a result, behavior, the self cannot adequately manage its choices. With no greater narrative and no substantial schema of virtues within itself, the self tends to choose self-protection, often by overpowering the other.[30] A striving for identity is evident in the self's default function to overpower a weaker other. Volf writes:

> The tendency toward violence is, moreover, reinforced by an inescapable ambiguity of the self. . . . I am who I am in relation to the other. . . . *A tension between the self and the other is built into the very desire for identity*: the other over against whom I must assert myself is the same other who must remain part of myself if I am to be myself.[31]

Because of the fear and resistance that coincide with sin, the self struggles against the other to establish its identity. If the created intent for the

28. Hauerwas, *Christian Existence*, 42; Volf, *Free of Charge*, 102, 193.

29. Volf, *After Our Likeness*, 3; Volf, *Free of Charge*, 34–35, 38–40, 56, 102–3.

30. Hauerwas, *Community of Character*, 126.

31. Volf, *Exclusion and Embrace*, 91, emphasis added.

self lies in a covenantal relatedness, the self disrupts this communion with the other. In this passage Volf refers to the relationship between the self and the human other, but a similar comparison can be drawn between the self and the divine Other. The self struggles because it cannot own its relation to God. By fighting for autonomy, it denies its created intent and remains divided from and unreconciled to the divine Other.

The conscience participates in this organization of the self. It upholds the self by maintaining a sense of authenticity and a continuity of identity—a sense that "this is who I am" from one event to the next—a role that requires a set of organizing virtues not inherent to the self. For the self to live virtuously, that is, undividedly, it must not only learn from the virtues of a truthful narrative, but also must join that narrative's community, which requires more from the self than the self (or any other structure) would.[32] For the Christian, this process of self-formation grows out of an ongoing relationship with God's Spirit, Word, and church.

Self-Deception

When sin released the knowledge of evil at the Fall, it also unleashed the second consequence of internal fragmentation: the ability to deceive. So long as it is self-deluded, the self remains divided. For example, Hauerwas points out this self-delusion when individuals are unable to accept their ignominious deeds as part of their life narrative. Since the acknowledgement of wrongdoing is required for an integrated self, those who overlook, ignore, or intentionally forget their wrongdoing deceive themselves. Hauerwas argues that if persons only acknowledge wrongdoing in order to set things right, they are still deceived because some wrongs cannot be rectified. When wrongdoing cannot be righted, it is often not recognized; when the self is unable to accept culpability, it fights to protect its divided story. It compensates for its wrongdoing by portraying it as beneficent, and the greater the challenge to its denial, the more strongly it fights to promote how good its story is. This defeating trap of denial, this fight for self-protection, leads to reinforced self-delusion and, worse, can lead to violence. For, as Hauerwas submits, wherever the self uses violence for protection is precisely where that part of the story is disingenuous. An individual who acknowledges personal transgressions without resorting to self-defense has, at least in part, faced one's self-deception.[33]

32. Hauerwas, *Community of Character*, 126–27, 149.
33. Hauerwas, *Christian Existence*, 37–39.

Herein lies the vitality of the other; it is essential to the self's pursuit of truth. No one is altogether innocent (Rom 3:20),[34] and the self must acknowledge its location within a cultural narrative and maintain a locus from which to evaluate reality. For the Christian self, the church is indispensable for the individual to live with less self-deceit. Since the story of Jesus overlays individual stories and teaches persons how to make sense of their particular narrative, the gospel guides the self from deception. Because of Christ's story, in which salvation is found, individuals are freed to own their lives, both their good and their shameful aspects. The self hides from what it fears, but without fear the self need no longer and must no longer hide. It need no longer be deceived. The power that deception holds over the self is broken by Christ.

This aberrant division of the self is temporal. Since the Christian's self and personal identity will not be fully known in this temporal dimension, the tension of division remains. One will not fully know who one is until the Eschaton when God's final revelation will be unveiled (1 Cor 13:12; 15:50–54). Volf distinguishes a "historical minimum" from the "eschatological maximum" as the ends of a spectrum for the unity of self.[35] This spectrum can also be aptly applied to knowledge about the nature of the new self.

IDENTITY OF THE NEW SELF

The following section develops a theology of identity that builds upon the common ground established by the writings of Volf, Pak, and Hauerwas. Once the Christian understands the covenant relationality between Creator and human, one can enter this narrative and form an individual manifestation of it. Since the Christian identity is multifaceted, several of its key aspects will be delineated here in order to later articulate a theology of Christian identity in migration (chapter 9): an identity of departure, belonging, and displacement.

---

34. Even victims possess culpability, although this in no way justifies violence. Volf, *Exclusion and Embrace*, 79–84.

35. Volf, *After Our Likeness*, 268–69. Hauerwas confirms the importance of eschatology in the Christian faith and for how Christians are to "negotiate the world" but does not discuss this at length in relation to self-understanding. Hauerwas, *Approaching the End*, ix.

Identity of Departure

The identity of the Christian self involves a departure, the primary departure of allegiance. This departure can take a variety of forms, but it is directed from a point (who one once was) to another destination (who one is in Christ). Those who believe the Christian gospel are swept up into its message and depart from their past beliefs.[36] Their allegiances change. The self, as determining agent, allows another authority to reign as superordinate, placing itself as God's servant. The outlook of departure is to consider one's life no longer one's own.[37] Obeying Jesus Christ means to follow him and submit to his leadership and direction.

Since the first migration from the garden of peace, God's people of faith have long demonstrated a pattern of pilgrimage.[38] Abraham's story perhaps best demonstrates this identity of departure based on divine directive; it serves as an example to all who would follow in his faith footsteps (Gen 12; 15; Rom 4:11, 16; Heb 11:2, 8–17). Not only was Abram called to leave his family's religion in a departure of spiritual allegiance, but he was also called by God to leave his family's country in a departure of circumstance (Gen 12:1–3).[39] God gave him a clear delineation for obedience: leave to bless and be blessed in return. Abraham, with no known assurance other than belief in a God whose word was reality, moved (Gen 24:7). Abraham's belief in this revealed God changed his spiritual allegiance and, in his case, this belief not only required a spiritual migration but also a physical migration. All who adopt the Christian faith are also called to an internal spiritual move and to begin a pilgrimage (Ps 84:5–7).[40] The journey itself is an indication and acknowledgement that the individual needs to be spiritually transformed.

As chapter 3 describes, after conversion an individual undergoes a transformation of self (Gal 2:19–20). This change does not signify a loss of

---

36. The message of the Christian gospel is primarily to believe in Jesus Christ. In believing in the Christ, one accepts that s/he has personally transgressed the holiness and goodness of God and, through Christ's physical crucifixion, burial, and resurrection which satisfied the wrath of God on one's behalf, one's sin has been propitiated, communion restored with God, and freedom to walk in newness of life following the way of Jesus has been inaugurated. Faith is the operating principle by which persons act and demonstrate the gospel narrative they have believed.

37. Hauerwas, *Christian Existence*, 91.

38. Eschatological hope includes, then, a finality where peace and home will be found. Confused roaming will end; exploration will not.

39. Migrating from the Ur of the Chaldeans, Terah, Abram's father, and his extended family set out for Canaan but settled in Haran (Gen 11:31–32). Upon Terah's death, God prompted Abram to leave Haran for Canaan.

40. See Volf's discussion, Volf, *Exclusion and Embrace*, 38–40.

the original self or of individual distinction, but a change—a movement—in relationality.[41] God inclined to redeem humanity, and this inclination made relation possible. The human self, for those who accept this relationship, is changed by that determination for relationality, which in turn shapes their identities. Gabrielson adeptly describes Saul of Tarsus's transformation as an "enlivening" of, rather than an eradication of, his self. Saul, who became Paul upon his Damascus conversion, was so completely deconstructed and reconstructed in his identification with Christ that he experienced an entire reorientation to his identity, way of life, and mission (Gal 6:14–15).[42] This kind of dynamic relationship is only made possible by the action of both parties, divine and human. The indwelling of Christ requires human movement, both invitation and participation.

This redefinition of the self in Christ culminates in an adopted identity. The core of the self redetermines and realigns to identify with Christ and his mission. A follower of Christ acknowledges one's old self-maneuvering as an invalid attempt to preserve one's independence from God. In a movement of exchange, one receives a new, redeemed self that the Son of God constrains into a new pattern of life: self-giving. This movement signifies an exchange of identity, of leadership, and of allegiance, but not an exchange of the individual person. The person as a being remains intact and recreated. "Putting on a new self" means that a change, a shift from dressing in the same way as before, is necessary (Eph 4:24). While individuals possess multiple identities of varying importance, they typically give precedence to one central identity and organize the others in relation to it. They pass all their decisions through the grid of one of these life themes—beauty, faith, family, ethnicity, sexuality, fear—which creates (inconsistencies notwithstanding) a semblance of internal coherence. For the Christian, Christ becomes this definitive agent that determines personal identity.

Upon spiritual conversion or *metanoia*, individuals experience a shift in identity, a change of being, and a turning from who they once were as they attempt to live as liberated creatures of God. This new acknowledgement of dependence indicates a migration. Conversion is a spiritual process in which God calls one to depart and to follow Christ, and this process

41. Williams, "Assimilation and Otherness," 265. Williams elaborates on this relationality within the Trinity, between God and humanity, and between persons. Individuals can choose to shift their definition of self and their identity by taking in some aspect of another and changing the nature of their relationality. A person's identity is changed by one's "determination toward another."

42. Gabrielson, "Paul's Non-Violent Gospel," 123–29. Gabrielson cites John Barclay that divine and human agency hang in "dialectical fashion" (124), alluding to Hegel's method of dialectics where two apparent or truly contradictory statements are held together, and even resolved, by their interaction.

reorients one's personal identity. Determinant factors of identity, such as relationships (including those with history, society, and family), habits, language, and motivations become subject to Christ. Jesus is the new "environment" in which the Christian moves, and, in this geographical sense, in which identity is restructured.[43] In this reconciliation of identity, a synchronous self-configuration occurs, and competing roles and behavior are brought in obedience to Christ. Diachronically, one's identity reconciles different historical experiences of the same self into categories of "before Christ" and "after Christ."[44]

When one identifies with Christ, one joins a collective identity that is comprised of every nation, tribe, and tongue and has been grafted into one group called by God to depart from polytheism (Rom 11:13–24). What is more, they claim allegiance to their manner of belief and living as revealed by Israel's history and its Messiah.[45] As it is their formal acknowledgment that they have been claimed, the emphasis of their departure is not so much in the perfection of their faithfulness (although that is an expected due course) but rather in the truthfulness of their lives. They claim their identity as followers in a resolute posture of dependence and trust.

Whereas this departure of allegiance is intrinsic to the Christian identity, one's physical departure varies by circumstance. A variety of factors drive individuals to migrate—God's particular calling, environmental disasters, family connections, and personal desires. Cultural expectations, family pressures, and competing desires can also influence the direction of the departure one takes. Given the human condition to err and even though they may seek to follow God's will on their journey, the path of obedience for each individual is by no means linear and is often circuitous. Their progress unfolds over time and often in hindsight.[46] Moltmann reinforces the teleological element of this departure in his characterization of nature. For the person set on pilgrimage, nature becomes one's "traveling companion." Both nature and the pilgrim yearn in faith with hope for the culmination of God's kingdom rather than the transitory present (Rom 8:18–22; 2 Cor 4). Moltmann writes that both humans and creation view "the world . . . as

43. Snodgrass, "Paul's Focus," 262–66.

44. I apply McAdams's theory of life-story identity configuration and integration to the Christian. McAdams, "Redemptive Self," 99.

45. Hauerwas, *Christian Existence*, 39.

46. Volf treats Gilles Deleuze's consideration of departure as nomadic (namely as without a beginning, destination, particularity or directing agent) as futile wandering and as unrelated to the Abrahamic example. A further charge against Deleuze's rendering is that his conception does not explain how one can "resist the evildoer." Volf, *Exclusion and Embrace*, 40–41.

a process moving in a unified fashion toward its redemption."[47] Beyond Moltmann's analogy, more significantly, the Spirit of God remains the Christian's traveling companion throughout the course of life (John 14:16, 26; 15:26; John 16:7; Eph 1:13). The fact that God accompanies and directs the transformation of the self on this journey assures its completion (Phil 1:6). This change is a complex, dynamic process that follows a unique path for each person in one's daily and ultimate conversion from behavioral and psychological darkness to light (John 8:12; Acts 26:18; 2 Cor 4:6; Eph 5:8; 1 Pet 2:9; 1 John 2:9).

Identity of Belonging

This departure indicates the commencement of a journey, but the pilgrimage of personhood is more than a departure and a beginning; it is a belonging. In order to create this belonging, the identity of departure requires that every part of one's being becomes identified with and found in Christ. The self's transformational journey culminates in a reunion with God. Ultimately, as Alpha and Omega, God is both the beginning of and the end of self-pilgrimage.

The first migration of identity for the self is one of belonging; the Christian undergoes a transfer of identity by adoption in which one is received into a new family. The self's new location becomes in Christ placed into his lineage; the Christian self lives outside itself and in God upon conversion.[48] This element of belonging—that the self is held in God—is crucial. Other stimuli continue to shape the person, but the self is defined by God. Experiences are subjected to this greater reality: who I am is defined by *whose* I am. Since God assigns meaning, one's personal identity "arises *extra se*," outside of oneself.[49]

The second migration that creates this identity of belonging concerns God's divine presence. God's Spirit condescends to indwell persons (1 Cor 3:16). Although the exchange is unevenly weighted, it still demonstrates reciprocity and mutual belonging between humanity and God. As the sacrament of baptism portrays, the Christian pilgrimage involves a daily journey of reconciliation with the triune God. The goal of this new life is to commune with God, and this communion directs the pilgrim. The intimacy of that communion allows the pilgrim to walk in obedience to God (Matt 5:48;

47. Moltmann, "Theology," 31–32.
48. Volf, *End of Memory*, 198.
49. Grenz, "Social God and Relational Self," 91.

1 Pet 1:16). The new self portrays God's likeness, and the character of the triune God determines the Christian's identity.[50]

The identity of belonging indicates a familial relationship. This relationship shows a positional belonging when Christians are reborn, adopted as heirs of God's kingdom, experientially belong to Christ, and join one particular narrative. Anyone born outside of a family has no permanent place in that family, but a son or daughter belongs to it forever. This permanent sense of belonging is a result of this family relationship. While parents can disinherit their children socially and legally, and children can emancipate themselves from their parents' authority, family members cannot become *unrelated* to each other. In an even deeper commitment, God has vowed to never disinherit those who accept their adopted identity (2 Tim 2:13). Herein is the dynamic exchange between parties—the steadfastness of God's loyal giving and the self's unpredictable receiving. Even if God divinely knows which children will stray, God wills not to control their actions. In addition to belonging to God the Father as children and belonging in God the Christ, the Christian identity of belonging also includes the last member of the Trinity: God the Spirit (Rom 8:15; Gal 4:6). Through belief in "the word of truth" in Christ, the Christian self is given God's Spirit, which is "a deposit guaranteeing [its] inheritance until the redemption of those who are God's possession" (Eph 1:13–14). God's accompanying Spirit serves as one's "chaperone" on life's journey until the final reunion and the ultimate fulfillment of the self.[51]

This identity of belonging relates to the eschatological promise of God's kingdom. Who one will be in the future informs one's present identity, and what will be in the future motivates one's present behavior. This teleological understanding of promised history undergirds an understanding of Christian identity.[52] God's promise to redeem creation and consummate its deliverance guides one's understanding of how to exist. When Christians believe that they belong to this promise, they understand who they are, where they are from, and how they should act and react.[53] One's identity—who one perceives oneself to be—is the birthplace of willed action and

---

50. Volf, "Being," 1–2.

51. Kevin McGill, Sermon on Ephesians 1, Fellowship Bible Church, Dallas, TX, October 7, 2007.

52. Volf and Hauerwas both deal with the eschatological implications of the church and how they relate to Christian corporate identity. Hauerwas and Willimon, *Resident Aliens*, 86–92; Volf, *After Our Likeness*, 127–35.

53. Volf, *Exclusion and Embrace*, 27; Volf, *End of Memory*, 108, 179–80, 199, 202, 207.

prescribes how that individual will interact with the other.[54] How does one accept the other yet differentiate the self from the other? How does one seek self-protection and also reconciliation? How does one fight injustice yet remember wrongs suffered rightly? How do warring communities pursue peace? God's eschatological promise and a Christian identity of belonging offer answers to these questions.

One's Christian identity comes from belonging to God, but it is also colored by one's culture. Who the self is and what identity it portrays primarily reflects its God-given nature within a finite historical milieu. Even though they are scarred by the Fall, cultures display God's creative imagination when it is placed in humanity's hands. Despite the presence of sin, cultures display wonderful ingenuity in their mores, infrastructure, communication patterns, art, and so on. The Christian self belongs to God fully and to its culture illustratively. As Campbell rightly shares, "Christ-identity can pervade all cultures, transforming them but not imperialistically obliterating everything as if Christian faith were an entirely independent culture which replaces, and is discontinuous with, previously existing patterns of life."[55] Cultural ideals do not trump the Christian's responsibility to belong to God (in manner of pattern, speech, and thought) when and where these conflict. Although people are born into cultural settings that deeply impact their patterns of thinking, speech, and behavior, their regenerated being creates a new identity that is formed by God's Spirit, Word, and church. This communal shaping evidences the self's identity of belonging.

Identity of Displacement

The redeemed self belongs to God in a new manner of living. The self after conversion possesses two qualities in greater fullness: an increased capacity to give of oneself and a new openness in oneself that allows the other a presence. These qualities lead to a rich, vibrant, ever-changing, and unpredictable construal of identity. This arrangement maintains the essential distinction of the individual, avoids the dissolution of the self, and allows the other to be identified in the self as part of its identity as a "non-identity."[56] Furthermore, the rapprochement of the self and the other disarms the power struggle within the self, which is practical in today's culture of power

54. One's internalized identity does not prevent the intrusion and presumption of the other to impose an identity on that individual which one would not own. Taylor, "Politics of Recognition," 25–26.

55. Campbell, *Paul*, 14.

56. Volf, *Exclusion and Embrace*, 178–80, 189.

politics, economic scarcities, gender wars, and ethnic rivalries. The self re-coils from injuring itself; when the self perceives the other as part of itself, it pauses. When the other is integral to one's identity and self, the other is no longer the enemy.

Because it belongs to God, the self gains the capacity to consider the other in a new way. If the other is no longer an enemy, the self feels a re-sponsibility to protect the other as a fellow creature of God. If Christian identity must reflect Jesus Christ, then a Christian will not only identify with his death, burial, and resurrection but with his displacement of self (Phil 2:3–6). Not only will the redeemed self acknowledge and receive the other, it will displace itself *for* the other and can choose to be alienated for the other.[57] Paul imitated Christ when he experienced and taught a consis-tent self-shifting for the sake of the other (Rom 12:10; 1 Cor 9:21–23).

The story of Joseph demonstrates these three facets of a Christian iden-tity. Joseph's kidnapping thrust him into a foreign world of Egyptian cus-toms and gods at an impressionable age. From approximately age seventeen through age thirty, he lived as a member of an ethnic and religious minority and suffered both antagonism and socioeconomic oppression (Gen 37:2; 41:46; 43:32). He learned, however, how to operate within this environ-ment, speaking their dialect and assuming their forms of appearance, to the extent that his own brothers did not recognize him (Gen 42:8, 23). While these years of Egyptian socialization could have influenced him to forget his people's faith in Yahweh, Joseph demonstrated an identity of departure from his surrounding influences. Joseph did not forsake his allegiance to, and identification with, this foreign God of the Hebrews. Secondly, Joseph feared and enjoyed a communion with God that demonstrated an identity of belonging, one that was so obvious that others attested to it (Gen 41:38; 42:18). Joseph derived personal meaning from relating to his God (Gen 39:9; 45:7–8). Most of all, Joseph's encounter with his brothers demonstrated an identity of displacement. After they betrayed him at such a vulnerable age, Joseph could easily have severed any further contact with his brothers when they were driven to Egypt by famine. Joseph created space within himself, displaced his personal wounds, and extended himself to the very ones who had sold him into slavery. After almost fifteen years apart, he could not have predicted how his brothers would respond to his kind overtures. Even though he risked incredible pain if his brothers were not remorseful, Joseph set aside his prior victimization in the hope of reconciliation.

---

57. This is not to say that those who do not possess Christ do not demonstrate great valor and sacrifice for the other. However, their motivation in doing so may not be *for* Christ's sake. Even those who do not claim God demonstrate the gifts and capacities that God has given humanity.

This willed displacement is a twofold migration of the self. The self makes a circumstantial choice to make room for the other and, in doing so, that very self is moved (shaped) internally. Although Bauerschmidt discusses alienation in relation to the distance of the self from the world, this same alienation can, in turn, form the individual. "The alienation of the viator from the world is not a radical rupture from an inherently sinful creation, but is rather a journey toward happiness along a distinctive path, a happiness that involves the *perfection-through-reordering* of the person."[58] This principal understanding of one's identity has profound applications for daily interaction; these are discussed in chapters 9 and 10.

58. Bauerschmidt, "Aquinas," 39, emphasis added.

III

Sociological Research
on Identity in Migration

7

Research Methodology

THE PURPOSE OF THIS study is to explore, describe, and, in part, explain the experience of identity change and maintenance in educated international migrants amidst multiple cultural and national transitions. Multiple methods were utilized to study these complex phenomena. The following describes the rationale, procedures, methods, and processes of data analysis that were employed to address the research questions.

RATIONALE

A critical realist/postpositivist stance was adopted for this project, meaning that the social research was based on the premises that an ontological reality exists, that researcher knowledge of that reality is perspectival, and that it is possible to judge, or at least attempt to judge, between differing accounts (see chapter 1).[1] The research design and the choice of a mixed methodology fit this theoretical paradigm because they do not reduce human behavior to "the physical or the mental, the material or the ideal, the corporeal or the spiritual."[2] This approach allows for the quantification of variables as well as

---

1. Smith, "Critical Realism." Research processes are rendered meaningless without these principles. The very discussion of criteria by which to judge the quality of inference a researcher can make relies on a realist ontology. See Greene, *Mixed Methods*, 167. Likewise, ethically, only if accounts are not equally valid as truthful representations, can a system of ethics for research practices be devised. See Lincoln et al., "Paradigmatic Controversies," 114–15.

2. Smith, *What Is a Person?*, introduction.

the employment of their qualitative aspects and for the socially constructed nature of human experience to be taken into account.

Further, a mixed methodology both allows and reflects the tension that can be observed in the objective and subjective natures of human life. Conclusive patterns of human behavior can be drawn while still allowing for contradictions, especially with cross-cultural research. As Greene and Caracelli argue:

> A mixed method[s] study that combines these two traditions would strive for knowledge claims that are grounded in the lives of the participants studied and that also have some generality to other participants and other contexts, that enhance understanding of both the unusual and the typical case, that isolate factors of particular significance while also integrating the whole, that are full of emic meaning at the same time as they offer causal connections of broad significance.[3]

Despite a strong historical positivist emphasis and a swing to qualitative research from the seventies, scholars have called for a due consideration of both methodologies within the social sciences.

Caution must be taken in removing an observable element from its social context because this step may change its internal structure and characteristics for study; what has been teased out and analyzed in a new environment can differ from the initial original element of study. Science that objectifies the study of human behavior in a solely quantitative manner can give rise to this dilemma. Because human action is creative to a certain extent but is also limited by structural constraints of power and interests, the investigation of human behavior can be furthered by qualitative research. Qualitative research is beneficial for observing the processes and meanings of persons in their contextual conditions, in "*how* social experience is created and given meaning."[4] Through exploratory study, significant elements in these processes may be observed, and these factors may then be isolated as variables for inquiry from a quantitative paradigm.

The mixed methodology of this study lends itself to adequate exploration and the generation of new data in qualitative inquiry as well as an assessment of associated factors in quantitative measurement. The quantitative portion strengthens the validity and reliability of the study while the qualitative component assists in identifying the nature and range of beliefs, attitudes, and values that relate to religious narratives in cultural adjustment and migration. The efficacy of a mixed research design lies in the use of

3. As quoted in Greene, *Mixed Methods*, 171.
4. Denzin and Lincoln, *Sage Handbook*, 8.

different methodologies for different purposes. Brannen, for example, summarizes Hammersley's original classification of how different methods (with different data sets) can improve overall data interpretation in three ways: through the triangulation of data across methods for verification, through the facilitation of one method informing the design of another, and through a complementarity of methods that reveal different aspects of the research subject. A mixed methodology allows an investigation of data from different and "cross-checked" angles to discern a more accurate picture of reality in lived experience.[5] While this study employs both facilitation and complementarity without a presumed intersection of data, these multiple methods open the way to different levels of description and the possible corroboration of data. The methods used in data collection were 1) semi-structured interviews, 2) participation in the setting, 3) direct observation, 4) field research notes, 5) email correspondence, and 6) questionnaire responses.

METHODOLOGY

Narrative View of Inquiry

Scholars have increasingly promoted a narrative approach in the study of human behavior since it allows an open study of how individuals make meaning and understand themselves. This study incorporates a narrative structure to examine how faith affects personal identity construction in migration. Rather than highlighting developmental stages of life, this study considers the identity experiences of international graduates in their migratory stages: the pre-departure from their country of origin, the period of study abroad, and the return migration to their country of origin.[6]

Qualitative: Case Study Design

This study explores how religious factors affect the construction of various personal identities in the context of international migration. To this end,

5. Brannen, "Working Qualitatively and Quantitatively," 314; Bryman, *Social Research Methods*, 635, 717. Triangulation *within* a method is an intersection of data vectors. Different kinds of triangulation are given in King and Horrocks, *Interviews*, 164.

6. All interviewees were return migrants to their country of origin. Survey respondents were graduates who remained in the United States, returned to their country of origin, or migrated to a third country.

it employs a multiple case study design which investigates a phenomenon within its present context.[7] Ideally, case studies generate fresh concepts and corroborate or contest existing theoretical claims.[8] Because they allow for life experiences to be explored in all their complexity over time and across cultures, case studies are well-suited to address research questions.[9] As parsimonious quantitative methods alone are not conducive to the collection of information about daily lived experience, they cannot effectively ascertain the complexity of embodied existence.

The study uses an interview guide approach comprised of three types of questions: initial open-ended, intermediate, and ending questions.[10] The semi-structured interview format was selected because it allows the introduction of a pre-determined set of questions (which yield coverage of similar material among participants) yet provides flexibility for both parties (participant and interviewer) to explore alternate routes during discussion. Since migration lends itself to certain types of inquiries (questions of departure, location, temporality, courses of action, turning points), interviews followed the biographical narrative interview sequence, which asks questions in a narrative form and order.[11]

This study investigated how international migrants interacted with various cultural transitions during different periods as well as how their religious faith affected their perceptions of their identities. Broader data was collected from participants' life stories to afford a better comprehension of the development, change, and maintenance of identity over time. Questions were arranged in a narrative form that followed the chronology of their migration experiences: their pre-departure from their country of origin, their period of study abroad, and their return migration. I deliberately avoided varying questions in order to maximize the ability to compare answers across cases and to prevent differences between participants in ordering effects.[12] Over the course of one year, twenty-two semi-structured interviews (with eighteen graduates and four spouses) were completed in person along with participant observation. This number was chosen based on the probability that theoretical saturation (where additional interviews are likely to

---

7. Yin, *Case Study*, 17–20.

8. Flyvbjerg, "Five Misunderstandings," 423–24.

9. Shim, "Marital Maintenance," 37–38.

10. Bryman, *Social Research Methods*, 470–79.

11. Rosenthal, "Biographical Research," 50–51.

12. Bryman, *Social Research Methods*, 220.

yield little new information) had been achieved, paired with the feasibility of the study to continue.[13]

Qualitative: Ethnographic Fieldwork

As an additional method of inquiry, I traveled to the participants' locations to observe their routines and engage in conversations on a daily basis. Although this effort did not constitute a full ethnography, these direct observations extended the type and reach of data collection and revealed a segment of their lived experiences. Observing their daily practices provided additional insights that were crucial for a clearer articulation of their embodied reality. Interacting with participants in real time allowed me to experience (and co-fashion) daily life as a shared experience. This co-construction provided me with a greater sense of ethical responsibility, enforced the value of reciprocity, and protected against a detached study of participants as objects.[14] Additionally, my longstanding rapport with the participants assuaged some discomfort they may have felt in being observed by an unfamiliar source or being interviewed in an unfamiliar place.

Quantitative

In addition to qualitative research, identity concepts can also be quantitatively measured. Particularly in cross-cultural comparisons, drawing conclusions and trends from associated factors requires the definition and quantification of variables. While some dispute that religion is an appropriate domain to be quantified for study, David Voas argues for its value and appropriateness.[15] This study used a questionnaire to explore specific variables related to the negotiation of identities and migration patterns. The graduates' location, migration, and correlated factors were assessed. Due to its forced-choice response format, this quantitative measure allowed an initial assessment of how participants evaluate their multiple identities by comparative strength and overall prioritization.

---

13. Ibid., 421.
14. Bowie, "Trespassing," 41, 44.
15. Voas, "Surveys," 144–45.

Reflexivity and Performativity

Since the researcher functions as both an observer and an interpreter, careful attention was paid to researcher reflexivity.[16] While reflexivity has been defined in multiple ways, that which is discussed here is "the process of reflecting critically on the self as researcher, "the human instrument."[17] As such, I spent considerable time contemplating and recording how my own presence interacted with the research process, from project development and data collection to analysis and interpretation. For example, I came to realize how my own political positions colored my opinion (and judgment) of various participants' choices. When I evaluated how my personal views were subtly influencing the way I told my participants' stories, I was able to make necessary revisions.

During the study I inhabited the space of both an insider and an outsider as researcher.[18] As an insider, I have personal experience as an international student and also identify with the participants' religious identity. Although I spent a decade directing an international office and developing considerable rapport with the participants, I remained an outsider. Since my participants and I were separated by unequal access to material resources by virtue of birth, gender and citizenship, my identification was largely vicarious. This representational ideation inevitably affects how the research is presented, but my awareness and contemplation will mitigate, to some degree, against misrepresentation.

The principle of performativity should also be considered in the research process, and interviews are performative. As an interview is conducted, the parties react to each other, altering their identities and thereby shaping their behavior and the very data that is collected.[19] Although my presence in the interview invariably altered interviewees' responses, our previously established trust and knowledge about each other helped to increase their level of comfort and to lessen misrepresentation on my part. Also, while my shared religious beliefs and relationship with them could have imported bias into the reading of the results, I attempted to temper any distortion of the data by 1) being aware of my vulnerability in rendering a descriptive and interpretive analysis and 2) attempting to replicate their original thoughts as they were intended. Lastly, I speak as one whose background has been materially privileged, which invariably colors my experi-

---

16. Wuthnow, *Meaning and Moral Order*, 52.

17. Lincoln et al., "Paradigmatic Controversies," 115.

18. Bowie, "Trespassing," 42–44, 61.

19. Razon and Ross, "Negotiating Fluid Identities," 494–95.

ence of life, affects the reporting of my research, and, in many ways, isolates me from the cold realities of others' experiences.

RESEARCH SITES AND PARTICIPANTS

Interview participants for this study had departed the United States in return migration. Research sites for this study were determined primarily based on availability, access, government regulation, and on the feasibility and funding available to reach those destinations.[20] The research sites were primarily located in areas of former Communist Europe, including parts of predominantly Catholic Europe, and in areas of South and Southeast Asia. Interviews were completed with persons living in Albania, Hungary, Poland, Romania, Italy, Spain, India, Hong Kong, and Singapore.

Because this research design seeks in-depth exploration and not broad generalization, the participant sample was obtained through generic purposive sampling. A generic purposive sample is a non-random sample whereby the researcher first defines criteria to address the research questions and then strategically selects the sample.[21] Criteria for interview participants were 1) a foreign-born citizen who entered the United States on a temporary student visa, 2) a graduate of Dallas Theological Seminary between the years 1983–2013, 3) a current resident outside of the United States, 4) a member of a religious minority identity in Asia or Europe, and 5) a verbal agreement to a doctrinal statement of evangelical beliefs. All the interviewees had signed a doctrinal agreement of Dallas Theological Seminary's basic evangelical beliefs at the time of their admission, which facilitated a study of evangelical identity over time. According to the maximum variation sampling strategy, demographic variation in age, gender, marital status, profession, city size, and country was sought to diversify the sample.[22] Eighteen interviews were completed with five female and thirteen male graduates, ages 28–53 ($M = 34.06$, $Mdn = 41$). In order to ensure that being observed or interviewed did not pose any risk of endangerment or

20. Citizens of countries, in which Christian membership is prohibited or poses greater risk, were excluded to avoid placing the participant in a compromising position with the government authorities and to ensure the author could truthfully state the purpose of her visit at the port of entry. Another feasibility factor was the safety constraints on the researcher, a Caucasian female traveling alone.

21. Bryman, *Social Research Methods*, 422. This is distinguished from *theoretical sampling*, in which cases are added as theory is conceptualized in a sequential manner.

22. Pak, *Korean American Women*, 46. See Appendix 1 for demographic information of interviewees.

illegal action for those participating, nine nationalities were selected from South and Southeast Asia and Europe.

The three inclusion criteria for questionnaire participants were 1) a foreign country of origin, 2) entry into the U.S. as a foreign student, 3) graduation from Dallas Theological Seminary. Questionnaire participants were not required to have maintained their evangelical identity, a caveat that offered unique insight into identity change over time. Rather, a survey question was added to ascertain current evangelical commitment. Of the 581 questionnaires distributed, 405 were completed, constituting 69.7 percent of the total possible respondents. Participants omitting more than 50 percent of the data in their surveys were removed prior to analysis. Approximately 96.5 percent of the participant questionnaires (N = 391) were retained for analysis.

At the time of the study, I had worked in the International Student Office of the institution since 1999 and had maintained personal contact with most of the graduates from the classes of 2000 to 2013. This long-standing personal connection established an important level of trust prior to a request for participation in the study. While no financial incentive was offered, our previously developed rapport assisted in questionnaire response and ease among interviewees. Respondents may also have had, however, a motivation to please me because of our prior relationship. Participants are susceptible to response bias, such as social desirability bias, which is the tendency to respond in a way that anticipates a desired answer, thereby distorting a truer account.[23] This bias is an even greater vulnerability when the participants know the researcher personally. On the other hand, the efficacy of total anonymity in research situations has also been contested.[24]

PROCEDURES

Approval was granted by the King's College London Arts and Humanities Research Ethics Panel (REP) prior to data collection. To obtain a list of potential participants from the institution, names of international graduates from classes 1983 to 2013 were gathered. All of the known international graduates from 1983 to 2013 were invited to complete the questionnaire, and interview participants were then selected and contacted. Informed consent forms were obtained from all interviewees; questionnaires submitted online signified consent as was outlined in the accompanying information sheet.

23. Bryman, *Social Research Methods*, 227–28.
24. Lelkes et al., "Complete Anonymity," 1291–99.

Interviews

An initial interview guide was prepared, which incorporated some of the narrative analysis questions that have been used by Pak and Shim in their previous research.[25] The list of questions was then further developed based on a review of the current literature, and five pilot interviews were conducted in order to test the guide. The pilot participants had each experienced return migration to their countries of origin although they currently resided in the U.S., which made them ineligible for the final study. Candidates were selected based on a range of demographic diversity that was commensurate with the foreign graduate body of the institution. Feedback from these pilot participants was critical in formulating the final interview guide. Upon completion of the pilot interviews, I reviewed their responses to discover what had emerged from our interaction that seemed most relevant to my research questions. Largely, I summarized each portion and added a title that matched its content. Some of the comments stood out as unusual, which led me to rephrase some of my interview questions.

Interviews were agreed to and arranged by email from the initial list of international graduates from the classes of 1983 to 2013. I presented information sheets and consent forms to the participants well in advance of the interviews so that they could give them careful consideration. Voluntary consent was obtained in each case. The researcher traveled to each of the participants' locations in Europe or Asia to conduct the interviews, except in the cases of four individuals who had already planned to come to the United States for other reasons. Participants were allowed to select the interview locations which included the participant's home or office, my office, or an otherwise undisturbed location. In two instances a public café was used due to time constraints. Each location was based on what the participants deemed would best serve their personal preferences and family needs. My goal was that any inconvenience be mine and not theirs.

Prior to the commencement of each interview, I summarized again the nature of the study and reviewed the possible benefits and risks of participation with each subject. Since each participant had already known me for years, we had an established rapport between us. I took time, however, to share current news about my personal life, my interest in the project, and the importance of their input in my research. I advised the participants not to offer more information than they felt comfortable sharing, to ask questions as desired, and to end the interview at any time they wished. As the participants were multi-lingual and had previously demonstrated a graduate

25. Pak, *Korean American Women*, 223–26; Shim, "Marital Maintenance," 291–92.

level of proficiency on the Test of English as a Foreign Language (TOEFL) for admission to the institution, the interviews were conducted in English. Furthermore, all respondents, since their graduation from a master's and/or doctoral program in the United States, had continued to use the English language in their daily lives. With prior permission obtained, interviews were audio-recorded and lasted 1.25–1.5 hours. A fifteen-minute break was given at the approximate halfway point (at forty-five minutes) per interview. To note initial impressions, observations and items for further consideration, post-interview reflections were recorded immediately upon completion of the interview. Interviewees were given a small, non-cash thank-you gift for their time.

The process of data collection, which began in November 2012 and was completed by August 2013, was comprised of five interviews that were conducted in Dallas and seventeen that were conducted overseas. After the first field site visit to Europe in November 2012, the second field site visit was to South Asia in March 2013, and the third field site was Southeast Asia in July and August 2013. Four interviews were completed with participant spouses as they were available and willing, in order to compare the transcripts of couples for commonality or difference, fact-checking verification, and gender effect. The content of the spouse interviews proved to be very similar to the graduates' responses and were not included in the final analysis.

An early decision was made regarding the potential offer of housing by participants during my stay. With supervisor approval, I decided I would neither request nor decline housing. Participants who offered me housing did so voluntarily. In all cases, I planned for separate hotel or hostel accommodations. Of the fourteen interviews that were completed outside of the United States, five participants did invite me to stay with them in their home. This invitation afforded a greater opportunity for prolonged engagement and for observation of the participants' daily routines. As several of the locations were not considered safe for a female traveling alone, a second positive consequence of these unpressured arrangements was researcher safety.

Since the interview recordings were intended to be anonymous, participants were coached to not give any personally identifying information during the taped interview. No physical evidence of interviewees' names matched to their interviews exists. Interview guides with researcher notes were numbered and kept in a locked, confidential location. As a further measure, digital recordings were encrypted on an Iron Key flash drive and kept in a locked, confidential location. These anonymous numbered interviews were professionally transcribed but not personally identifiable. I reviewed each interview for transcription accuracy.

Questionnaire

A portion of initial survey questions were adapted from previous research.[26] After two-thirds of the interviews were completed, the qualitative data was assessed to formulate additional survey questions. The questionnaire was drafted and sent to multiple expert researchers for outside review. It then went through five rounds of revisions; each new draft was sent to a new expert for comment in successive fashion. A pilot study was then scheduled. Current international students from the institution, who participated on a volunteer basis, were recruited based on a range of demographic diversity that was commensurate with the foreign graduate body. Pilot participant feedback was critical in formulating the final questionnaire for linguistic clarity and comprehension. Following the completion of the survey, I led the participants through each question in a guided discussion, probing for possible misunderstandings and suggestions for better phrasing. Participants' responses were further instrumental in formulating the initial list of multiple choice responses. Once the final list of questions was created through Survey Monkey and uploaded, a second pilot study was performed. Five different individuals then completed the online questionnaire for further review and to determine the approximate time required for participation.

The final online questionnaire contained thirty-six questions (Appendix 3). A potential list of 699 international graduates from the classes of 1983 to 2013 was compiled; of these, 594 had available email addresses. Most email addresses were known already from my personal knowledge or were otherwise listed by graduates in the alumni database. A supplemental search was made through Internet search engines (e.g., Google, Facebook, etc.). Of the initial 594 graduates, five graduates were determined to be deceased, and eight emails were undeliverable. The final count of graduates with available emails was 581. The questionnaire was sent on 5 June 2013 and was accompanied by an information sheet that detailed the research available for review at http:///questionnaireinfo.blogspot.com. No incentives were offered, and the completion of the questionnaire served as the participant's voluntary consent to participate. Two graduates responded but declined to participate. Participants spent approximately 10–30 minutes to complete the survey.

26. The survey questions adapted from other research studies are noted in Appendix 3.

Questionnaire Measures

Participants provided demographic information such as gender, age, country of origin, marital status, type of entry visa into the U.S., year of matriculation at Dallas Theological Seminary, length of residence in the U.S., religious background, and ethnic background. The following were assessed in the questionnaire:

Religious Identity. Attitudes about religious identity were assessed (α = .54). Participants used a 5-point Likert scale to indicate the perceived importance of their own religious identity to themselves (1 = not important at all, 5 = extremely important), the strength of ties they felt to members of their religious faith (1 = I strongly disagree, 5 = I strongly agree), and the extent to which their religious faith related to their geographic place of residence upon graduation. (1 = not at all, 5 = very much).

Ethnic Identity. Attitudes about ethnic identity were assessed via self-description (α = .72). Participants used a 5-point Likert scale to indicate the perceived importance of their own ethnic group (1 = not important at all, 5 = extremely important), the strength of ties felt with members of their ethnic group (1 = I strongly disagree, 5 = I strongly agree), and the extent to which their ethnic group membership related to how they felt about themselves (1 = I strongly disagree, 5 = I strongly agree, reverse scored).

National Identity. Attitudes about religious identity were assessed (α = .70). Participants used a 5-point Likert scale to indicate the perceived importance of their national identity (1 = not important at all, 5 = extremely important), the strength of ties felt with citizens of their country of origin (1 = I strongly disagree, 5 = I strongly agree), and the extent to which their citizenship related to how they felt about themselves (1 = I strongly disagree, 5 = I strongly agree, reverse scored).

Negotiation of Identities. Participants were asked which identity (religious, ethnic, or national) was most important to them in a forced-choice response format that included an Other category.

Challenges in Country of Origin. Perceived challenges to Christians in their country of origin were measured by a series of questions regarding their personal experiences, their level of concern for their children and how they cope with that concern, and how they estimate the amount of discrimination toward Christians in their country of origin.

Adjustment Factors in Migration. Participants reported the most important factor in cultural adjustment when studying abroad, the item they most needed during their period of study abroad, and if applicable, the item they most needed in returning overseas.

Home Visits during Study Abroad. Participants reported the number of trips taken to their country of origin during their period of study.

Graduation Plan upon Entry. Participants' initial migration intentions were assessed when they provided their original graduation plans upon first entering the U.S. to study.

Cognitive and Behavioral Change. Participants assessed if and in which area(s) they had experienced personal growth due to their study abroad.

Current Geographic Location. U.S. residence or non-U.S. residence was determined.

Motivation for Choice of Residence. Participants reported their motivations for remaining in or departing the United States.

Ethnographic Fieldwork: Participant Observation

Participant observation occurred in three two-week segments with approximately four to five days in each interview location. I kept daily notes of conversations, participants' comments, and practices that were relevant to my area of inquiry. Often, participants and their spouses offered further comments after their interviews were completed. These insights often nuanced and informed what they had told me in the formal, staged interview. Additionally, recording their observations allowed me to later review this material and notice some elements that I may have otherwise overlooked. At the time of record, I was unsure if certain details were pertinent but later found my notes helpful in forming my final analysis. Thorough field notes, impressions, and data management procedures were recorded. All notes were numbered and contained no personally identifiable participant information.

In each location, I joined the participants in their various daily activities: church services, neighborhood visits, community Bible studies, Bible Institute events, social events, English classes, and after-school programs. Additionally, I toured their various places of work, which included church buildings, offices, campuses, and classrooms. During all of these events, I had numerous informal conversations with participants, spouses, neighbors, colleagues, church families, and ministry leaders.

QUALITY OF RESEARCH DESIGN

The researcher's background is pertinent in establishing one's credibility since the researcher is the primary instrument in data collection and analysis (see chapter 1).[27] Beyond my background, my numerous interactions and conversations with the participants during their years of study and since their graduations added to my knowledge regarding their identity management over time. In addition to the research interviews, I engaged in field-site observation of the participants in their family, religious, public, and professional environments. Interviews were transcribed, reviewed for transcription accuracy, re-read for NVivo coding, and re-read multiple times over several months to grasp the length and breadth of the material. My recordkeeping of all research stages, an "audit trail," was thorough, and I maintained an awareness of reflexivity and avoidance of intentional bias.[28]

Regarding the quantitative portion of this research, previous research does suggest that self-identifications of one's religious, ethnic, and national self-understanding are relevant measures of those identities.[29] Considering the Cronbach's alphas for religious, ethnic, and national identity, the reliability of these constructs was considered acceptable for this study.[30]

DATA ANALYSIS

Using Greene's summary of what is needed in mixed methods studies, data analysis strategies included data cleaning, data reduction and transformation, data correlation and comparison, and analysis for inquiry conclusions and inferences.[31] This study includes a qualitative as well as a quantitative analysis of data. The interview and survey analysis will be described along with additional comments on field notes and email correspondences.

27. Pak, *Korean American Women*, 46.

28. Bryman, *Social Research Methods*, 392.

29. Alwin et al., "Measuring Religious Identities."

30. Cronbach's alpha was lower for the religious identity construct. However, reliability is considered adequate for reasons explained in the limitations section of chapter 8.

31. Greene, *Mixed Methods*, 144–45.

Interviews

A multiple case study of eighteen semi-structured interviews was analyzed for uniqueness within cases as well as uniformity among cases. NVivo software was utilized to collate conceptually-related material. Narrative analysis is differentiated from an analysis of narratives. Narrative analysis requires multiple interviews with each participant with each case described at length. While this study does not offer a full narrative analysis, several techniques were incorporated from that methodology such as "narrative configuration" (combining data into a chronological integrated story) and "narrative smoothing" (judging which events to highlight as meaningful).[32] Narrative analysis requires that each case be compiled into a detailed, complete story, which limits the total number of cases that are possible. In the spirit of narrative inquiry, I studied each case for its unique and individual complexity. To accommodate a much larger number of possible interviews, however, I did not report the full within-case analysis in the final results.

Analysis of these narratives was completed in three stages or levels: descriptive coding, interpretative coding, and thematic coding.[33] Firstly, the interview transcripts were read thoroughly to gain an overall understanding. Sentences and paragraphs of the raw data were coded conceptually. For each line I asked, "What is this about?"[34] Category titles reflected a general connection to the research questions, but I remained open to new categories that I had not anticipated emerging from the data. The portions that seemed not to relate to the research questions were not coded in particular. I had not created any categories prior to or during my pilot interviews. Upon completion of my first five interviews, I coded all five comprehensively within one week to increase indexing similarity.

Codes were then grouped together under larger subject headings of main ideas. I created the most categories from the first interview with modifications after each additional interview; I saved a node summary report in NVivo to show my indexing development as the coding progressed. A majority of codes were assigned within the first five interviews. Subsequent interviews spawned additional codes but at a much slower rate of addition. A minority of codes were added with each successive interview that reflected any divergent information from each respondent or any alternative train of inquiry from the previous interviews. My categorical indexing was transferred interactively from my research questions to the data and back

32. Shim, "Marital Maintenance," 47–48.

33. King and Horrocks, *Interviews*, 153–74; Rubin and Rubin, *Qualitative Interviewing*, 204–7.

34. Ritchie and Lewis, *Qualitative Research Practice*, 224.

again.[35] The coding and grouping levels of analysis were completed individually for each transcript, leading to forty category headings or indices. During this second phase, both within-case and cross-case comparisons were made, and potential themes that encased larger sets of indices began to emerge. Upon reflection, I realized that I may have created too many categories initially. No harm was incurred, however, other than wasted time; in fact, this extra effort may have helped me to better study the material.

The third stage of data analysis included a thorough review of all interview material with a view to finalizing themes. Coding decisions were checked and rechecked for appropriateness and accuracy, uniqueness and comparability. I especially looked for anomalies that stood out from the coded data. The third stage solidified the initial themes.

My approach to data organization was a combination of cross-sectional and non-sectional strategies.[36] Cross-sectional analysis sorts information categorically while non-sectional ordering is more holistic and mindful of the "life cycle" of narrative. I used both strategies to consider the same data in different ways for different purposes. In addition, I chose to perform literal, interpretative, and reflexive readings of the data to discover 1) the participants' understanding of their social reality, 2) my interpretation of their accounts, and 3) my participation in their data construction.[37] For example, literal indexing categories included Personal Demographics and Description of Study Abroad Experience. Interpretative indexing categories were titles such as Stigmas, Resistance, and Sense of Calling.

From the initial themes, four main themes were chosen as the most salient upon which to elaborate and further analyze. The final data analysis from these interviews and questionnaires is presented in chapter 8.

Questionnaire

Questionnaire results were compiled for a quantitative analysis of data, and particular attention was paid to the three identities assessed (religious, ethnic, and national). The quantitative results were also considered in relation to the inferences drawn during qualitative analysis.

Preliminary analysis. The data were first re-coded in Excel before being analyzed in SPSS v.18.0. Questionnaire items were regrouped and re-coded for clarity based on participant responses. Before analysis, variables were checked for impossible values, duplicate cases, and missing data.

35. Mason, *Qualitative Researching*, 121.

36. Ibid., 107, 129–31.

37. Ibid., 109.

Distributions of continuous variables were examined to determine if normality assumptions were met or whether non-parametric statistics needed to be used. Extreme outliers were investigated in order to check for technical or clerical errors. If the size of a measurement could not be attributed to such an error, it was included in the analysis, and the effect of deleting the observation was reported. Descriptive statistics were then calculated for all variables. Specifically, for continuous variables, means, standard deviations, medians, minima, and maxima were calculated. For categorical variables, frequencies and percentages were calculated. This preliminary analysis was also used to examine research questions 1, 2, and 4. An alpha level of .05 was used to determine significance levels for all analysis throughout the study.

Primary analysis. For the first research question, frequencies and percentages of participants' perceptions of the most important identity were examined. In other words, participants' rankings of the importance of religious identity, ethnic identity, and national identity were assessed.

For the first part of the second research question, percentages of the extent to which religious faith determined location after graduation were assessed.

For the second part of the second research question, a chi-square test was used to determine whether individuals who cited religious reasons as the primary factor in determining their location were more likely to leave the U.S. after graduation. Specifically, individuals were classified as citing religious reasons for their location after graduation or not citing religious reasons. These two groups were then compared by their decisions to stay in or leave the U.S. upon graduation to determine whether individuals who cited religious reasons were more likely to live outside the U.S. than individuals who did not do so.

For the third quantitative research question, a Friedman test was used to examine potential differences in individuals' ratings of their religious, ethnic, and national identities. If the Friedman test showed an overall difference between the three scores, a series of Wilcoxon-signed rank tests were used to determine specific differences between each of the three identities. Nonparametric statistics were chosen for this analysis due to the non-normality of the data on religious identity.

Additional Data: Field Notes and Email Correspondence

Email correspondence and participant observation notes augmented the data collected through interviews and questionnaires. These notes were determined to be relevant and collated into the data analysis.

8

Field Research on Identity in Migration

How AND WITH WHAT resources did my evangelical respondents construct their social worlds? This chapter includes findings from and analysis of the qualitative and quantitative data that was collected in the course of this study: the relationship between religion and the construction of personal identity, the relationship between migration and the individual, the negotiation of multiple identities for this educated migrant population, and the relationship between religion and individual migration.

Prior to a discussion of these findings, a few introductory comments should be made. First, beliefs cannot be essentialized as static. Beliefs certainly can and do change, as demonstrated by these respondents who experienced both a religious conversion and multiple cultures. Core beliefs can also remain relatively consistent over time. Because persons are always incorporating new information and experience into their beliefs, these beliefs do evolve and deepen.

Secondly, from a sociological point of view, constructions of identity can only be understood within particular and intersecting social contexts. Richard Jenkins deftly summarizes these contexts (which are particular to a discussion of ethnic categorization but broadly applicable) in order of increasing formality: primary socialization, routine public interaction, sexual relationships, communal relationships, membership in informal groups, kinship relationships, life-course transitions, healing and medicine, secondary socialization, market relationships, marketing, employment, administrative allocation, social control, organized politics, social policy, official classification, and science.[1]

Thirdly, three contexts (geo-historical period, religious socialization, and foreign educational training) significantly influenced my respondents. By their own admissions, however, a reality exists outside of themselves that directs the process of their identifications. Their references to the supernatural, while they do not offer the empirical evidence to form a sociological theory, must be included to explain the motifs and motivations of human behavior.[2] How these individuals credit the supernatural in the development of their identities in migration is of particular interest. Bearing in mind the complexity of human behavior due to the multiple contexts mentioned above and other factors, as well as the interaction of these factors with one another, this discussion will describe the relationship between religion, migration, and the dynamic construction of personal identities.

CONTINUITY OF IDENTITY: PERSONAL FAITH AND IDENTITY CONSTRUCTION

As I observed my participants in bustling metropolitan cities and quieter country towns, they talked about themselves most often in terms of their religious identities. Their self-descriptions involved their relationship with God and, particularly, the person of Jesus Christ. Of those I interviewed, 39 percent had a nominal Protestant or Catholic upbringing, 22 percent had been raised by practicing Protestant parents, and 11 percent were second-generation Christians whose parents had converted from a different faith. Almost one-third (28 percent) were first-generation Christians from other religious or non-religious backgrounds (atheism, Buddhism, Hinduism, or Islam). All claimed to have experienced a spiritual conversion, most of them during their late teen years or early twenties. Their self-constructions of personal identity seemed to be rooted in this singular conversion experience as well as in their ongoing relationships with God and with their religious communities. Religion can connect the individual to the group as a "basis of association" and also offer "expressions of sharing meaning."[3] Since many religious processes occur outside of a traditional congregational context, this study investigates religion in the daily lives of these graduates—especially in their educations and return migrations—and offers one possible interpretation of the importance of their religious identities.

1. Jenkins, *Rethinking Ethnicity*, 65–73.
2. McGuire, *Religion*, 8.
3. Ibid., 25.

How did aspects of these graduates' personal faith relate to identity construction in their migration experiences? All of my interviewees reported that their faith provided them with a coherence of meaning and purpose.[4] According to their accounts, they claimed their relationships with a divine being determined their identities and formed the basis of everything else in their lives. My respondents described their identities as something they believed was given to them and was strongly related to the person of Christ.[5] Despite their differing cultural contexts, this emphasis on the centrality of Christ to their identities was clear. For instance, a participant (#4) who was raised as an atheist in formerly Communist Europe reported:

> I am a person who has given his life to Christ . . . understanding the identity that He has given.

Others described similar self-conceptions:

> To be a Christian is to change the core of my desires in my heart. Before I was a Christian, I desired different things. . . . I am extremely happy that His presence changes me continuously and helps me to be a different person. . . . It's a reality that I am different. . . . I know I'm not the same person. . . . It's an experiential thing when Christ becomes my life for real. #7

> I am what I am because of Christ, and Christ is the one who produces fruit in me. That's my identity. #10

> My identity [is] how I see God seeing me or how God looks at me or how God sees me. And then how that impacts me to then assess wherever I am. #12

> My Christian identity . . . is something that really doesn't have to do with cultural things or with political things. It's something that really has to do with the core of who I am and how nothing—not even my relationship with my spouse or with my child—even my religious identity hasn't gotten to that core. And the only one that has gotten to that core is God. #13

> It was during my first year of university where particularly, my Christian faith . . . I felt that, no, there's something real about that, and it needs to be central in my life. #15

---

4. For related findings, consider Lee et al., *Heart of Religion*; Mooney, *Faith*.

5. The processes by which identity is made, constructed in discourse, are described in Bamberg et al., "Discourse and Identity Construction," 178–79, 186–87.

A graduate living in Singapore, a comparatively affluent nation, asserted his realization that humans are not "self-sufficient beings" but depend on something more than food—in his terms, by "every word that proceeds from the mouth of God"—to be sustained in life (Matt 4:4). While religious identity was perhaps the most crucial factor in guiding these graduates' lives, it was not the only sociological factor. Multiple sources of socialization (family, education, historical period, cultural context, etc.) combined to form different processes for each of these graduates, and the alterations to their personal identities were continual.

These graduates further believed that their interactions with a supernatural being directed their daily embodied practices. I observed this approach to their daily tasks as summarized:

> I am purchased. I am no longer my own, I mean, property of my own. I am owned by God. He has plans for me. He has purposed things for me to do from before I was even born. And that's what defines my way. #1

> [My identity] is refined and changed through my spiritual beliefs, which in many cases contradict those first and initials steps towards creating my own identity. So I had to refine it through meditation and through reading Scripture and understanding, okay, who I am now as a person without all these things that I just mentioned, and who does God make me or want me to be? #7

In each of the six countries I visited, participants displayed many similar practices. Their families prayed before meals in both private and public settings. Each of their homes was decorated with religious works of art and wall hangings of Bible verses. They interacted on a daily basis with like-minded believers, even as they otherwise functioned as a religious minority within their local communities. I joined them in their regular activities: Sunday church services, home group Bible studies, lunch meetings, social events, and neighborhood outreach events. For example, Tirana, the Albanian capital, hosts an annual National Book Fair where groups set up booths to present their publications. I attended with my participants, who took turns representing their organization alongside other booths such as multiple Islamic associations and the U.S. Department of State. Of the one hundred booths present, only four were Christian, an indicator of the minority status of Christianity in Albania. While my participants differed from one another by their contextual constraints, they conveyed to me that they chose their daily practices in relation to the God they worshipped.

My respondents described their constructions of God as a deity who relates personally to them and directly affects their material and immaterial existence. This God is their personal caretaker in life's journey, and they strived to seek God's desire for their decisions, which they ascertained primarily through the guidance of God's Spirit, the Bible, and their church communities. The participants certainly also discussed uncertainties in their lives and concerns about their present circumstances; the doubts they expressed about the futures of their ministries, schisms with co-workers, and concerns for their children's schooling illustrate that their faith did not exempt them from the complications of daily existence.

In addition to providing a sense of purpose and direction, their religious faith seemed to offer the participants significant contentment. Notwithstanding circumstantial hardships, each of them claimed that their Christian faith fulfilled them. In the context of their studies abroad, 94 percent described their dependence on and contentment with God during the arduous process of relocation.

These individuals, however, still faced stark economic realities. How did one relocate as a religious minority to a community where ministers are often unpaid and are often, at best, bi-vocational? Sixteen of my eighteen interviewees had paid ministerial positions in their home countries arranged either before leaving to study abroad or prior to graduation. Of the remaining two, one returned to a secular profession. The other became the primary caregiver for his children as his wife had an employment contract to fulfill. What happened to the sense of God's provision when adequate financial resources were not present? In their dependence on God, these individuals also depended heavily on human participants. Financial provision was credited to God when it had been received from other donors, as one gentleman shared:

> For thirteen years, we have seen God provide for us. We raised
> our own support, and we've never been without food or shelter
> or clothes, so he has always provided. And this faith, that he
> will provide, encouraged us to go, even though we didn't know
> much. #4

In fact, 72 percent of my interviewees were substantially supported by financial donors from the United States. Interestingly, this provision fell along geographical lines for my interview sample; those living in Singapore and Hong Kong did not receive such support. Still, as respondent #10 confessed, religious faith was required to relocate before provisions were procured:

> When we come back, we have to bring only four suitcases. Trust God for the rest. And so where we are going and what we are going to do, a lot of questions. But again, with faith only we took a step, and we came here.

The quantitative survey further assessed the reported importance of the graduates' various identities (religious, ethnic, and national). Frequencies and percentages of the international theological graduates' perceptions of their most important identity were examined. Of the participants who answered this question, 96.6 percent rated religious identity as the identity most important to them. Approximately 1.6 percent rated national identity as the most important, and 0.5 percent rated ethnic identity as the most important. Approximately 1.3 percent of participants believed another form of identity was the most important. Participants also conveyed varying amounts of concern for their children's educational, economic, and social opportunities in their countries of origin. Of those who responded, over two-fifths were not concerned at all (23.3 percent) or concerned very little (19.5 percent). Almost three-fifths were somewhat concerned (22.1 percent), very concerned (22.1 percent), or extremely concerned (13.1 percent). Their responses also indicated that the amount of discrimination toward Christian adherents in their countries of origin was present but less pronounced. Of those who responded, over three-fifths considered discrimination not at all present in their country (25.5 percent) or not very much present (37.9 percent). The remaining two-fifths judged discrimination to be somewhat present (20.4 percent), a considerable amount (11.1 percent), or very much present (5 percent). These responses demonstrate that even a strong religious identity does not absolve other life concerns, which is consistent with similar findings from interview responses. How this correlation varies by country suggests another avenue for further research.

No survey question directly assessed a sense of dependence on God in migration. Of those who did leave the United States, however, almost one-fourth (24.4 percent) named funding as the item most needed to return overseas. Those without pre-established funding prior to their departures, therefore, may have relied in part on their religious faith when they chose to leave. Moreover, those who remained in the U.S. rather than returning to their countries of origin (27.5 percent) reported that they did so due to an offer of employment in the U.S., one which they may not have been able to procure overseas no matter their level of spiritual desire to return home.

Considering the prior religious commitment of these individuals, these reports are not surprising. Rather, they hold value in establishing the strength of the perceived importance of their religious identity relative to their other identities. Still, why did these respondents describe themselves in this manner and construct their personal identities primarily in spiritual terms? Scholars have asserted that it is in human nature to construct personal worlds in a narrative manner; to be human is to be storied.[6] Sociologically, which public narratives are available crucially determine how people view themselves.[7] Certainly, my respondents were recipients of local social schemas being written onto them, so to speak. I propose further that they expressed considerable agency by placing themselves into a particular religious narrative that was not as easily sustained in their local contexts. From their reports, they perceived themselves as active participants in this biblical Christian narrative and its continuance. One's chosen system of meaning is applied to explain one's reality.

How could these return migrants have adopted a social narrative that was not encouraged locally? Despite their minority status as evangelical Christians, their global ties provided the sufficient "plausibility structures" for them to maintain a strong sense of their religious identities.[8] Several of those I visited lived under much harsher environmental conditions than they might have faced if they had remained in the United States. Despite this hardship they were empowered by their global religious ties and by conversations with Christian colleagues via Skype, church services, and seminary chapel messages streamed via the Internet. For example, in India where no Christian radio station exists, my participants played Christian music from CDs every time we drove in their vehicle. The reinforcement through Facebook should also not be minimized; during my stay I observed each participant referencing email, Facebook, blogs, and other web pages to connect with other Christians around the world. Even if their local contexts might have discouraged their minority religious identity, their established global religious ties compensated for this shortcoming. Identities are deconstructed and reconstructed every day, and what these participants could access continued to form them. They seemed to maintain their religious identities by depending on these resources.[9] Social factors, not the least of which were organizational connections, global ties, and a spiritually formative graduate education, greatly supported the effect of their religious faith on the construction of their personal identities.

6. McAdams, *The Person*, 405–11.

7. Park, "Ethnic and Religious Identities," 9.

8. Plausibility structures, coined by Peter Berger, are social relations and processes creating structural support and a social base for a system of meaning to exist. McGuire, *Religion*, 36–37.

9. The ability for self-election in identity-making is not ubiquitous. Ibid., 57.

DISCONTINUITY OF IDENTITY: MIGRATION AS MOLD

After returning overseas, these interviewees re-joined the ethnic majorities of their countries of origin and became members of a religious minority as evangelical Christians. Even as cultural insiders, 94 percent of those interviewed felt like outsiders at times in their local communities for their faith or for their adopted habits from studying abroad. How did international migration affect these individuals? This question afforded my participants an opportunity to explore and to reflect upon their experiences. How they described personal changes within themselves as a result of their migrations will be highlighted, namely their changes in perception and practice as well as the forging of new partnerships and trajectories.

Changes of Perception

Seventeen of eighteen interviewees commented that their experiences abroad led to changes in their personal perceptions of reality. In other words, studying abroad provided them with a sufficient period of time to be exposed to and absorb different patterns of thinking about life. One student illustrated this well in his political shift:

> I would categorize myself as a staunch free market person before coming here, and I thought it's a biblical view. My understanding of the Old Testament gained here actually corrected this view in such a way that I understand God took care of the weak and poor and put some limits on the rich and powerful and how can they use their position of power toward—in relations with the weaker and poor. So I no longer so pure or free market person. I actually believe that the Old Testament, as a social model, actually suggests that we should be very careful about not leaving people who are helpless help to themselves, for example. . . . That's ironic in a sense because of [my country's] socialist background, you were pushed maybe mentally more to capitalism, but then [I am] in a capitalistic society studying the Old Testament. #1

Exposure to new cultural contexts led to a myriad of new conclusions regarding gender equality, family relations, the value of humanity, racial discrimination, personal care, and politics, among other areas. The most frequently mentioned change, which was described by 61 percent of interviewees, was a transition from legalistic to grace-oriented thinking.

Changes of perception did seem to coalesce based on each participant's country of origin. Graduates from India more often discussed the
influences of the ideas they adopted in the U.S. about the value of individual
human life, whereas respondents from Hong Kong more often mentioned
shifts in their personal views regarding the benefits of democracy. A pilot
participant from South Korea mentioned how his view of marriage dramatically changed as a result of his studies abroad. The man had grown up in
a rural area, and he described how Confucian thinking and his work as a
police officer in a "more macho or male-dominant organization" had taught
him to see men and women as unequal:

> I didn't have a sense of husband and wife, as a family, you're a
> separate entity, with equal position. And wife has same right to
> talk as a companion. . . . I didn't have any good chances to learn
> about that kind of thing. So my marriage was kind of suffering.
> My wife was under that kind of pressure. So when we moved
> here, not culturally in general, but especially by the professors
> here and by the examples of their life and humility and how they
> deal with their wives. . . . That really changed my, you know,
> perspective on my marriage and about my relationship with
> my wife. So I think that was the grace, the gift, and the change
> we—I—actually I experienced. Pilot interviewee #4

Regardless of the participant's background, the most responses re-
volved around one particular perceptual change. This was a transition
from a legalistic type of thinking to grace-oriented thinking. Many of my
interviewees came from conservative evangelical communities (Brethren,
Baptist, etc.), and their studies in the U.S., even at a conservative seminary,
broadened their views about what they had previously considered to be
inappropriate. For example, an Indian graduate, prior to his stay in the
U.S., had thought that only communion bread without yeast could be used,
movies were forbidden, and that the Bible must be read first thing in the
morning. By living in a different cultural context of Christian believers, he
determined that these behaviors were prescriptions, not requirements, for
Christian conduct.

Many participants also shared, however, that some of their personal
views did *not* change with international migration but were instead fortified and became more "rooted" (#7). They claimed that their religious faith
was their plumb line from which they assessed their ways of thinking. The
perceptions that were reinforced rather than changed, however, are not
easily categorized; they did not clearly pertain to moral issues, nor were
they clearly *not* of a moral nature. Some graduates' views regarding racial

reconciliation and the treatment of women—both deeply moral issues—
did change, but their views about traditional sexuality and marriage, for
instance, did not.

My respondents tended to differentiate between cultural mores (beliefs they reported had changed) and essential tenets of the Christian faith
(which they reported had not changed).[10] For example, interviewee #3
stated:

> Of course, there are some basics, some essentials about Chris-
> tianity, but there is not [only] black and white. There is a wide
> area of gray area, you know, where people can live out their own
> Christianity in a good way and not necessarily the same way
> you do.

Even this differentiation is slippery, for what they once believed was
fundamentally important—such as a style of worship or a particular de-
votional time—did shift over time. None of my participants, however,
reported that any of their Christian doctrinal beliefs as expressed in the
historical church creeds had changed. What seemed to change more than
their perceptions of Christian ideals was their perception of the appropriate
behavioral approach toward responses to others who did not share their
views. As one graduate (#2) quipped:

> Do I still hold to our theology? You bet . . . and I understand
> these things much better now. But, you know, to be there theo-
> logically, I do not have to be a griping, fundamentalist, legalistic
> fanatic.

Participants most often used the biblical text as the central factor to
determine the validity of their views. A graduate (#12) explained:

> [Studying in the U.S.] has helped me to not just take something
> on just because a good personality is saying it, but to really
> check it against the lens of the Scriptures and see, okay, will it go
> through the lens of the Scripture and still hold true?

Strikingly, the issue of gender in senior church leadership was one that
did not change for my interviewees; the views they held prior to their studies abroad did not alter. Interviewees of both genders considered women to
be either eligible or ineligible for senior church leadership.[11] In South Asia,

10. Paul Hiebert referred to this distinction as "critical contextualization." See
Hiebert, "Critical Contextualization."

11. Some evangelicals contest whether women are allowed a position of final authority, such as elder or senior pastor, over an entire congregation. Whether women

where some conservative churches permit females to be senior ministers while their counterparts in the U.S. or Europe do not, some of my female Asian interviewees were *more* conservative than the culturally dominant view. Despite Europe's greater liberality regarding gender roles in general, conservative churches there hold to more traditional views, as tended my participants. Given the lower female percentage of seminarians in general, the sample was insufficient to draw strong conclusions, but the question does demonstrate that opinions obviously differed—even among women—on this matter, and that these opinions did not change after a period of international migration.

Additionally, graduates reported that they needed to re-evaluate their cultural mores after returning to their countries of origin and had to decide which practices to keep, discard, or resume. One gentleman described this need for assessment:

> In a sense, you are innocent to your own reality that you grew up in. You are not aware of your own cultural biases or your own culture, and unless you make a really hard effort to exegete your own culture, then you are doomed to think what, you know, mass media tells you to believe. #7

Several of the female interviewees, for instance, after experiencing certain personal freedoms in the U.S., described having to modify their behavior after returning to more traditional cultural contexts such as India, Hong Kong, and Singapore. As participant #11 noted:

> But in our culture, very often I have to keep quiet [or else] then people will think [my husband] is not a good leader.

Participant #10 further apprised:

> It's definitely more challenge to be in ministry as a woman in [country] because more of our work is our identity with our husband. And whatever we do, it's in connection, and we do it together. . . . I think the way we are structured, the way [this country] still is structured.

The male graduates with more egalitarian views also faced considerable resistance upon their return if *they* crossed prescribed gender boundaries by doing duties culturally assigned to females, such as washing dishes or by having their wives handle financial transactions. Returning home, therefore, often required a partial reversion to the original cultural context,

---

can serve in ministerial positions or in senior leadership in any capacity is sometimes misunderstood as the issue.

which one participant described as "removing this [mind-set of] American-ization" (#3).

Changes in Practices

Seventeen of the eighteen interviewees commented that their experiences abroad led to changes in their personal practices. These changes fell into two main categories: organizational and individual. The organizational practices that the interviewees reported discovering or adopting in the U.S. were teamwork, delegation, worship service style, authenticity, and goal prioriti-zation. Individual behavioral changes included changes in structuring their day, skills, communication style, procedures, and personal growth. Nearly 40 percent of participants described how they adopted a more structured lifestyle, particularly in punctuality and planning. New skills that they ac-quired often related to their areas of study (such as teaching, linguistics, or exegesis) but also included more broadly applicable skills such as projecting confidence, emotional independence, creativity, objectivity, critical evalu-ation, and intentionality. Various participants approached their daily tasks with new habits. Regarding trash disposal, participant #9 relayed:

> Like throwing trash everywhere, we wouldn't think twice before that, before coming to the U.S., you know? Throw it anywhere in the street. But now, we know we can't do that. I have to put it in my bag and bring it and put it in my trash can.

One third of those interviewed expressed that they found resistance to their new practices by some in their home communities, but as an inter-viewee shared:

> We had to . . . just kind of hold our ground . . . because we know they're a good thing, regardless of the fact that they don't really come from our culture. #13

One graduate explained how some nationals who had converted to Christianity were still benefiting from their caste designation even though they had left Hinduism:

> The pastor has to teach people, you know, "You are Christians now. Go and change your certificate, or don't claim those privi-leges. It is fraudulently claimed because you are Christian now, but you are claiming the privileges of the caste that you used to be." A lot of Christians do, in the rural area, and particularly, they are going for college admissions and all those things. #10

Although these individuals underwent processes of change, their behavioral patterns did not necessarily remain static once adopted. Interviewees described instances where they would, depending on the context, fluctuate back and forth between cultural practices. I visualize this process of cultural flexing as an image of an accordion. Just as an accordion can be pressed or released by the musician, individuals can expand or contract their cultural patterns to meet the perceived demands of a situation. Regarding simple linguistic or cultural habits, these participants mastered a set of cultural cues in one context (the U.S.) but reverted to their previous patterns of behavior after returning to their countries of origin. Sometimes which habit to employ was not always clear. For instance, I was dining one evening in the home of a respondent while visiting his country. While it may be acceptable in that culture to use one's utensil to pick a piece of food from one's teeth, when the husband moved his knife toward his teeth, I saw his wife gesture an undeniable message: using your knife in this way is inappropriate in this context. A flood of realization or even embarrassment, as I perceived it, washed over his face as he quickly lowered his arm. Even though I was in their country, an American in the room trumped a cultural habit that may have otherwise been permitted. At other times, participants expressed surprise at how much they had forgotten of their native patterns. Take language, for example, as one participant revealed:

> I used Google to get my English into Hindi word. Now, I have to get my Hindi to English. Can you believe what's happening to me? #9

For cultural patterns that were infused with substantial moral meaning, however, participants communicated that they intentionally chose which behaviors to practice. The choices they described seemed to fall into three categories: alignment with the predominant culture, an amalgamation of cultures, or an opposition to the predominant culture in which they were present. For any practice that did not pose a personal moral conflict, they usually aligned with the contextual mores. This accommodation of fitting in tended to fall into areas of daily living such as eating or accomplishing domestic or business tasks.

Some of my interviewees capitalized on their intercultural experiences to formulate a combination of practices from both contexts. This amalgamation led to mixing cultural patterns. For example, one of the Hungarian graduates affirmed that he used teaching methods from his U.S. education yet differed from the U.S. customs in some ways. In Hungary, introductions before public speaking are not common and usually consist of no more than giving the speaker's name, whereas in the U.S., introductions tend to "sing these long odes about you and your great achievements." This man followed the Hungarian style of introduction but incorporated it into a teaching style adapted from the United States.

The participants chose a third response, opposition, when they perceived that a cultural pattern morally conflicted with their religious beliefs. This practice of maintaining difference despite the cost of appearing to be a cultural anomaly grew out of strongly held values that the participants were unwilling to forgo. These choices often set them at odds with other social actors. For my respondents in Hong Kong, Singapore, and India, for instance, this meant that they did not participate in cultural religious festivals as detailed earlier. Even among evangelical Christians within one country, however, opinions about what to oppose differed. For instance, a graduate expounded on how Christians should respond to the custom of bribing physicians in Albania. Before a woman delivers a baby, her family commonly pays the doctor in addition to what is normally charged. According to this graduate, Christians differ on whether or not to pay the doctor in advance, and even Christian doctors disagree on whether or not to accept this payment. When asked what he had done personally, my respondent said that when his wife was leaving the hospital after childbirth, he gave a gift to her doctor. If the doctor had demanded extra payment, the husband said:

> I think I would still pay the money because otherwise I'd risk the life of my wife. I think they'll be responsible before God for doing what's wrong. I would see myself as doing everything I can to save my wife and protect her. So it's not an easy thing.

Another shared:

> There's a lot of corruption [in home country], and I think our faith really keeps us from kind of feeding that. Maybe something like bribing a police officer out of a fine, you know, that you were really guilty of. We would go ahead and pay [the ticket, not the bribe]. However, things would be different if we had to give a gift to, like, a government official to let us accomplish something for the church, which he would have had to do anyway. It's not something illegal, but we know that, unless we give him that a thank-you gift, he's not going to do it. I would say for illegal things, not, but for the things that are legal and that they should be doing and that are good, personally I feel like it's okay. #13

Lastly, my interviewees reported that the changes of perceptions they experienced due to studying abroad often led to significant changes in their moral and political practices. This information highlights the value of international migration in that multiple perspectives were shared and appraised. For example, in regard to political principles, graduate #16 surmised:

> I think a little influence is the U.S. [having] a high regard towards democratic ideals, and this is something [my country] is growing. And I think by living in the States, it does help me to also think more in terms of this area.

This graduate struggled with his government's course of action and had voted for more democratic changes in his country.

Experiencing multiple perspectives does not simplify decisions about how to live, but it does draw attention to the complexity of social interaction and the need to draw conclusions carefully. Sometimes the benefits of exposure to cultural variation are more apparent. Consider this graduate's description of how his perceptions changed:

> Previously, I had no idea of Africans. You know, I come from a caste discriminatory society. Everything is discriminated based on color. Caste is an English word, but you know, it comes from a Sanskrit word, *varna*. *Varna* is color, so you are in a society based on your color. . . . And until I came to America, I did not know that I can work towards breaking down the barrier. But America definitely gave me that opportunity because the church that I was part of was an African-American church. And I stayed on the church for twelve years, and I was able to see how they look at the world. And now I'm able to look at the society as God's beautiful creation. White, black, yellow—they are not inferior, superior. And I can actually work towards unity of people while we celebrate our distinctives. So both the churches, the church we started in [the U.S.] and the church that we are now starting in [Asia], the number one value is breaking down the barrier. [In the U.S.] it was the class, racial barrier. Here it is caste, color, and regional barriers. #6

Individuals within different societies, then, can evaluate varying standards of conduct and manners to promote a more peaceful way and, hopefully, a more peaceful world.

Analogies from Survey Results

After the qualitative analysis revealed this theme of change in perception and practice, two survey questions were created to assess if any changes were also reported by the larger questionnaire sample. Frequencies and percentages of which ways studying abroad had changed their thinking the most and their behavior the most were examined. Of the participants who answered how their thinking changed, encountering a different worldview (28.9 percent) and learning to think critically (23 percent) were ranked highest, followed by learning new ways of interacting with people (19.4 percent) and thinking creatively (14.5 percent). Of the participants who answered the question of how studying abroad had changed their behavior the most, 34.3 percent cited that they related to people differently. 30.8 percent cited that they had new values they had not lived by before. 13.2 percent said they had become more tolerant, and 7.0 percent said they were more patient. Another 8.4 percent cited other ways in which their behavior had changed the most. 4.6 percent cited they became better citizens, and only 1.6 percent experienced no behavioral changes or were not sure if they had.

In summary, both samples of participants described how their views had been greatly challenged and broadened by their study abroad experiences. Their thinking had become more critical and nuanced when they were faced with multiple interpretations. These changes highlight the fluidity of personal identity, as personal opinion or self-perception is contextually influenced and changes over time.

While international migration broadened the participants' views in several areas, the kind of socialization—a conservative graduate theological education—that they received while in this new cultural context (the southern U.S.) greatly affected the types of perceptual changes they encountered. While a conservative theological education would be expected to reinforce previously held opinions on morality and ethics, the cultural differences of the U.S. expanded these interviewees' views in other ways, namely from a legalistic way of thinking to increased open-mindedness. It is not clear if this open-mindedness reflected the influence of the conservative evangelical seminary culture or the democratic, liberal American culture. Presumably, both were influential.

In considering the relationship of migration to personal identity, migration led to both an increased fluidity and a strengthened rigidity of beliefs and practices for this sample. A new cultural and educational context gave them the opportunity to actively question their assumptions. This process expanded some of their previously held beliefs and practices. Notably, these shifts occurred more often for beliefs and practices that they considered non-essential to their theological "meaning-content."[12] They carefully distinguished cultural conventions from transcultural biblical principles.

12. Ting-Toomey, "Matrix," 119.

Lost and Found: Changing Partnerships, Networks, and Trajectories

How were my respondents received by their religious leadership and congregations when they returned to their religious communities at home? As previously stated, half of those interviewed resided in Singapore, Hong Kong, and India while the remaining half lived in six European countries (Romania, Poland, Hungary, Albania, Italy, and Spain). Given the number of geographic, social, and personal variables, it is difficult to draw strict conclusions about how they were received; several patterns, however, did emerge from the data. Three of these are particularly significant: the respondents' receptions by local religious leadership, their emerging transnational networks, and the personal trajectories of their life paths.

The receptions of these returnees by their local religious leadership seemed either positive or negative, with very little in between. Surprisingly, reports of reactions from their home ministries did not fall between these polarities, at least for these respondents. With one exception, the returnees reported negative or positive perceptions but not both. The nature of their receptions was not particular by country but rather reflected their previous organizational connections. The religious institutions that had maintained continuous ties with students during their sojourns tended to welcome them home with enthusiasm and respect. They were eager to "capitalize on [their] experience" (#1) in the U.S. and placed them in new positions of leadership upon their return. One of my interviewees from Poland was promoted from local to national leadership as a strategist and human resource manager upon his return due to his intercultural experience and training. Each of the graduates (from Albania, Hong Kong, Hungary, India, Poland, or Spain) that maintained an organizational relationship during their period of study received similar recognition (50 percent), and all of them still worked for these same organizations at the time of their interviews. The other half (from Hong Kong, India, Italy, Romania, or Singapore) reported a more negative reception and difficulties in reconnecting upon their return. Two-thirds of this latter group established new ties during their studies abroad with U.S. organizations; these groups have largely supported their work overseas since graduation. Again, the negative reactions from these religious groups did not seem to differ by country, nor did they seem to differ for any other apparent reason. No factor, such as type of local ministry or gender, seemed to be associated with the way the participants were received by local religious leadership.

While a general sense of esteem was reported by those who studied abroad across the nine countries, the respondents also admitted that their international experiences *created* tensions at home. In Italy and Hungary, graduates reported being perceived as "the Americans." Other graduates from Spain and Albania shared that their suggestions were often discounted because they were seen as "a little Americanized." Another elaborated:

> These four years were very important for me, but they didn't want to listen what I learned, you know, who I am now. They just wanted [who I was] four years ago. I felt like they communicate to me, "Just forget about this. Nothing happened." Just go through, we live together. That's why it was hard for me, and maybe I did something wrong or communicate wrong. I didn't want to say, like, I had *better* experience. I just *had* this experience. It was hard for them to listen. That's why I stop do this. Sometimes I regret say anything because it's not create a good atmosphere. Spouse of interviewee #1

Some said that they were treated more tentatively by their local religious organizations. One of my interviewees from Albania claimed that his ideas were met with discomfort, even pessimism. More than once, if his proposed idea was not favored, the claim that this was "an American idea" was the reason for its rejection. Another graduate elaborated:

> It's hard to say if you can know these kind of things. If we stayed in a better communication with our people back there, that would be possible, but these people change. The guy who took us to this responsibility stepped down two years later, and now there's someone else who is leading the organization. They also had their own view or vision on how things function. #1

More significantly, some interviewees' return sometimes posed a threat to local religious leadership. Upon returning to his home church in Italy, one pastor surmised that he was perceived as an intruder:

> I didn't go there with a view to take back my position. I was aware that now there was a new leadership. I want to be just resourceful. And they decided—this is my guess—they were scared that I want to overcome them, and so they don't want to make room for me.

Another graduate from India faced a similar reticence among some colleagues in his denomination. He described several incidents where certain leaders, even pastors, within his denomination inquired what he was going to do upon his return and if he would join the same denomination because "they thought that our coming back may jeopardize their position."

One-third of the graduates interviewed did not return to their home locales, but rather settled in different regions or countries. In the first case, my respondents were perceived at times as outsiders or strangers despite their similar national and cultural ties. For instance, South Indians faced regional prejudices upon relocating to North India. In another case, one of the graduates in Singapore encountered outdated stereotypes of his U.S. alma mater. Conversations over time allowed him to correct these assumptions, and his acceptance was finally gained by another legitimizing factor—his adjunct faculty status at a local seminary in the country.

Another noteworthy pattern was that of emerging religious transnational networks. Almost two-thirds (61 percent) of participants mentioned forging new partnerships due to their migration experiences. Because of the graduates' experiences abroad and their new American contacts, they created new pathways among themselves, their local churches, and ministry organizations for transnational collaboration. Their American contacts included seminary professors, fellow graduates, ministerial leaders, churches, mission agencies, businessmen, and lay members of their congregations. My respondents from Hungary, Italy, India, and Albania mentioned that they were hosting a steady stream of guest speakers in their countries—whom they had met during their time in the U.S.—to lead Christian conferences, marriage seminars, seminary courses, and more. U.S. organizations partnered with my participants to not only provide resources, but also to collaborate on foreign ministry strategies, events, training, conferences, and publications.

These relationships were reciprocal, as U.S.-based organizations also gained foreign resources that supplemented their needs, such as information, education, mission leaders, and public speakers. My participants were consistently invited to speak in the U.S. at conferences and churches, to lecture at universities, and to form collaborative research teams with former colleagues and professors. Several of my respondents, for instance, were flown back to the U.S. by churches that had invited them to speak at their annual missions conferences. These partnerships varied but benefited graduates with an enlarged financial support base, a circuit of guest lecturers for their institutions abroad, or membership in American missionary organizations that operate worldwide. For instance, one graduate was employed by a U.S. ministry agency to work in his own country. These relationships evolved into multidirectional networks as individuals traveled, proposals were shared, and new connections were solidified.

The graduates' migrations allowed them to plot new trajectories for their lives as well as for their children's futures. One-third of interviewees shared that, while their studies abroad did not lead to residency in the

United States upon graduation, they were open to the possibility of their children studying or residing there.[13]

The respondents' migration experiences and their access to new forms of capital (social, financial, and spiritual) on my respondents' ministries were significant. These international relations, forged during their studies abroad, effectively bolstered these migrants' re-adaptations to their home countries, and in some cases provided the economic opportunities to make return a *possibility*. The prospect of returning to a country that faced depressed economic conditions led some to remain in the United States, according to the survey. Within the quantitative sample, 27.5 percent of those who stayed in the U.S. listed an offer of employment as the reason they remained while only 11.8 percent of those who departed the U.S. listed employment as the reason they left. Interestingly, 18.1 percent of those who stayed in the U.S. listed religious reasons for remaining while 39.4 percent of those who departed reported their departure was for religious reasons.

Despite the lack of access to social resources as religious minorities, the interviewees and their ministries were in large part maintained by global networks as an alternative form of social capital. Their international ties provided substantial access to resources that helped to sustain their alternative religious practices. Also, their migrations—even though temporary—forged new avenues for prolonged fellowship with other Christians via technology. For example, for the past four years I observed these graduates share their life experiences with one another and request support and prayer on a daily basis through Facebook. They enjoyed significant kinship ties, even for members of a religious minority in isolated contexts. These global ties sustained ministries that may not have survived otherwise. At the same time, foreign individuals, communities, and organizations gained substantial new material resources—financial, educational, social, and legal—as well as psychological, social, and cultural resources—prayers, corporate unity, and a sense of belonging—through these migrants when they returned home.

A cost remained, however, for those who migrated. Even as new partnerships were formed, former connections were lost over time and with physical distance. This prolonged physical distance both attenuated and strengthened previously salient identities, again depending on the particular geopolitical narrative of their new locations. While these respondents gained much in perspective and practice by living in different locations, no strong alternative superseded the importance of physical presence in forging longstanding relationships. For example, while some students were abroad,

13. Children who were born during the parent's study gained U.S. citizenship.

some home churches lost touch with them, changed their leadership, and altered their ministry goals among other shifts, making it difficult for the student to remain connected. One student who returned to South India lost his denominational connection during his absence abroad but established a new relationship with a U.S. organization through which he now receives donations, accountability, guidance, and administrative support.

Graduates' responses on the survey questionnaire rated the items they most needed when they returned overseas: 24 percent needed a ministry network of local Christian churches, leaders, and groups, 24.4 percent needed funding, 11.6 percent needed encouragement, and 11.2 percent needed a ministry mentor. This conveys that, upon returning home, they did not reintegrate as easily as might be expected. Those graduates, who visited their countries periodically or came from home churches that maintained contact with them, seemed to sustain their transnational connections more successfully. Similarly, their newly minted U.S. partnerships might in the future become endangered if they are not renewed by periodic visitation. There is no replacement for "being there," and for migrants who attempt to maintain transnational partnerships, sustaining a sufficient presence in multiple places is a stressful challenge indeed.

NEGOTIATION OF IDENTITY

From a myriad of possible identities, three were considered in this study. How did these graduates negotiate their religious, ethnic, and national identities in different contexts? How did these migrants, having lived in multiple cultural contexts, describe how they viewed themselves? As discussed above, they ranked their religious identities as more important than both their ethnic and national identities. Not only was their faith the most important aspect, but it also seemed to function as a paramount organizing principle for their other identities. One interviewee remarked:

> My identity doesn't come from my nationality as Indian, although that says I'm an Indian. But my primary identity, I would say, I'm an object of God's love. God loves me. That is my—the whole destiny is changed because of Jesus Christ. #6

This privileging of faith seemed to re-prioritize my participants' various identities.[14] They organized their other identities to align with their self-assigned primary identity. For instance, interviewee #11 stated:

14. The *centrality* of identity as the "individual's normative perceptions of self over time with respect to" a given identity is distinguished from the *salience* of a particular

> Because of my conviction—my religious convictions, I put them above all my other identities.

Another respondent summarized:

> I'm firstly a Christian, and of course, Singaporean, Chinese, of a certain background.

That they prioritized their religious identities, however, did not lessen the significance of their ethnic or cultural identities. Indeed, they esteemed and respected their heritage. For instance, one graduate shared:

> Being Chinese in some ways actually defines me. It's a large part of my identity. #18

Also apparent was their affinity toward their languages, literature, arts, history, heritage, and the shared idiosyncrasies of their cultures.

How did the ethnic identities of these participants relate to their national citizenship? All of the interviewees identified with their ethnic and/or cultural groups based on a shared history of experiences, but they did not describe their identities in national geopolitical terms. Not until I asked them did some of them articulate between their sense of ethnic and national identity such as this graduate:

> I would say it's more like a local sense of duty, like the community I'm in, the people around where I live or where I work . . . but in terms of a bigger like national, it would be more like ethnic sense of duty more than a national sense of duty. It would include like overseas Chinese, people from—ethnic Chinese. . . . I just don't normally think of the national duty. Yeah, it's local, ethnic, and then it's worldwide. #16

This gentleman's sense of ethnic identity, then, was less clearly tied to his nationality and stretched beyond national boundaries. A graduate from India insisted that there is no such thing as an "Indian" in the national sense and barely in the ethnic sense of shared identity. Within India, multiple ethnic groups and fifteen official languages—not including English—exist. This person tended to differentiate people by region as South or North Indians. On the other hand, later in his interview, he did explain what he deemed to be "Indian Indian," that which all Indians share in common: respect and care for elders, teachers, parents, and for the wider family.

---

identity in a given situation. Centrality involves a "hierarchical ranking of different identities relative to their proximity to the individual's core definition of self." Identity salience at a particular moment or event is a function of both person and situation combining to create a third outcome. Sellers et al., "Multidimensional Model," 25.

The religious identities of my respondents seemed to give them a sense of citizenship that was not based on any nation-state or demarcated by human boundaries. As participant #2 observed:

> We are eventually, you know, citizens of a different world. And probably that's the primary identity.

This alternate citizenship was not merely a matter of exchanging a national citizenship for a global one, although interviewee #1 did mention feeling like a "citizen of the world" because studying abroad and "meeting people from other countries helped to develop this kind of thinking." Rather, this citizenship was other-worldly and created a sense of belonging to a new world unmarred by human leadership.

Often, my interviewees relayed their country's political events, whether positive or negative, in terms of their religious beliefs. In other words, they narrated their political views with an overarching sense that the powers involved were not merely earthly. One graduate explained how her faith provided the motivation to obey political law despite her disagreement:

> I think of that verse that, you know, we are to submit to authority [Rom 13:1]. You know, and so in our country, the party is not of the same faith as I am, but I choose to submit, although I don't agree with all the policies and all of the different things that they have. #11

Interviewees emphasized what stood out to them as God's provision for their countries and, similarly, how they believed God had blessed the United States for its Christian heritage. In giving me a tour of Tirana, one graduate relayed how God had protected Albania through Woodrow Wilson and his Christian friend, Phineas Kennedy. Kennedy studied at Princeton, where Wilson was a professor and who later served as the school's president. When Wilson became president of the United States, Kennedy influenced Wilson's protest against the partitioning of Albania among Italy, Greece, and Yugoslavia in 1920.[15]

On another occasion I attended a church service at which one of my interviewees was speaking. In his discussion of the country's annual national celebration, he highlighted one of Albania's religious and educational leaders, Gjerasim Qiriazi (1858–1894) and quoted several of his remarks during the sermon. Before his untimely death, Qiriazi founded the first school for girls in Albania under the Ottoman Empire, and his writings as well as the Qiriazi family were instrumental in establishing the Protestant

---

15. Pearson, *Albania*, 140–42.

movement in Albania and the Albania National Awakening.[16] The speaker exhorted his audience that to be a good Christian also meant to work for the good of the nation, referencing national identity in relation to religious identity. For these participants, hope for their nations was tied to their religious faith. This connection appeared in interviews from each of the nine countries. Indian interviewees credited Christians with introducing an educational system and bringing it to both men and women, citing William Carey, Frances Xavier, and Alexander Duff among others as examples. One respondent from Hungary felt that he made a significant difference for his nation because he filled a "gap" in biblical teaching and evangelism in his country. This man had led camps every summer for the past twenty years, and by his estimation, over 20,000 young Hungarians have been told the message of the Christian gospel in this setting.

Even with their sense of other-worldly citizenship, my interviewees spoke positively in reference to their nations and their people. During my stay in Albania, preparations for its centennial national independence celebration were underway. Tirana seemed alive with excitement with bold red and black flags flying from many tenements. In the middle of Skanderbeg Square, the main city plaza, stood an enormous national flag that served as a backdrop for residents' family photos. My interviewees participated along with their neighbors in many of the activities leading up to the centennial. They hoisted a flag from their bedroom balcony and joined the national parade through the city. This pride in their national participation seemed to pose little conflict for them in regard to their religious beliefs. In regard to national events, their religious faith did not isolate them from community participation. Likewise, I noticed a similar response from my interviewees in India. So long as the national events did not involve a religious purpose, they participated in these national occasions enthusiastically, such as when they cheered for India in worldwide cricket competitions. I observed this enthusiasm first-hand in their living room as we watched India defeat Australia to reclaim the Border-Gavaskar trophy that spring.

In those countries where national, ethnic, and cultural identities *were* integrated into the majority's non-Christian religious identity, however, my interviewees experienced increased levels of tension. As members of a religious minority in the diverse political contexts of South and Southeast Asia, Western Europe, and former Communist Europe, only 6 percent reported little to no conflict between their religious and national or ethnic identities. 94 percent reported that being noticeably different in their daily practices

---

16. Elsie, *Dictionary of Albanian Religion*, 210–11.

from the mainstream population and encountering significant social pressure to conform caused them considerable tension.

How my interviewees negotiated their ethnic and national identities in relation to their religious identities varied more by geographical location and culture than by gender or age. Some of them, for example, avoided some national festivals in India. One Indian respondent explained that many of the Indian festivals have religious ties to Hindu gods and that Indian Christians respond differently to this association. Some refuse to participate altogether, while others participate, contextualizing the celebrations as cultural. His response was more nuanced. If a given festival posed no offense to other Christian believers, he considered attending. For him, bridegrooms wearing garland, *rangoli* (a decorative art form drawn on courtyard floors), and *Holi* (a spring festival of colors) were permissible. If the event promoted Hinduism directly by the wearing of the *bindi* or the worship of gods (as in *puja*, a prayer ritual), however, he and his family abstained. He stated that he would have to inform his neighbors:

> No. I am a Christian, and I don't do idol worship, and I cannot come.

Another described catering to her neighbors' Hindu religious identity whenever it did not pose a conflict to her Christian faith. For example:

> When you are Christian, people assume that you eat beef. We don't bring it in our house, and we don't eat beef out of respect for our neighbors. I mean, of course, we could bring it and cook it and eat it, but just so that we would have, you know, an access to our neighbors, [we don't].

Another of my Indian interviewees added that, as Christians, they were perceived to be "less patriotic" due to Christianity's association with British colonialism.

My Chinese respondents also differentiated between traditional festivals in their homeland. As Christians, while they participated in Chinese New Year celebrations as a "celebration of the season" (#17), they declined to take part in others, such as the Festival of *Mazu* (or *Tianhou*), the Sea Goddess. The ritual of ancestor worship posed an additional challenge. While this practice is very common among the Chinese, my Christian respondents hesitated to take part. In general they practiced the respect for and remembrance of elders but refrained from fully participating in worship. These brief examples illustrate the difficult task of forging personal identities when the complicated facets of history, religion, ethnicity, and nation converge.

Other graduates faced little difficulty in maintaining and negotiating between their religious and other identities. My Polish interviewee stated that not being a Catholic in his country is no longer "a big deal" since the population is diversifying. As a part of the European Union, Poland has experienced increased mobility and his community has become increasingly aware of other ways of life. He also commented, however, that he had not seen more conflict as a religious minority simply because he had not been particularly involved in his city's local affairs. Another participant from Hungary reported little difficulty in negotiating his various identities, part of which may have been due to his ministry's location at an all-inclusive campus (with its own lodging, offices, and cafeteria) in the countryside.

My participants' negotiations of multiple identities did not always lead to a reconciliation of personal values. In Hong Kong, one of my interviewees relayed the story of his struggle voting in political elections. Candidates who supported more conservative moral ideals tended to lean politically toward communism. My respondent supported candidates with more democratic ideals. However, the more democratic candidates tended to take a more liberal view on moral issues, which he did not support. The dilemma tempted him to abstain from voting altogether. When asked which candidate he ultimately chose, he said he voted for the more democratic leader despite his moral views.

Another European graduate specified:

> Like here [in the U.S.] people feel very strongly about a certain political candidate or party or whatever, and they really think how maybe, God is very, very supportive of that one particular candidate. In [country of origin], we just think that, you know, some are less evil than others. But we don't think that any of them are really good. So I can be okay with some of the expression of that thought. . . . I don't feel like I need to have it all worked out in order to feel like I'm a Christian. I don't feel like I'm not a Christian if I don't agree with this or if I don't agree with that. #13

My respondents reported that they were motivated by their faith to promote the communal good for their countries of origin, but this goal came with its challenges. For example, the Indian graduates who directed educational programs did so without proselytizing, as required by state law. During my stay in India, I observed how they meticulously compiled statistics to fulfill their government reporting requirements for their organization. One of the graduates shared a further example with me of how he negotiated between his faith and his responsibility to the state. As a ministry director in India, he was approached by local leaders with Maoist backgrounds who came to him for pastoral support.[17] They had become Christians but still had unresolved police cases regarding their past Maoist activities. This director was careful before supporting them as he desired to fulfill government regulations and did not want to be perceived a Maoist supporter.[18] Before he endorsed their ministry, he suggested that they approach the authorities to settle an outstanding police case, even if it meant serving a jail sentence. His standard was unpopular, but he felt strongly that serving as religious leaders meant abiding by government laws as much as possible.

As members of a religious minority, these graduates struggled to live by their faith in a dynamic balance of discernment and interaction among a diverse community. This was a difficult balance, as one graduate verbalized:

> [We are] socially seeking harmony, though we need to spread our faith, we need to be in harmony with other people. . . . That is very difficult thing to do because of opposition and everything. On the way, we will offend some people because gospel is offensive for somebody. Some people will reject it. But as an [nationality], our responsibility toward our country is keeping the harmony—and helping this nation reverse. And as a Christian, we have responsibility to spread the gospel. #10

Others summed:

> Living out my faith should work toward impacting my country in such a way that it would set an example of what living out the Christian faith would look like and how that would be so magnetic to other people that they would want to follow. They would want to do it. They would want to become a part of it. #12

> The real way we see change in society is kind of at the grassroots level. It's one person evangelizing to another, and then when they're born again, they have the Holy Spirit come and give them a new life and that really changes them. So if you want to change society, yes, it can be done through like political laws and stuff like this and that helps bring, if you like, some of the blessings that God would have for people to society at large. . . . We really need to do it sort of in a personal level through evangelism to sort of still bring out that change at large. #15

17. The term Maoist refers to their participation in the Communist Party of India, also referred to as Naxalite.

18. "CPI (Maoist) Included."

Several participants mentioned that they struggled to live according to the principles of their faith, a faith that was incompatible with their social systems. In India, for example, the practice of caste and the Hindu concept of *maya* (a Sanskrit word meaning that the material world is illusion, an "art" by which "appearance is produced") are pervasive.[19] This participant shared how countercultural it was to resist this frame of mind:

> There's always like a million people in anything . . . like a million people waiting in line for that, for a job or for a school or for something . . . so that plays in our mind. Even when we stand in a queue, we are always looking, like, *How do I get ahead?* . . . so that's built into our system . . . so that motivates people to go to any means. They will be corrupt, they will use their influence, they will pay bribes, they will cheat. . . . A lot of stuff that we teach, it's to help them think that there is an option. It is not just the rat race. . . . There's always a—God-given opportunities, and when we look for God, He provides. He does stuff. And that's a very unlearned—that kind of a thing. #8

In Albania, according to my interviewees, bribery and government corruption are likewise embedded into the social system with little recourse for their contestation. The prevalent cultural belief is that "to get ahead, one must take," and my respondents shared how challenging it was to "do right in the eyes of God." Overall, while my respondents communicated trying to abide by their national laws as part of their national identity as citizens, they found it harder to abide by their countries' cultural precepts.

How did the quantitative results relate to these graduates' negotiations of multiple identities? A Friedman nonparametric test was used to test for differences in the strength of religious, ethnic, and national identities among these graduates. Results revealed a significant difference between the strength of the identities, $\chi2 (2) = 432.54$, $p < .001$. A series of follow-up Wilcoxon signed-rank tests were used to test the combination of pairs for differences. Results indicated a significant difference between their perceived significance of their religious and ethnic identities,[20] $Z = -15.84$, $p < .001$. Their perceived significance of religious identity was greater ($M = 3.47$, $SD = .62$, $Mdn = 3.67$) than that of ethnic identity ($M = 2.26$, $SD = .85$, $Mdn = 2.33$). Results also indicated a significant difference between their perceived significance of religious identity and that of national identity, $Z = -14.87$, $p < .001$. Their perceived significance of their religious identity

19. Zimmer, *Myths and Symbols*, 24–26.

20. The strength of the significance of their perceived identities was measured rather than the concepts themselves.

was significantly greater than that of national identity (M = 2.44, SD = .81, Mdn = 2.33). Lastly, the results indicated a statistically significant difference between their perceived significance of ethnic identity and national identity, Z = -4.60, p < .001. Specifically, their rated significance of national identity was significantly greater than their ranking of ethnic identity (see table 5).

Table 5. Means, Medians, and Standard Deviations
for Strength of Religious, Ethnic, and National Identities

	N	M	SD	Mdn	$\chi2$	p
Identity					432.54	.001
Religious	385	3.47	.62	3.67		
Ethnic	385	2.26	.85	2.33		
National	385	2.44	.81	2.33		

All identities are socially constructed. In these cases, one central identity—their religious identity—seemed to function as a filter to guide daily decisions, even their migration patterns. By what process is that centrality determined? The identity that serves as the filter is the most salient for an individual at a given time.[21] The identity deemed most important to one's self-understanding seems to determine the ordering of and priority given to other identities. Given their choice of education and profession, that their religious identities were ranked as most important at the time of assessment is unsurprising, although it was necessary to establish. Given continuing international ties with other Christian believers that offer both social and financial resources, it is expected that their religious identities will be sufficiently maintained.[22] How did this religious identity, however, become initially prominent, especially for those in a social context where Christianity was the local religious minority? Investigating the social factors that surrounded their conversions would be fruitful for further research.

Perceived American Negotiation of Identities

Interesting patterns emerged regarding my interviewees' perceptions of how those in the U.S. negotiated their identities. Although all of the graduates had also traveled extensively to other regions of the U.S., they tended

21. This assignment can be self-assigned and/or ascribed by others, making the fashioning of identity a powerful, and potentially dangerous, social construction.

22. McGuire, *Religion*, 37–39, 57–58.

to focus their observations on the local residents of North Texas. As afore-mentioned, my interviewees were members of the majority ethnic groups in their respective countries of origin but members of religious minorities. As Christians, they gained membership status in the religious majority during their stay in the U.S.[23] but became members of an ethnic and cultural minority.[24] This temporary inversion in status may help to highlight the processes of identity construction since their observations were extremely beneficial in exploring intercultural patterns. They addressed questions such as, how do Christians from various countries differ in their understandings and constructions of their personal identities? Do certain trends and idiosyncrasies emerge?

In another benefit of international migration, my interviewees' outsider views of the U.S. offered important insights and held up a mirror for national and self-evaluation. Two reflections in particular were the racial divide within the American church and the conflation of evangelical religious identity in the U.S. with its national identity. The international students first commented on the racial tensions they noticed in the United States. For example, one graduate raised in the multicultural context of Southeast Asia shared:

> One thing that surprised me more strongly than I expected was the segregation of the different ethnic groups even among the Christian community. You have the famous saying quoted by [Martin Luther King Jr.]. He say, "The eleven hour of the Sunday is the most segregated hour," right? . . . I mean, to me, as an outsider, I would imagine segregation by language is natural and more obvious. It happens. You know? For example, in [my country of origin], we do have Tamil-speaking churches, congregations, in other words. We do have Chinese-speaking congregations, English-speaking. So the segregation is because of the language, which seems more natural but not so much by ethnic groups. #14

While this graduate was accustomed to a blending of ethnicities within the same religious community in her country, her comment points to a

23. 78.3 percent of the U.S. population identify as Christians. *Global Religious Landscape*, 54.

24. The racial composition of the county in which they studied is 68.7 percent white, 22.9 percent African American, 5.5 percent Asian, and 2.9 percent other. Those of Hispanic origin are included in each of the previous categories. Separately, 38.9 percent identified as Hispanic or Latino, 32.2 percent identified as white alone (not Hispanic or Latino), and those identifying as non-white, non-Hispanic were not assessed. See "Quick Facts."

striking difference in her American experience. In the U.S., she perceived new ethnic barriers that even one's religious identity did not necessarily overcome. A pilot interviewee expected more assistance upon his arrival from those who shared his ethnic and cultural background. To his surprise, white individuals, with whom he shared religious but not ethnic ties, however, aided him more. He not only sensed that his presence created racial tension for Caucasians, but also that this tension was relieved once they determined that he was from Africa and not the United States. He elaborated:

> I was disappointed though because I expected that more African-American blacks to welcome me more than the brothers—Caucasians, white—but it was different. So that was a shock first. Anyway, in general, yes, I was welcomed. . . . Especially when some [instances], maybe because of the culture, because of the history of this country, in some places I will go, and people were actually, I would sense the tension between white and black. And then I began to speak, then people say, "Oh, okay, I thought you were from here." So then when they know I'm international, then they change. So I felt that uncomfortable level of, people believed, begin to exclude me, but as soon they know I'm just a foreigner, and international who just came, that I am not an African-American, then they welcome me. Pilot interviewee #5

Considering their racial backgrounds were primarily Euro-Caucasian or Asian, my other respondents did not refer to any mistreatment based on their racial/ethnic ties. One interviewee from India, however, did share an experience that took place after the events on September 11, 2001 in which she was singled out for her appearance. She reported that while she was wearing her *salwer kameez*, a woman stopped her in a store and asked if she was from Pakistan. After confirming that the student was from India, the inquirer then stated that if she had been from Pakistan, she would have had to shoot her. The graduate supposed the lady was joking but relayed to me how much that encounter frightened her. Upon sharing this experience with an American friend, she was told that it would be better for her not to wear such traditional dress. These examples illustrate the racialization of ethnic identities in the United States.[25]

Several interviewees also commented on how strangely they perceived conservative evangelical Christians in the U.S. conflating their national identity with their religious identity. Those that had been raised in communist contexts had always seen religion as antagonistic to the state. One comment illustrates:

25. For a conceptualization of racialization, see Ponce, "Racialization," 11–14.

FIELD RESEARCH ON IDENTITY IN MIGRATION

> In [country of origin], they're not really connected at all. That's
> one thing that's very different here. Here [in the U.S.], Christians
> kind of integrate their patriotic feelings with their religious feel-
> ings. In [home country], not at all. There is a very clear separa-
> tion of the two, maybe because of the legacy from communism,
> but we feel like the government's always going to be corrupt, no
> matter what we do, and we can't expect anything good to come
> from the government. So a lot of us are—don't even bother un-
> derstanding it. #13

Considering the history of a particular nation and its government's relation to religion is vital to understanding its constituents' socialization and the formation of their religious and national identities. One respondent warned against the close identification of political views with religious ones. He noted that this tendency in American Christians gives them unrealistic hope:

> This kind of right-wing conservatism that so many times, evan-
> gelicals are, like, hand in hand with actual politics. . . . I saw
> that here [in the U.S.] . . . that kind of idealistic patriotism that
> "*ours is Christian nation chosen by God for this mighty task.*"
> Christians do the same in our [home country]. . . . Ultimately,
> it's the expectation that political leaders or Caesar is going to
> Christianize everybody. . . . Christianizing comes from the heart
> of an individual. . . . America is not going to be more Christian
> under Mitt Romney and not be less Christian under Obama, if
> you really want to make it this simple, because it starts with the
> heart of the individual. It doesn't start with Caesar. #2

As he noted, this practice is not limited to the United States. Several of my participants observed that the tendency for individuals to conflate religious and national identities occurs in their home countries as well. As one interviewee from India described, India has several religious constituencies, and these memberships are used to vie with one another for political power. According to her report, political races could be won or lost if religion is made the issue, and she recognized the use of this tactic in both the U.S. and India.

Identities are not cleanly segmented, and how they interrelate depends on the multiple narratives of which an individual is part. Members of a minority population can be distinguished seemingly solely by their identity as other in some social aspect. One's historical, political, and social narratives largely determine which identities are differentiated as other. As Cresswell summarizes, "The close connection between place, identity, and morality creates a world that is difficult for some of those who are apparently 'without place."[26] New identities emerge from each historical movement and its unique factors such as the proliferation of international migration in the last two centuries. When different aspects of identity intersect, some identities become more important within certain contexts. Thus, for my interviewees, their sense of ethnic identity and, to a lesser extent, their national identity, was highlighted because they were perceived as the other in the U.S. during their stay. Their Christian religious identity, however, was received as acceptable in this local context and was even strengthened by their theological study.

DIVINE CALL AND MIGRATION AS WITNESS AND BLESSING

The religious identities of my interviewees were integral to their self-understanding, so much so that they reported that their faith moved them, literally. Other motives to relocate—such as the desire for higher education or the provision of a scholarship—may have wielded additional influence. My interviewees attested, however, that their personal sense of God's leading was their principal motivation to migrate around the world. For instance:

> My coming here was a resolve of strong conviction that this is God's way for me; this is God's leading for me. [I'd] been considering seminary studies for probably seven or eight years before I eventually got here. There was a tension because on one hand I thought God wants me to do it. On the other hand, it was a big financial challenge, and I did not have enough faith for a while to really seriously try to accomplish this goal. . . . Even in coming and then surviving . . . it was always an issue of what God wants me to do. We had a faith perspective on what was going on and why we are doing this. I was here on a mission. #1

The participants described a sense of knowing how God was leading them—through prayer, consultation with trusted advisors, and the unfolding of circumstances (such as the provision of financial aid, help with family needs, visas, and material resources). As #14 stated:

> It was through, you can say, God's providence in the network of people that I got to meet in [country of origin]. . . . I believe it was the Lord speaking.

---

26. Cresswell, *Place*, 117.

For two-thirds of the participants, their reports of the circumstances that surrounded their migrations were remarkable:

> We had no personal connections to [name of school]. And to just Google "[name of school]" and start from there and have a monthly income of $100 and to actually arrive in [the U.S.] with only $250 in your pocket—that was all the money we had—and what happened in between, just that chain of miracles and things that made it possible, I mean, for us, it was very clear that it was God that was making it happen. #13

Their faith was not only central to studying abroad, but it was the crucial factor in deciding to leave the United States. Of my interviewees, 89 percent reported that they primarily returned home due to their religious faith. They expressed their religious commitment, however, in various ways. Some described that they had held an initial religious intention to return from the beginning. Others had already arranged an organizational or contractual agreement, so returning was the ethical response according to their faith. Others shared a sense of religious desire and/or duty. The interviewees' descriptions of their religious motivations were expressed primarily in two ways, in terms of stewardship (19 percent), as a spiritual calling (56 percent), or as both (25 percent).

Stewardship denotes a sense of responsibility for something, and these participants felt responsible to invest in and appropriate their educations for their home countries. As #10 shared, "That's the reason we came—so that we can be useful to so many people." Consider another respondent's testimony:

> God has invested in us this education. And because of the lack of this kind of education back there and because of also how much we understand the [home] culture versus maybe some Americans who would want to go be missionaries there, I really feel that that's where we're most used right now. #13

In observing my participants' daily routines, I noticed that their forms of stewardship varied. Those in Poland, Romania, Hungary, Spain, and Italy, Albania, Singapore, and Hong Kong were involved in theological education, church planting, or ministering to members of more educated groups such as university students and business professionals. In India, these forms of service were also undertaken, but the most striking form of outreach was the developmental assistance and the physical care given to local residents, especially in remote villages. Several graduates led non-profit medical camps, literacy programs, deaf education programs, and general hygiene classes at the grass-roots level for their communities, especially for women and children.

Despite their religious minority status, these Indian graduates had met little resistance in their countries of origin when they offered this assistance. In autumn of 2013, regional newspapers including *The Hindustan* showcased one graduate's work: her community hygiene classes for illiterate rural women. Attendees were taught how to make a nutritional health powder to fight malnutrition and also about empowerment through moral values. Another graduate described her work in a center for HIV-positive children:

> None of the other religions want to do anything with these kids. You know, even if they want to give something—you know, as a donation as a good karma—they will just hand it out from the door and leave and have nothing to do with the kids. But one of the churches in our city has some of their young people go and teach them songs and read the Bible with them . . . because nobody else comes. . . . They just give things, but don't spend time with the kids or teach them anything
>
> . . . and they invited me to speak to the nine through the eighteen-year-old girls. And they asked me to speak about puberty, about adolescence, and about, you know, sex. And you know, expose them instead of them being shocked. #11

These services came at no small cost to some of my respondents. I saw them forgo basic conveniences like running hot water and electricity in order to serve their neighbors. In attending a literacy class, for example, I surveyed the room in which one of my interviewees was teaching. It was a hot stone sweatbox that was surrounded in blackness. Literally, the class was learning in the dark. A small window had been hewn into one wall but was insufficient to light the room. The temperature was sweltering, and the class constantly swatted away mosquitoes. These graduates risked the hardships of disease, pollution, and religious discrimination. Many basic tasks were dependent upon outside forces, such as showering, which is subject to the availability of electricity to heat the water. Access to material resources and comforts, which my graduates had experienced in the U.S., were limited. As a participant observer with Western sentimentalities, I wondered, "They obtained a master's or doctoral degree for *this*? Why?" In fact, almost half (45 percent) of the interviewees also mentioned how greatly surprised their fellow nationals were when they returned. Their family and friends had been "convinced" that they would remain in the United States.[27]

27. Statistics on return graduates are rarely available. The rate of student return to China ranged from 14 to 42 percent for years 1995 to 2002. As of 2011, considering

In addition to returning to where their Christian faith was held in less popular regard, my interviewees accepted non-profit ministerial positions. Since the completion of master's and/or doctoral degrees from an accredited graduate school in the U.S. provided access to employment in many locations other than their countries of origin, why had they left the affordable luxuries of the United States when a pathway to permanent residency was obtainable for them? Their choice to return home, while not to be romanticized, raises many questions for investigation. Why were they motivated to leave despite opportunities to remain in the U.S., despite familial encouragement to do so, and despite the financial cost of returning home? Did family ties, the cost of living, faith, culture, employment, or a combination of these factors offer them the motivation to return?

My participants explained that their sense of *calling* from God motivated them to return home despite any obstacles. In addition to their sense of stewardship, respondents described this calling as a purposeful mission that God had bestowed on them individually.[28] For example:

> One thing that was very clear in our mind was that we are being led by the Lord to go and take an education and then come back. So even though there were lots of, I would say, luxuries that we got accustomed to being in the U.S., my father-in-law uses the word "hamburgerized" [laughs]. So we were in a sense a little hamburgerized being in America, but knowing that that is not what God's purpose in our lives is, for us, helped a lot. That was something that God had helped us understand and helped us grow. And to believe that, you know, God had sent us to U.S. to get equipped so that we can come back and be His instruments here in [home country]. To know that, even though it is hard with many different things, God is going help get us acclimatized back. #12

the 2.64 million Chinese studying abroad from 1978 to 2011, the return rate was 36.5 percent. See Donald and Benewick, *China Atlas*; Luo, "Returning Overseas Students." Finn found that international science and engineering doctoral graduates who entered with a temporary visa have an averaged return rate of 36 percent. The return rate of this research sample of theological master's and doctoral graduates was 64 percent. Finn, "Stay Rates," i.

28. Weber asserted that the religious conception of calling (defined as a "task set by God" or a "defined area of work" (28), and in particular, a "fulfillment of duty within secular callings as being of the absolutely *highest* level possible for moral activity") developed only from and after the Protestant reformation (29, his italics). See Weber et al., *Protestant Ethic*, 28–33. A religiously motivated vocational calling is described as "central to identity construction" in Williams, "God's Global Professionals," vi.

Their expression of this divine call to move and to bless is reminiscent of such biblical characters as Abram, who understood God to direct him to move in order to be blessed and to bless many others in doing so (Gen 12:1–3).

This sense of calling did not differ based on the respondent's nationality. Despite their varying cultural contexts, their reported motivation was quite similar; they moved based on their understanding of God's will for their lives. Several graduates shared:

> God's call was very clear, and I want to obey His call. . . . That call and that vision just did not leave us. . . . Some of the choices I've made is only because I follow Christ. Otherwise, there's just no way I would have done some of these things I'm doing. #8

> The verse that comes to my mind is about how Mordecai says to Esther, "Who knows. God may have had you in this place for this time," not the exact words, but just my paraphrasing [Esth. 4:14]. And when I think about myself being [nationality], I think God had a special reason for me to be born in [country of origin] and this culture among these people in this period of time. I feel privileged to be born here and even more privileged to know that God has a special reason behind it. . . . I know that my significance is not in belonging to a special culture, but knowing that God has me here for a special purpose, a special reason. #12

> We felt like while we were here, nothing had changed enough in God's calling to us to make us change our plans. Again, that sense of understanding for sure that God had planned – had called us to this made a really huge difference in putting up with the cultural differences that we had to go through. And just the lack of comfort that is involved in living in [home country] vs. [U.S.]. #13

My respondents further considered their calling to return to their countries of origin as an opportunity to share their faith with their family, friends, and acquaintances. How they shared this information differed according to their cultural context and its level of hostility to Christianity. One graduate from India described how she responded when her Hindu dietician asked with incredulity why she had come back. She carefully shared her calling to return and serve the people of her country. Another graduate, from Hungary, used this question as an opportunity for direct evangelism. He explained:

They [would ask], "Why did you come back?" That was a great conversation starter about our call, what motivates us to come back to our country. So that was always a great starter because that's not the usual pattern.

While the graduates described their main motivation to return in terms of stewardship or calling, other factors may have accompanied this decision (such as the desire to be near family). They did not emphasize these reasons, however, in the interviews. Only one graduate from Singapore stressed that it was just "natural" to return home rather than remain in the United States.

The graduates' religious commitment to return overseas did not assuage their accompanying doubts about their calling or any difficulties in returning. One interviewee (#18) described that her transition to the U.S. was easier than her return because she had a clear goal in the U.S.—to study and graduate. Once she returned, however, she wondered if she should have stayed in the United States. She believed God did want her to return home, but the fact that her goals were less clear upon her return troubled her. "Things are like open-ended, so what am I going to do next?" Another interviewee expressed doubts about his job transition when he returned to Albania. His organization had assigned him a new position with which he was unfamiliar and had initiated new strategies during his absence. These changes led him to grow concerned about the direction of his ministry. Other participants also described their difficulties in returning to pursue non-profit ministerial professions. The reality of raising the financial support to fund their activities added a great deal of pressure to their decision to return.

To what extent did these graduates' religious faith play a reported role in determining their locations after graduation? The questionnaire assessed the frequency of and the extent to which their religious faith determined location upon graduation. Of the participants who answered this question, 60.1 percent claimed that religious reasons very much determined their location upon graduation, while 20.5 percent responded that they determined their location to a considerable degree. The remaining participants rated religious reasons as somewhat (9.7 percent), not much (4.1 percent), or not at all a factor (5.6 percent). On the scale from 0 (not at all) to 4 (very much), over four-fifths of the responses ranged from 3 to 4.

While religious reasons may have been related to their decision-making, they did not inoculate participants from remaining in the United States. In fact, of the 405 survey respondents, 36 percent of the graduates did stay. While all of my interview respondents did depart the U.S., 44 percent of them admitted that they had contemplated staying. Their deliberations were based on the material opportunities in the U.S. and their acclimation to its culture. For some, the draw to stay was simply because they had "settled into living in the States" (#17). Even those interviewees who were part of an established organization abroad did not avoid this deliberation, as half mentioned that they too considered staying. This internal debate of whether or not to return may be an inevitable part of migration, as one graduate shared:

> Although there were several distractions here, we kept our focus, and our primary commitment was to go back. #6

Another elaborated:

> While in America, I may have thought about, what if God wants me to stay here? What if—you know—what if He wants me to start a church here? Life is easier here. Better future for my kids. Why not stay? But I understand that God made it that I was born in [home country]. . . . I believe that He has a special place for me here. He wants me to impact my country with the gospel, so I take it as a calling from him to invest in my people and in my country. . . . I believe every student that comes from a poorer country, I think those things go to their mind. . . . I kind of saw how [students] were finding ways to find a job and to get integrated into the churches or the culture there, so that maybe they could continue to work and not go back to their countries. #4

To further investigate, a Pearson's chi-square test was used to determine whether individuals who cited religious reasons as the primary factor in determining their location were more likely to leave the U.S. after graduation. As shown in table 6, these individuals were significantly more likely to leave the U.S. after graduation, $\chi 2 \, (1) = 16.12, p < .001$, Phi = -.21. Specifically, a greater proportion of the participants who cited religious reasons as the primary factor in determining their locations left the U.S. (78.5 percent) when compared to participants who did not cite religious reasons as the primary factor (57.3 percent). Similarly, a greater proportion of participants who did not cite religious reasons as the primary factor stayed in the U.S. (42.7 percent) compared to participants who did cite religious reasons as the primary factor (21.5 percent).

Table 6. Frequencies and Percentages for Location
after Graduation by Religious Reasons

| | Religious Reasons | | | | | |
| | Yes | | No | | | |
	N	%	N	%	χ^2	p
Current Location					16.12	< .001
U.S.	26	21.5	111	42.7		
Not in U.S.	95	78.5	149	57.3		

In discussing the association between religion and migration, one would expect personal faith to motivate students to study theology. Less apparent is the role their faith played in their decisions to study abroad and in post-graduation. The data, however, showed that the decisions of where to study and where to reside after graduation were highly related to religious beliefs. Both qualitative and quantitative measures demonstrated that those graduates who left the U.S. did so primarily from religious motivation. Even when given a choice of other reasons, such as family or employment, they cited faith as the central reason for their departures. In fact, their faith more strongly determined their choice to leave the U.S. rather than to remain. Does this pattern hold true for international graduates in other fields? Few studies have assessed the stay rates of international students, and they are limited to students who obtained degrees in economics, science, and engineering.[29] This study is the first to assess stay rates and motivational factors of theological graduates. Do other factors correlate to geographic location after graduation besides religion? Do such factors as age, gender, length of time lived in the U.S., country of origin, or initial intention upon enrollment determine migration outcomes? While the principle of inertia (what is settled tends to remain settled) may be a factor in why people stay, a sense of commitment, religious or otherwise, may be a salient factor in why people move. The determination of which factors make a difference in migration is an avenue for future study.

This research lends support to the idea that religious faith is linked to the course of personal migration. A sense of calling as a providential directive, and a sense of identification with the larger biblical narrative, may have served as mechanisms for how my participants made sense of their lives through a narrative construction of identity.[30] Individuals make com-

29. Aslanbeigui and Montecinos, "Foreign Students"; Finn, "Stay Rates."

30. See McGuire, *Religion*, 25–32. That meaning is the pursuit of religion is contested. See Bender et al., *Religion*, 7–9.

mitments, however, within cultural narratives. These public narratives, into which individuals are written by virtue of birth and socialization, produce plotlines along which persons are partly defined and to which they partly adjust.[31] Migration, then, offers the opportunity to engage with multiple and sometimes conflicting cultural narratives.

LIMITATIONS OF STUDY

Since the questionnaire sample was not selected at random, its external validity is weak. While the results could reflect outcomes of similar populations, I did not draw generalizations of this nature. Also, the low reliability of Cronbach's alpha score for religious identity was expected, in part because of the low number of items that assessed this construct. Additionally, the third question regarding religious identity did not tap into the construct in the same way as the first two items (see questions 9–11 in Appendix 3). This shortcoming, however, is not grave for the purposes of the present study. Despite the difficulty in using quantitative methods to delineate identities, quantitative measures were crucial to evaluate data from the total graduate sample rather than from the smaller interview sample.

AREAS FOR FUTURE RESEARCH

This exploratory research offers several directions for further study. The most immediate possibility is an investigation of what other factors predict migration outcomes. Voluminous questionnaire data were collected and analyzed but, because certain portions were not central to the current project, their results will be published separately. While this study focuses on evangelical Christians, comparative studies of return migrants from other religious faiths are warranted. The interaction of identities and identity configuration in migration are additional areas that are ripe for investigation, especially in consideration of reintegration for returnees. Lastly, while this study was largely qualitative in nature, quantitative and longitudinal measures in future research could address causal mechanisms that explain certain types and pathways of identity configuration.

---

31. Somers, "Narrative Constitution," 618–20.

SUMMARY

As discussed in chapters 1–6, religion and migration factor significantly in the construction of personal identities. This sociological research project both qualitatively and quantitatively offers contemporary support for that claim.

These international evangelical Christians found their religious faith to be indispensable to their constructions of personal identity. In fact, their religious identities outweighed other personal identities (ethnic and national) in perceived importance. For the majority of my participants, their religious faith was highly related to migration outcomes. By their reports, their personal faith moved them to leave their homes to study abroad and also to return home afterward. These results support the view that personal belief in and identification with a religious narrative can prompt physical movement. Interestingly, those who remained in the U.S. did not cite religious reasons for doing so while those who returned overseas did. In other words, their personal faith was not associated with their motivation to remain in the United States once there, but it was associated with their decisions to depart the U.S.

International migration also molded their identities, and the ways they negotiated the interaction of their religious, national, and ethnic identities changed according to the social context in which they found themselves. Migration reshaped the beliefs and behavior patterns of these sojourners. Their beliefs, even those of a religious nature, did not remain static but were altered or fortified based on the diverse experiences they encountered. They gained alternative ways of thinking, doing, and being. Also noteworthy is the benefit that the international migration of visitors brought to the host nationals. That is, the presence of these foreigners and their reported observations significantly guided the host country members to new meanings and methods as well. Noted in particular in this chapter were their observations of racialization of ethnic identities and the conflation of religious and national identities in the United States that should be carefully evaluated.

Considering this specific cohort of educated evangelical international graduates, this study illustrates a complex negotiation of multiple personal identities (religious, ethnic, and national) that are further complicated by international migration and highly differentiated by local contexts. As globalization and technology advance, the implications of international migration on the construction of personal identity are vast. How we as human beings write and rewrite ourselves remains rich soil to till and cultivate.

IV

Toward a Theology
of Christian Identity in Migration

9

Transformation: Identity in Migration

INTRODUCTION

Setting aside the debate regarding the existence and nature of the self, the following is a theological reflection on Christian identity in migration. Specifically, this chapter explores the premise that God develops and reconstructs human identity through the process of migration. How does this process change one's views of one's self? What might be migration's theological purpose in this regard? This project seeks to describe how God uses migration as a tool to shape Christian identity. It further investigates what principles from the process of migration can be drawn to form an initial theology of Christian identity in migration. It asks, how does a theological understanding of migration and identity relate to how one lives in the world?

One's sense of who one is changes according to the social spaces one is placed in or chooses to inhabit. This chapter offers a theological perspective on the construction of human identity through certain biblical characters and contemporary social research. It does not offer a study of the identity of God per se but rather a theological consideration of how God might construct human identity through migration. Toward that end, it weaves together a biblical overview of narrative threads rather than presenting a systematic treatment. As expositions of biblical texts regarding migration are prevalent, this work illustrates how God might use migratory events to shape human identity. This description attempts to "reveal truth as it is experienced by individual selves" and how that understanding applies to human experience, standing as a testimony "for the mending of life."[1] This work, then, seeks to offer an intercultural description of one embodiment of an evangelical religious identity and leaves open the possibility that this description may point to a shared commonality of the human condition.[2]

Any theological interpretation or attempt to convey the meaning and implications of the Bible originates from one's set of theoretical presuppositions. Methods of biblical interpretation have varied over the centuries and can be loosely categorized into the traditional approach, the historical-critical approach, and the literary approach. While each of these approaches has merit, none can claim superiority. A method of interpretation tends to focus on or prioritize one of four elements: the text, its author(s), the world to which the text refers, and its readers.[3] Any interpretation risks overlooking and neglecting the other facets that are vital for a thorough understanding. While acknowledging the textual variance that engages biblical scholars worldwide, I consider the Bible a reliably preserved document for documented reasons.[4] Nevertheless I approach it critically and with a scholarly consideration of the text, its social location, and an awareness—albeit inadequate—of how my own social location affects my interpretation. The historical-critical approach (including textual, source, form, and redaction criticism and historical and cultural reconstructions from archaeological and social-scientific analyses) are valuable as are literary approaches that inspect the actual forms of the text. My methodology in this work, however, emphasizes its narrative context and a historically traditional understanding that the biblical text offers multiple levels of meaning, that is, a historically literal sense of meaning (*peshat* for Jewish scholars) and a homiletical sense of meaning (*derash*, rabbinic extensions of the text for application to their present audience).[5] I describe (that is to say, interpret) the biblical events as presented within their canonical framework[6] and offer insights as to how these events may relate to contemporary migrants.

This theological discussion of identity construction in the context of migration is viewed narratively, as the nature of meaning is story-formed.[7]

---

1. Taylor, *Theology of Blessing*, 3.

2. Smith, *Moral, Believing Animals*, 3–4.

3. Tull applies the four elements that M. H. Abrams assigns to a work of art to exegesis. Tull, "Methods of Interpretation," 682–83.

4. Wallace, *Revisiting Corruption*, 27–33.

5. Tull, "Methods of Interpretation," 682–93.

6. This method is further described in Wray Beal, *1 and 2 Kings*, 36–37.

7. Ricoeur, *Figuring the Sacred*, 308–10.

Because of the nature and the limitations of this project, I examine identity formation on the individual level but set aside a discussion of how migration might affect this process at the collective level. Since relational negotiation is complex, this examination seeks not to create a "linear correspondence" from scriptural texts for application[8] but rather to consider the negotiation of identities in various contexts to highlight both the commonalities and diversities of the human condition.

Migration is "a site for the reconstruction of the meanings of the human condition . . . [bringing] . . . socio-cultural and religious identity de-formation, re-formation, and trans-formation."[9] How does God, then, seem to use migration to shape human identity? A tentative theology of Christian identity in migration must encompass 1) an exploration of how God might use migration in the construction of identities and 2) a description of the principles that migration elicits for a theology of Christian identity.

This theological project conceptualizes identity in light of three factors: the effect of original sin, the involvement of God in this world, and the mysterious nature of identity. The doctrine of original sin dictates that humanity is born with a corrupted nature and that each individual sins by one's own volition (Isa 53:6; Jer 17:9; Rom 3:23). This corruption skews human perceptions and shrouds human discernments of reality (Col 3:3–4). We misconstrue human identity in significant ways and are unable to fully know ourselves. Volpe describes this "incompleteness" as "our total incapacity to 'finish' our individual selves."[10] Identity, therefore, is God's project to complete, and Christ's followers depend on God for "one's sense of wholeness." Since we cannot discern ourselves fully, a theological understanding of identity is provisional.

Secondly, the grace and workings of God that precede human activity must be borne in mind. The triune God innervates this present world and sustains humanity from its first breath to its future life (Gen 1:3; 2:7; Ps 33:9; Col 1:17). God the Father forgives sin and daily provides (Matt 6:11, 26; Luke 23:34). The Father's love sent forth the Son to forge a path for humanity's adoption (John 3:16; 6:44; Rom 8:15–16). God the Son, as the Word (Gr., *logos*) of God, narrates Christian existence as both its creator and redeemer and is the "one whose body Christians become" (John. 1:1, 14; Rom 12:5; 1 Cor 12:27; Eph 1:23; Col 1:18; Rev 19:13).[11] The Spirit of God superintends human development (Rom 8:15–16, 26–27; Eph 1:13–14).

---

8. Ruiz, *Reading*, 6–8.

9. Cruz, *Intercultural Theology*, 121, 152.

10. Musekura, *Assessment*, 58.

11. Ibid., 59.

The Godhead makes possible the diversity, dynamism, and integration of human identities in their construction.

Thirdly and most importantly, any theological analysis of identity construction is, at best, partial. For as we are hidden in Christ, the construction of human identity is a mystery, bounded by our finitude to be able to comprehend this transformation (1 Cor 13:9–12; Gal 2:20). Because of the limitations of sin and the mystery of our location in Christ, a Christian must depend on God's interceding grace and goodness to reveal who one is. Movement toward one's identity in Christ is due to God's prevenient grace in constant, if invisible, operation, and "who we *truly* are as God sees us" remains shadowed.[12] Of course, God is not the only agent in the construction of human identity. A dual agency consists of both God and humans as actors (which constitutes another divine mystery of God's working and human involvement).[13]

Theology is "intrinsically linked to the ethnic and national contexts in which the religious experience occurs" and thus is localized, even "ethnocentric," as Peter Phan claims.[14] The multicultural nature of this research means that its array of religious experiences are somewhat broadened. Each articulated theology reflects a single contextual theology, certainly, but it is possible to form a "locally responsive and, at the same time, globally intelligible discourse" in various theologies.[15] As the local context becomes increasingly intertwined with the global, each contextual theology speaks in some way to the larger landscape of reality. Any theology should be intercultural and based upon the quotidian experiences of migrants, and studying a sample of evangelical members across a number of countries offers a broader view of lived experience across contexts.[16] This project draws from these similarities and particularities described in chapter 8 for an initial theology of Christian identity in migration.

Vast differentials also exist between the experiences of voluntary and involuntary migrants. The themes I discuss regarding how to think theologically about identity construction in migration, however, might offer insight into both the forced and free migrations of Christians. While power dynamics are inherent in the construction of identities and are influenced by institutional structures and chief power players, those will not be delineated

---

12. Healy, *Hauerwas*, 106.

13. The concept of "active reception" according to Volpe's description of John Milbank's term relates here. Volpe, *Christian Identity*, 123–34, 143–44, 154–55, 219–20.

14. Phan, *Ethnicity*, 255.

15. Cruz, *Intercultural Theology*, 159.

16. Campese, "Irruption of Migrants," 6, 17–18.

at length here. This study does not seek to glorify migration or the status of migrants but rather to highlight how God might use migration in the construction of human identity and how migrants might view themselves in relation to God and one another. This compilation utilizes multiple sources; biblical accounts and research results are used in a discussion of divine involvement in identity configuration. In a discussion of how the migrant participants in this study negotiated their identities, principles are drawn from various psychological and sociological theories, primarily narrative and identity negotiation theories (see chapter 2).

The enactment of Christian identity, which is narrated in multiple ways, involves a transformation. The noun, which originates from the verb *transformare* (from the Latin, *trans* "across" and *formare* "to form"), means to change in shape or metamorphose. Oliver Davies offers an act-based account of Christian transformation when he argues for a unity of mind/body and self/world in non-reductive materialism.[17] The freedom to act as a conscious subject is neither detached from materiality nor reduced to it but is made within it. Transformation occurs as "embodied cognition"; the act transforms the individual. Davies explains, "In every deliberate act, there is a moment of becoming and so also a moment of risk. Who shall I become when I do this?'[18] What we do in the body transforms us and transforms the world. Because Christ is living and exalted in history, those who are "received, [are] made anew, into the newness of world that comes about in him."[19]

When this transformation is analyzed, the act of migration aids the theological conceptualization of identity construction. Metamorphosis indicates a "from-to," an intentional directionality, a *telos*. The processes of migration mirror this. Moreover, those who understand their own creaturely status accept the contingency that derives from "being mortal material in an unpredictable world."[20] Migrants acutely experience this vulnerability.

Another theological consideration of identity construction benefits from drawing upon the processes of human change within the context of migration. In the first section of this chapter, I investigate five aspects of how God may reconfigure personal identity through the process of migration. In the second section, I draw upon these five aspects of migration in

17. Davies, *Theology of Transformation*.

18. Ibid., 50. See also 43–49, 169–71.

19. Ibid., 143. "We can act directly upon the material shape of our brain through resolution and will . . . in a process which involves the redirection of neural pathways. . . . Far from being autonomous and above our bodily life, human self-awareness is in fact strongly embedded in bodily processes which are orientated to our acts" (49).

20. Ibid., 170.

order to develop six principles for an initial theology of Christian identity in migration. These two parts ultimately connect to demonstrate how migration develops Christian identity formation.

MIGRATION AS GOD'S IDENTITY-CONFIGURING INSTRUMENT

The Old and New Testaments are replete with narratives of migration and the movement of peoples. Whereas the divine purpose of human migration for Christian mission is described elsewhere,[21] I focus on the divine purpose of human migration for Christian identity, referencing biblical and empirical examples. How might God use migration to shape human identities? What might people learn about themselves and God through the process of migration? In fashioning human identity, God seems to employ migration as an introduction, disorientation, chisel, witness, and blessing. These tools will then be related in part two of this chapter to develop principles for an initial theology of Christian identity in migration.

Discontinuity of Identity: Migration as Mold

Based on my research study, the process of physical migration shaped the formation of the graduates' personal identities. In this, identities have migration patterns of their own. Migration can change identities by the introduction, disorientation, and chiseling it offers the migrant. I now consider how my research participants and the biblical narrative illustrate these specifically.

Migration as Introduction

Migration can serve as a divine tool of introduction, both to who God is and to one's own self. Despite the effects of globalization, cultures, to some extent, remain localized, and their inhabitants are socialized according to deeply-ingrained social structures, pointing to the given and related nature of identity described in chapter 6. If physical movement promotes cultural understanding, then migration spreads intellectual wealth. Migration brings an amalgamation of ideas into a particular culture; exposure to a globalized mix of cultural practices, spread through their human products, leads cultures to be in conversation with one another on individual, social, and collective levels. Migration across cultures, then, can potentially mitigate the

21. Hanciles, *Beyond Christendom*; Walls and Ross, *Mission*.

particularizing influence of any one culture in understanding oneself and in constructing one's identity, as my summary of Pak's research in chapter 4 evidences. This exchange of ideas can be instrumental in providing new ways of reading reality, viewing the world, and seeing oneself.

Gemma Tulud Cruz submits that migration offers the option for the re-imagination of identities.[22] By introducing the individual to other human life narratives, migration can bring difference into the self. It encourages the undulating modulation of self, and who one thinks one is, to be challenged and potentially reframed. Kwok Keung Chan touches on this in his description of leading young adults from Hong Kong to mainland China for mission work. He describes how these trips were "life-widening" for the participants as they encountered each other and the "enzymes" which served as catalysts for ongoing personal change.[23] Similarly, in my research study, 94 percent of interviewees and 98 percent of survey participants reported experiencing new practices and ways of thinking that changed their perspectives and behavior in areas such as gender, interpersonal relations, discrimination and tolerance, critical and creative thinking, and organizational principles.

Migration also introduces the body of Christ, when faced with members from differing cultures, to an opportunity to analyze Christian practices. Practices once thought to be vital may be legalistic by adding to the requirements of true faith. In fact, the most commonly mentioned change for my interviewees was their shift from legalism to "grace-oriented" evaluations of what practices and perspectives were considered Christian. Interviewees shared specific examples, but one graduate expressed this more generally:

> I grew up in a certain Christian culture that was good, but limited. When I came here, I saw much broader world, people from different Christian backgrounds, from different Christian theologies, and very different experiences. So that helped me to see things wider and in a more open way. I tended, before coming here, to view Christian life as an assembly line a little bit, but you grow according to certain pattern that is quite, well, fixed. I saw that there is much more diversity. #1

What is more, migration offers the migrant the possibility to draw connections between one's self and the other in the identification of both difference *and* commonality. As one of my international graduates shared:

> People have the same issues. It's a little bit of different covering, but everyone has the same problem. But on the outside, the

22. Cruz, *Theology of Migration*, 7.
23. Chan, "First Mark," 23–25.

way we expose those problems, the way the culture expose those problems, it's a little bit different. #5

Luiz Carlos Susin posits, "The process of identity is made up of a going out from oneself, a journey through difference, and a return to oneself."[24] The potential of losing one's distinct identity, however, in order to engage difference (or the other) remains a central tension in identity construction. The Israelites, for instance, were thrust into various polytheistic environments in which they negotiated their enslaved, exiled, or minority status within dominant cultures and power structures. Daniel is a common example of such faithfulness[25] despite the persistence of apostasy and the loss of the Israelites' recognizability as God-fearers (Gen 35:2–4; Exod 34:15–16; Deut 12:30–32; 1 Kgs 11:1–2).

Jehu Hanciles argues convincingly that the exiled population retained their Israelite identity in forced migration more faithfully than those who remained settled in Judah (Jer 24:4–7).[26] The identity configuration that God may have in mind is sometimes aided by the harshest of environments. Migration can suddenly introduce a Christian to living as such a minority. Interestingly, my participants were accustomed to the challenges of being members of a religious minority in their home contexts. Some of the difficulties that they noticed with Christians being a majority in the United States are highlighted in chapter 8. Religious faith, when it is too closely identified with a majority group or power, can struggle to remain genuine, supple, and translatable.[27]

The introduction of difference in migration can also positively shape personal identity. Human identity was most radically confronted by the migration of God to earth in Jesus Christ. Daniel Groody sees migration as a central metaphor for the image of God (*imago Dei*), the Word of God (*Verbum Dei*), the mission of God (*missio Dei*), and the vision of God (*visio Dei*).[28] His comments elucidate how migration relates to the Christian faith and, further, to Christian identity. One's Christian identity includes a connection to all of humanity who has been born into the *imago Dei*. Being Christian necessitates treating everyone, however they are perceived, as dignified and worthy of respect. Human dignity, then, is evaluated by virtue of being created by God rather than by the market "criteria of efficiency [and]

---

24. Susin, "A Critique," 79.

25. Carroll R., *Christians at the Border*, 77–78.

26. Hanciles, *Beyond Christendom*, 147.

27. Ibid., 105–7, 141–42, 148.

28. Groody, "Homeward Bound."

productivity."[29] Several of my research participants, particularly those from Asia, mentioned a new understanding of human dignity upon migrating to the United States:

> Some of the values have broadened . . . the value of humanity. The value of life that a person gets, how you view other person, the kind of respect you need to give, and about your cultural perception, [thinking] "Oh, this is a guy of lower caste, or he means nothing. I don't need to care about him," rather than seeing other person as a human being equally valuable and important. #12

> I understand more about the doctrine of human [*sic*], like, all people are created in the image of God, so we ought to have that kind of respect for other people. I think I understand it more just by living in the U.S. #17

In assuming foreign flesh, God clothed the Word of God (*Verbum Dei*) with a vulnerable identity and willingly embraced difference in order to identify with humanity (Heb 2:17–18). To follow the Lord's example, Christians must migrate physically, emotionally, and personally from within themselves to extend themselves to a different other. This act means risking who one thinks one is, risking what one thinks one cannot lose, in order to relate to and be reconfigured by the other.

Because God overcame the impasse of sin, Christ's followers can migrate across the human-human divide in reconciliation according to the *missio Dei* and cross the rifts that neighbors and nations so quickly wall between each other to recreate communion. God intends to be revealed to all of the peoples of the world, and migration introduces, as it did God to the world, God's servants to the world and the world, in turn, to God (Ezek 20:41; Matt 28:18–20). While the *missio Dei* overcame the chasm, new divides will be raised because not all will accept God's message (Isa 8:14; 28:16; Matt 21:42; Rom 9:32–33; 1 Pet 2:7). Groody does not discuss the implications when human migration is a journey *away* from God. How, then, should Christians respond to barriers they did not erect? As Volf describes, however, occasions may arise when divisions must remain.[30] Chapter 8 notes how my interviewees handled such divides and exemplifies how, as far as the Christian is able or allowed, one should pursue the other (Rom 12:18).

---

29. Francis, "Migrants and Refugees."
30. Volf, *Exclusion and Embrace*, 63–68, 90–96.

Finally, God intends to restore all of creation. The *visio Dei* (vision of God), the experience of seeing the face of God, is foretasted when Christians live in view of this vision of re-creation on the present earth (Ps 24:6; Matt 5:8). The belief in God's coming kingdom relates directly to how Christians can identify with others; their allegiance is ultimately to God and not merely to the provincial legislation of nations. For Groody, the way Christians treat migrants—living in purity for the sake of another—demonstrates this new identification. Rather than distorting God with our chaotic vision, *visio Dei* requires a radical re-identification and re-formation according to the ordering of God (Matt 19:30; 20:16; Mark 10:31; Luke 13:29–30). Seeing God requires bringing oneself to *see* those who are marginalized (Matt 25:34–46; Luke 16:19–31).[31]

In his series of four divides, Groody does not focus on the remaining person of the triune God (see table 7). His metaphor of migration to understand God and what it means to be human, however, can be extended to include the *Spiritus Sanctus* (the Spirit of God). God's Spirit leads the Christian in one's migratory path in two ways: through the physical journey upon this earth and through the journey of identification to see who one is when made anew in Christ. The Spirit remains with all who believe, given as a seal that marks who belongs to God and their down payment of inheritance, and who accompanies each person on one's journey to meet God (John 14:16–17; Eph 1:13–14). Travelers on this route walk according to the ways of God's Spirit (Rom 8:1–17; Gal 5:22–23). Those who lose their way and wonder if they have lost their sense of identity in God can rely on the Spirit to complete their identity reconfiguration (Phil 1:6).

Table 7. Migration as a Metaphor for Theology and Christian Identity

	Type of Divide	Identity Response
Groody		
Imago Dei	Inhuman | Human	Affirmation of Human Dignity
Verbum Dei	Divine | Human	Reception of God's Word
Missio Dei	Human | Human	Participation in God's Mission
Visio Dei	Country | Kingdom	Envisioning God's Kingdom
McGill		
Spiritus Sanctus	Death | Life	Reconfiguration of Self

31. Groody, "Crossing the Divide," 659–63.

Insofar as migration introduces difference among people, Christian sojourners can participate in "authentic social transformation" by the ethics of the knowledge and kingdom of God (Matt 5:13). Sojourners (Gr., *paroikos*) may serve as "social agents" who influence the world by understanding the multiple ways people can coexist, as my research participants demonstrated.[32]

Migration as Disorientation

The migratory experience away from what is familiar brings a valuable sense of disjointedness. This feeling of dislocation positions one to recognize one's humanness and reminds the sojourner how easily one can become helpless. Without one's usual social and physical support, one is jolted from what is normally taken as given, and the process of migration affords an opportunity to experience change and loss. Far from glamorizing the migrant's journey, these losses can be excruciatingly painful and life-threatening.[33]

The concept of disruption has been discussed in terms of identity formation and is relevant to how God uses migration to disorient one's self-understanding. Susannah Ticciati argues that it is when Job wrestles with God through his historically constructed "socio-symbolic" identities that his true self emerges.[34] It is precisely and only within these disruptions that his self exists and transforms. He is the "process of [his] probing."[35] The integrity of one's self, which is eschatologically structured by God in election, deepens as one is disrupted in one's historical embodiment. Migration is one historical reality that offers disorientation for the self to be transformed.

The Korean female immigrants in Pak's study, for example, reported that their fathers had left South Korea because of its lack of economic opportunities. Upon reaching their destinations, these fathers struggled with the new challenges of occupational alienation, cultural adaptation, and language acquisition.[36] This sense of disorientation on either side of migration deeply socialized these women in their views of themselves. They reported experiencing pressure to achieve academic and professional success, even at great personal sacrifice. These women struggled between their sense of collective duty and the sense of individual freedom that had developed in

32. Volf refers to victims as social agents in Volf, *Exclusion and Embrace*, 118.

33. Groody, *Border of Death*.

34. Ticciati, *Job and Disruption*, 162–74. "Not to wrestle with God, therefore, would be on Job's part a denial of the truth of his existence" (173).

35. Ibid., 167.

36. Pak, *Korean American Women*, 210–17.

the American context. Migration also confronted and confounded identity construction in new ways among my participants, and God seems to use this disorientation as a tool to reconfigure one's self-understanding. Consider what a European international graduate shared with me. His disorienting difficulties encountering the U.S. health care system allowed him to consider himself from a new perspective—one of poverty:

> I was burdened with the costs of health care. Having your kid in the emergency room brings bills that are unimaginable for a person coming from my background. I just didn't really know what to do with that. I was taught to pay my bills, and I just couldn't because I didn't have money to do that. It was really an experience that helped me to put myself in the shoes of people who are not privileged in economic sense. #1

Migration's disorientation also highlighted a state of lostness and neediness for these graduates. An interviewee describes his sense of helplessness and yet sustenance:

> Through these experiences, you know, learning compassion and watching, because money was always tight . . . depending on the promises of God for His providence. That was something that was very descriptive for our four years. For example, for us to come home each year, that was a miracle. We never had the money for it, but God always provided. #2

Fenggang Yang, in his research on Chinese immigrants who had converted to Christianity, found that migration increased their sense of homelessness.[37] Without a stable sense of geographic location, migrants can become more open to new identities in which to ground themselves.

While such an experience might deconstruct one's previous identities, as it did for these international graduates, the disorientation of migration also brings constructive possibilities for identity formation. Sojourners may experience the opportunity to embrace one's givenness from God, a concept elaborated in chapter 6. This disorientation not only provides an opportunity to reflect on the rootlessness of one's identity but also the possibility to find one's rootedness as a creature of God. Philip Sheldrake confirms that the "hunger for roots is fundamental to our deepest identity."[38] While migration uproots its participants, therefore, it also presents them with an opportunity to realize their need for rootedness in something more substantive and enduring than their physical location. This assertion does not

37. Yang, "Religious Conversion," 123–30.
38. Sheldrake, "Human Identity," 48.

dismiss the importance of the particularity of place; it rather suggests that one must be located in and from God. Similarly, Volpe argues the need for a re-orientation and transformation of human desire for the development of Christian identity.[39] To the extent that migration disoriented my research participants, it encouraged a questioning of their previous desires and an exploration of alternate desires.

The migrants in my study found themselves in a heightened position to search for and seek God's aid. The challenges of migration offer them the precarious opportunity to rely on God through dependence on others. This means the placing of trust in fellow humans while placing ultimate dependence on God. Multiple participants shared how they were provided for in studying abroad. One graduate recalled:

> There were a lot of generous people that didn't know me or knew me very little and helped me a lot, which was a really step of faith for me because every single semester it was like $5,000, and I had zero money. . . . I had this lady who met me *once* in [country of origin], and I never even asked her for a penny, but she knew I was in the States, and that I was going to seminary, and she sent me $3,000. Another time, it was my first semester, and I was supposed to pay for everything by four o'clock, and I was lacking $996. All I had in my checking account was like $1200 and that was all I had to live for two years. Two weeks before I had shared with a guy during prayer requests in class that I needed prayer for my finances, for my tuition payment in two weeks. Two weeks later, he shows up on that very same last day and says, "Hey, how are your finances? I want to help you out." So I'm thinking, well, he's going to give me $50. He writes me a check for $1000 that very same day. And three minutes later [she] walks in with a check for $75. The $1000 and the $75 was the exact amount of money that I needed to pay for my tuition and books for that semester. #7

Additionally, the disorientation experienced in migration can lead to a realization that the new location is no more oriented than one's original home. This discovery can encourage the imagination of new possibilities for who migrants might become, as Emmanuel Katongole has argued for Africa.[40] The disorientation of migration discourages a feeling of settledness and can foster an identity of departure and displacement I describe in chapter

39. Volpe, *Christian Identity*, 64–67, 224, 230–34.

40. Katongole argues against the McWorld and postcolonial Africa as assessed by Philip Jenkins in *The Next Christendom* and the Pentecostal-Evangelical movement taking shape in Africa. Katongole, "Hauerwasian Hooks," 150–52.

6. The Christian, most of all, should maintain a mindful readiness to move, both within one's person and for God's mission. Whether or not one moves one's place of residence, the Christian must seek ways to disorient oneself to sharpen and challenge one's sense of identity in movement toward the other. Insofar as migration disrupts one from settling into a single cultural particularity, it precipitates a re-identification with who one thought one was. In both a physical and a spiritual sense, God's people have been and should be on the move (Gen 12:1, 4; Matt 28:18–20; Rom 12:1–2; Gal 2:20). Humanity, however, has been prone to settle—from the first son of Adam who was ordered to wander to the early church that was forced to scatter (Gen 4:16; 11:4; Acts 8:1). On the contrary, God as migrant embraced the disorientation of indwelling human form to forge a change for the identity of humanity. Christians are so called to move out toward the different other, for this is integral to the understanding of one's self in God.

Migration as Chisel

Human migration, of course, varies in form, but God seems to use each scenario to create and recreate one's self-understanding. Robert E. Goodin describes the human condition as a necessary vacillation between "striving" and "settling," a perpetual desire toward ceaseless movement and a simultaneous "quest for fixity."[41] "Purposeful agents with temporally extended projects, identities, and commitments" pursue dwelling in a way that demonstrates a desire to "cohere well enough both simultaneously and over time to form a tolerably coherent whole" while also changing dimensions and locations intermittently.[42] Similarly, in my research study, my participants expressed a vacillation in their self-understanding in migration. Migration chiseled a change in their self-perceptions and personal practices. Their views sometimes remained rooted and unchanged; others shifted dramatically in migration.

In the biblical setting, God seems to use migration to shape human identity, even forced migration. For instance, God's removal of Adam and Eve from Eden started them on a journey of discovering what it means to live separated from the presence of God (Gen 3:21–24). Movement which heretofore had been in concert with their Creator had become the method to teach them their necessary separation from God. In the same way, for

---

41. Goodin, *On Settling*, 1–5, 29, 62–73. Goodin elaborates on five types of settling: "settling down," "settling in," "settling up," "settling for," and "settling on."

42. Ibid., 74.

Cain's grievous sin, God accorded him wandering status and separation from others (Gen 4:10–16).

Likewise, after the Israelites' sin of unbelief at the waters of Meribah in Kadesh Barnea, God determined that the community should wander in the Wilderness of Zin for nearly four decades (Num 20:1–13; 27:14; Deut 1:31–36; 2:14; Ezek 20:10–26, 36). More than mere judgment, God used this movement to instruct them and shape their identities over time, as a father cares for his children (Deut 1:31). God's attention to and provision for them proved their intrinsic value and God's sincere concern. Their identity also intimately reflected God's identity (Ezek 20:41–42). Again, as the wage for unrighteousness (such as oppression of the poor), God exiled God's people, for example, to Babylon and to Assyria (2 Kgs 17:4–6; 18:9–10; Jer 50:17, Ezek 23:9–10).[43] Disobedience—attempting to maintain an identity improperly related to God—is costly. Self-understanding of individuals constructed on false premises necessitates movement.

In using migration to separate parties, God seems to teach God's people that dwelling is more about an identity of being than a location. God abides only in righteousness, so for humans to dwell with God requires their movement (Ps 15:1–2). Such migration in the Old Testament instructed God's people that, despite their best self-assessments, they could be wrong. When the Israelites desired to construct their identities and self-understanding apart from God's instructions, God used migration to discipline their thinking (Exod 20:13; Ezek 20:30–44).

Ben Quash describes this dwelling as mobile and mutual for both God and God's people. Dwelling is "a presence that moves."[44] Abiding requires movement in order to establish intimacy and peace, as God demonstrated toward humanity in Christ. So too, Christians are called to walk with God, a journey that indicates continuing movement. To this end, migration is a tool that shapes one's understanding of one's Christian identity in this world. Home is wherever God resides—which is anywhere and everywhere and also nowhere in particular—no place is fixed as the right place (Ps 139). There is an "at-homeness," then, in God-directed transience.[45]

Considering my study, God powerfully used migration to shape participants' identities in relation to God. One graduate, for example, described his experience in voluntary migration:

---

43. Assyria conquered the northern kingdom (Israel) in Samaria in 722 BCE. Babylon seized the southern kingdom (Judah) in 586 BCE and organized three deportations (2 Kgs 24:1–25:21; 2 Chr 36:10; Jer 52:4–16, 29–30).

44. Quash, *Abiding*, 155.

45. Ibid., 158–60.

I just said, "Okay. I'm going to leave everything." I did not save anything. I had no money, and I left the States. . . . It's now ten years since I made the decision. And I can tell you even Yahoo or Google cannot take care of me the way God takes care of me. He has met every need. He's taken care of my life. He has been a good boss. And I tell that to my friends, too. There's just no way anybody can match what God is doing. #8

Joseph's experience in forced migration exemplifies this point (Gen 37, 39–50).[46] Joseph was Jacob's favored son to the dismay and jealousy of his half-brothers (Gen 37:4). The biblical text records only a few of Joseph's thoughts about himself as an adolescent. How does Joseph's self-understanding change when he is sold into slavery and transported to Egypt? What were his thoughts while abandoned in prison? While little can be said definitively, the biblical record does show a different emphasis in Joseph's speech thereafter.[47] Instead of drawing the glory of attention to himself (Gen 37:6–7, 9), Joseph gives glory to God (Gen 39:8–9; 40:8; 41:16).[48] Those who were not of the Israelite faith also noticed Joseph's transformation in captivity (Gen 41:38).

Joseph seems not to have blamed God for his mistreatment. Rather, during this time, Joseph grew in close communion with God, perhaps because his destitution in being forcibly removed from his home left him with no assurances but the presence of God.[49] As Quash explains, exile can be a gift, for "God's people *have* what they long for in *not* having it. They have it in one way by not having it in another. They are home *when* they are in exile, not just afterwards."[50] In the naming of his children, Joseph considered his circumstances in light of his relation to God, not to excuse the wrongs done to him, but to view himself in relation to the one true God (Gen 41:51–52).[51] Throughout his journey, even when he enjoyed positions of power, Joseph did not forget his creaturely relation to God (see chapter 6). From an understanding of God's sovereignty and his corresponding po-

---

46. I am not advocating forced migration, but even in forced migration, God miraculously draws redemptive good from evil (Gen 50:20).

47. Joseph trusted that even in slavery, God would come to his and Israel's aid (Gen 50:25; Exod 13:19).

48. Longacre notes Joseph's emphasis on "divine providence" as the "macrostructure" of his story. Longacre, "Joseph," 473–74. Joseph experiences continual attention from his God (Heb., ḥēn, "favor, grace," v. 21).

49. Roberts, "Homilies," 447–48.

50. Quash, *Abiding*, 142, original emphasis.

51. That Joseph gives his sons Hebrew names demonstrates that while integrated culturally into Egyptian life, he maintained his religious heritage. *Net Bible*, footnote 99.

sition of humility, Joseph was able to identify with the needs of those who were responsible for his forced migration (Gen 45:5–8; 50:18–19). Joseph, through his years of sojourning hardships, went from declaring himself a ruler over his brothers to redeeming his brothers.

Divine Call to Move: Migration as Witness

God seems to utilize the migrations of people, voluntary and forced, to shape the identity of God's people and the identities of those who do not know God. Joseph's success by the hand of God caught the attention of Pharaoh's captain of the guard, his prison warden, and Pharaoh himself (Gen 39:2–5, 21–23; 41:38–41). While this testimony may not have swayed them from their gods, Joseph's influence challenged their preconceived notions. One might also claim that Daniel's captivity in Babylon strengthened his minority religious identity in the same manner as Joseph's (Dan 1:6).[52] In addition, Daniel's odd diet and minority religious habits created conflict within the community, especially with his success before the respective king (Kings Nebuchadnezzar, Belshazzar, and Darius, successively). This presence of difference disrupted the status quo of the community's assumed identities.

Second Kings 5:1–3 further demonstrates how migration can shift one's identities. A group of Aramean marauders had kidnapped a young girl from Israel, and this terrifying event led to her enslavement by Naaman, the commander of the army of the king of Aram (Syria), to serve his wife.[53] Despite her own suffering, this girl did not seem to have abandoned her Israelite faith, and she boldly offered to Naaman, through his wife, an opportunity to be healed of his skin disease by the prophet of God.[54] Paul House compares her to other exilic heroes (such as Daniel and Mordecai) who "care for the spiritual and physical well-being of their conquerors."[55] The text reveals less about the girl's fate and more about how her witness, despite her forced migration, effected the identity construction of her pagan master. Despite Naaman's proud short-sightedness, the maid's testimony led

52. Being a minority in this context would have increased the salience of his religious identity. Sellers et al., "Multidimensional Model," 23–24. Sellers holds that "identity within the working self-concept at any moment is determined by the core identity and the immediate social context" (23) and some situations (such as an African American at a Ku Klux Klan meeting) are sufficiently acute to make a particular identity (racial, religious) more salient for almost all individuals (24).

53. Lissa Wray Beal considers the king to be Ben-Hadad II "by narrative context." Wray Beal, *1 and 2 Kings*, 43–45, 261–63, 333.

54. In a striking "initiative for a slave girl" says Baker, "1 and 2 Kings," 204.

55. House, *1, 2 Kings*, 273. See also Luke 4:27.

to his religious conversion. "Now I know that there is no God in all the world except in Israel" (v. 15, see also vv. 16–18). While she remains nameless in the text, the servant girl is historically remembered for her influence on a political leader to reveal the identity of the one true God. An element of individual choice can be noticed here in her identity configuration. Even within the confines of her oppression, her meekness had a tremendous voice. She exercised personal agency in choosing to aid her master and to testify to God's goodness even in her captivity. In God's economy of identity formation, the little often schools the great.[56]

Considering my research project, international graduates testified to living their Christian identity in unique ways. Many, for example, were pastors but also publically spoke at schools, conferences, and seminars. Others considered it their ministry to work in the public sector as therapists, teachers, lawyers, etc. One graduate from India, the only Christian in her subdivision, decorated for Christmas and held a special party for her neighbors to explain its meaning. Other graduates ran specific para-church ministries, for instance, to promote literacy in their community or reconciliation between rival ethnic groups. Above all, they considered their migration an opportunity to witness their Christian faith to others.

Christian witness has been spread by the vehicle of migration since the first century when persecution scattered the early church throughout the Roman world (Acts 8:1).[57] The nineteenth century saw a great increase of European and American missionaries. Although heavily Eurocentric for a time, the church's "polycentric nature" can be seen today with countries from Latin America, Africa, and Asia sending missionaries abroad. The countries in Europe, Britain, and North America that predominantly sent missionaries to Latin America, Africa, and Asia in the nineteenth and the first half of the twentieth centuries now receive missionaries from those areas.[58] In addition to missionary endeavors, the movement of Christian migrants spreads God's witness. The U.S. Pew Research Center reports, in its assessment of the religious affiliation of international migrants, that Christians comprise roughly 49 percent of all migrants who have left their countries of origin.[59]

While migration is a physical maneuver in service of God's mission, it is also inextricably tied to personal identity construction. Ultimately,

---

56. Long, 2 *Kings*, 70.

57. The spread of Christianity by migration mirrors the preceding spread of Jewish faith throughout Mesopotamia, Babylon, Persia, and Greece.

58. Walls, "Missiology as Vocation," 234–36.

59. "Faith on the Move," 24.

God employs migration as witness to make the identity of God known. The repeated chorus throughout the Bible reflects God's desire that humans understand who they are in relation to God in order to know and worship God (Exod 6:7; Ps 46:10; Mic 5:4; John 4:23). In addition to God's own migration to earth to reveal the very nature and identity of God (Phil 2:5–8), God seems to entrust those who have received salvation (and the reframing of their own identity) with the carrying of its message to those who remain uninformed (Rom 10:14–15; 2 Cor 4:4; Eph 6:15). Insofar as God's witnesses migrate throughout the world, this mission is possible. Insofar as this witness is authentically transformed and alien to this world, according to Hauerwas as I summarize in chapter 5, this mission is accomplished.

Divine Call to Bless: Migration as Blessing

Involuntary migration is a grave injustice to be rectified; migration, however, should not be thought of as an evil in and of itself, even when it seems to be a punishment. On the contrary, movement is a tool that carries out God's chief design to restore human identity and renovate this scarred world. One might consider Adam and Eve's expulsion from Eden a punishment, but death was their punishment for disobedience (Gen 3:23; Rom 6:23). While exile was certainly a consequence of their sin, their banishment was not punishment, but preservation. God removed Adam and Eve from the garden to set into motion a grand redemptive plan to *save* them (Gen 3:22). Moreover, God commanded the first couple to cultivate the earth and mandated human movement to do so (Gen 1:28). God did not retract this command to them after the Fall. After the flood account, God reiterated this same directive to Noah's family, and Noah's sons did indeed "spread out over the earth" (Gen 9:1; 10:32).

God's blessings that are experienced through migration relate to a greater theological discussion of blessing. John Brian Taylor traces this concept (Heb., *barak*) through the Old Testament in his theology of blessing.[60] The biblical writers describe different facets of the concept, but all send this overarching message: blessing is a way of being and a gift from God that declares God's purpose for humanity through an "offer of relationship."[61] It is a celebration of God's activity in the world. All things interrelate due to God's omnipresence in the world. Blessing is that which "contributes to the

---

60. Taylor, *Theology of Blessing*.

61. Blessing is contextually determined in each place as to what its specific content is. Ibid., 245–46, 294–95, 300–307.

flourishing, prosperity, and well-being of God's creation" and God invites humanity to cooperate in this endeavor.[62]

What is more, God moves to divinely initiate this covenant (Heb., *berith*; Gr., *diathēkē*) of blessing. John Milton outlines God's concrete movements throughout history: the call of Abraham, the Exodus redemption, the Sinai covenant, the conquest of Canaan, and the Davidic kingship.[63] In a unified "covenant purpose of blessing," God means to bless not only the people of Israel, but through them—and fulfilled in Jesus Christ—the whole world.[64] God acts to bless, to retrieve, and to restore humanity in its journey.

Migration, as an activity, is a blessing from God in the construction of human identity. It can, for one, challenge pre-established identity lines drawn by political powers.[65] Likewise, migration helped reorder such arbitrary lines for my international cohort and prompt a renegotiation of identities, as described in chapter 8. Migration also introduced these internationals to new vulnerabilities through which they reconfigured one's identity, potentially in relation to God. When disrupted from familiar cultural routines and faced with the unpredictability of migration, they were challenged to act, think, and feel in new ways. These adjustments shifted and shaped a person's self-understanding, especially when negotiating among various identities. Migration offered each student the capacity to extend who one thought one was.

The unpredictability of migration offers a context in which persons may change their self-assessments based on God's intervention. The story of Hagar, for instance, demonstrates this important theological purpose. While the text does not reveal Hagar's self-perceptions prior to her flight from her masters, some observations may be made from Genesis 16:1–16. As an Egyptian slave to Sarai, a Hebrewess, in Canaan, Hagar held a low social status and was likely demeaned on a daily basis. The power-playing tables were turned, however, when Hagar was found to have conceived the patriarch's firstborn, and she exploited this opportunity (v. 4b).[66] The established power, however, resided with Sarai, so much so that Hagar risked running away. For an unmarried female to flee at that time—pregnant without livelihood or male protection—seems unthinkable, but Sarai's treatment of her seems to have been sufficiently uncomfortable for Hagar to risk such

---

62. Ibid., 254, 302.

63. Milton, *God's Covenant*.

64. Ibid., 223–27.

65. Vertovec, "Transnationalism and Identity," 579.

66. Keil and Delitzsch, *Commentary*, 1, 140.

a journey (v. 6b).[67] It was during this journey, when she was removed from what daily provisions she might have otherwise experienced, that God pursued Hagar (v. 7). Whatever Hagar's perceptions of herself may have been prior to these events, she must have undergone an identity reconfiguration in this divine encounter.[68] The foreign god of her masters offered to protect her and her unborn child and promised that her line of descendants would not only continue but exponentially multiply (v. 10). After being tormented by Sarai, Hagar was valued and promoted by God.[69] Perhaps the experience of being valued by God on this haphazard journey led Hagar to see herself in a new light. Hagar, newly sustained by God, obeyed God's instruction to return to her slave master (v. 9). With the understanding that she had seen the "God who sees me"[70] and lived, Hagar returned with an altered identity. She returned, although still a slave, as one who had been uniquely honored by God (v. 10–13).

God can bless even in forced migration.[71] While Hagar's first journey was voluntary, her second departure was not (Gen 21:8–19).[72] Expelled by her masters, Hagar left with Ishmael, who was at least thirteen years old. This time her journey was aimless, and she and her son nearly die (v. 14–16). Hagar is approached by God again in the desert. God repeats the promise previously given to her and sustains their lives (v. 18–19). God's provision for Hagar encourages all migrants that God is a God who sees and cares for them even as they suffer in their sojourns.[73] As Hanciles states, "God's plan of salvation and redemptive action repeatedly unfold within the trauma and travail of displacement, uprootedness, and migration."[74]

67. Niditch, "Genesis," 17.

68. Hagar is the only woman recorded to be approached by Yahweh in the Hebrew Bible (v. 13). Morris further notes how extraordinary and similar God's promise to her was to Abraham's (Gen 12:1–3). See Morris, "Hagar."

69. Despite her cultural mistreatment, Hagar is identified as valued by God, and in their interchange of identity-making, Hagar is the first woman to name God. De Groot, "Genesis," 11–12.

70. "God of my seeing" (Heb., el roi). The pronominal suffix in 16:13 could be taken as objective ('who sees me") or subjective ('whom I see"). Net Bible, footnote 40. Beer Lahai Roi means "well of the Living One who sees me" (21:14). Overland, "Hagar," 376.

71. This is not to excuse, however, the forced migration forged by human hands. God sees and will judge injustice.

72. Some scholars combine these two accounts as one event. For reasons to the contrary and a review of various interpretations, see Overland, "Hagar," 377–78.

73. Hagar may mean "flight" from the root "to flee" and came to mean fugitive, immigrant, sojourner. Smith and Cornwall, Exhaustive Dictionary, 92.

74. Hanciles, Beyond Christendom, 378.

My research, focused on voluntary migrants, evidenced similar testimonies of God's care in personal distress as outlined in chapter 8. One European graduate described how he and his family were blessed through the difficulties in migration, by being tested and seeing God provide for them:

> I mean, we prayed and we prayed every day and just, you know God tested us right up front. My wife got very sick, and we were having $3000 in our pocket, we ran into a $12,000 medical bill. And we started praying, so it was a test of prayer, you know. And so it wasn't a school exercise. And we trusted in God's promises and the experience that people in our church really took the Christian call seriously. #2

In studying abroad and resettling, my interviewees reported their sense of calling and purpose from God to be blessed and to bless through their migration journeys.

> On a level we were living in States, life is much easier than here, so when you come back, and you start to have a real, every day, practical questions, you need some faith to survive in the environment. What I mean by "faith" in this context, it's knowing that we believe in God, and He has us here for a purpose. So if I wouldn't have that, it would be very hard to make a transition I think. . . . And then also when we go through different challenges it's like, okay. God will take care of this. #5

> [When first arriving to the States], I was so much stressed out that I was ready to leave right then (laughs). But I think knowing and taking time to spend with the Lord and knowing, God has brought us here for a reason, for a purpose, and we need to finish that. . . . God has just helped us through different ways in which he has shown himself to be faithful no matter whatever the situation will be. . . . One particular crisis was at the end of my three and a half years, the scholarship that we were under got stopped. And so the last semester and the following year of internship, we didn't know how we were going to go and do that. And then that was one of the very critical situations to trust in God. #12

The biblical accounts of Abraham, Daniel and his friends, Naomi and Ruth, Nehemiah, Esther, and Ezekiel further demonstrate the intervention of God in their lives despite the hardships of migration or exile. Migration blesses insofar as it enables the person to experience God and thus experience a change of self-understanding (Gen 32:22–32; Exod 3). The nearness of God is perhaps no more acutely felt than during an experience of physical displacement, and this nearness is always a migration on God's part, for God intimately identifies with human suffering (Isa 63:9; Heb 2:14–18). Moltmann, in relaying where the *Shechinah*—God's presence—went when Israel was forced into exile, proposes that "God followed her."[75] God's companionship in suffering signifies that humanity is deeply cherished by God. What does this do for the human construction of identity? God's migration on our behalf indicates the immensity of human dignity, a fact that those who believe can apply to themselves and others. Acknowledging self-worth is the foundation for a healthy construction of personal identity.

From a self-worth grounded in the migration of God, the Christian is freed to then move to serve others according to the displacement I describe in chapter 6. Whether the research participants remained in the U.S. or returned overseas, they communicated how they strove to no "longer live for themselves, but for him who died for them and was raised again" (2 Cor 5:15). Migration multiplied blessing since these migrants, who had received the blessing of God, became agents to bless others in their journey.

Summary

Supported by biblical narrative excerpts and contemporary social research, these five aspects demonstrate how God seems to use migration in identity construction and are pertinent in building an initial theology of Christian identity in migration. Identities if isolated can remain relatively unchallenged. Catalysts test current constructions of identity, and the first such catalyst is exposure to new identity options. Migration can function as this catalyst to introduce sojourners, as it did in my research, to multiple methods of meaning-making. Awareness of difference in one's new setting is insufficient, however, for identity reconstruction; overcoming the inertia of these graduates' current identity formations required a second catalyst. The disorienting process of migration caused these internationals to be so thoroughly shaken that they began to question and re-evaluate who they once thought they were. While a single encounter, unless peculiarly marked, may be insufficient to sustain significant self-reconfiguration, the catalyst of continued disorientation in migration consistently chiseled self-understanding and resulted in protracted identity change for those in my study.

While the first three aspects of migration catalyzed individual change for my research participants, the latter two functioned on a larger scale for collective change among these graduates in their local communities. God utilizes migration as witness to spread the gospel message of identity

75. Moltmann, "Theology," 17.

transformation in Christ. While migration is also described above as a cata-lyst for individual blessing, the grander scheme is how God might employ migration to bless humanity and even to recreate the world's identity (John 3:16; Rev 21).

PRINCIPLES FOR A THEOLOGY OF CHRISTIAN IDENTITY IN MIGRATION

In this second part, I consider the previous five aspects of how God uses migration, drawn from various biblical texts and my empirical research, to ask this question: How does God use migration to develop a theological understanding of what Christian identity should entail? To this end, I dis-cuss a theological consideration of Christian identity in migration. Namely, Christian identity is continuous and discontinuous, contested, migrational, and is characterized as witness in foreignness and as blessing in keeping.

Continuity and Discontinuity of Identity

Identities are both continuous and discontinuous—a fact that one's physi-ology illustrates. The compilation of physical atoms holding one's body together represent the same person over time. These atoms, however, that constitute a human being at one moment in time completely alter over time, thus demonstrating a "continuity of form, but transience of matter."[76] Not one atom in the whole of the body remains in its origi-nal location, although turnover rates vary by body part. These changes in physical matter do not forfeit one's sense of personhood. Stability and dynamism are both part of the created order and are held together by the divine Word of God (Col 1:17). Likewise, personal identities are both continuous and disparate over time.

The process of migration, physically and spiritually, demonstrates this duality of identity formation. Migration, as both an introduction to and a disorientation of one's identities, is the experiential catalyst for the conti-nuity and discontinuity of identity formation. While migration marks the discontinuity of a journey—disjointed cultures, multiple locations, loss of identity, it also marks a remarkable continuity—a mindful destination, a remembered self, a possible hope, a sense of direction.

---

76. Wright, *Surprised by Hope*, 157. Wright quotes C. S. Lewis's powerful descrip-tion of this process from Lewis's *Miracles*. A person is "like a curve in a waterfall."

McAdams's and Pak's narrative understanding of identity described in chapter 4 fits its continuous and discontinuous construction. Both migration and one's self-understanding contain narrative structures that include a story's beginning, route, and end, and, as such, constitute a narrative journey in the experience of life.[77] Even as one's identities alter over time, the sense of one's person endures as a whole. One participant described this sense of continuity in migration:

> I bring myself wherever I go. . . . I know who I am. I'm the same whether in China or the U.S. If I believe in integrity or in honesty, if I believe in truth, in sincerity, you know, in genuineness or friendliness, or in the general concern for, say, another person of the humanity regardless of who they are, you bring that with you everywhere you go. #14

My interview participants described themselves as experiencing identity coherence over time and significant identity ruptures in their migrations, both in a literal and spiritual sense. In addition to their spiritual conversions, they were members of the predominant ethnic majority and a religious minority in their countries of origin. Upon studying abroad, they were catapulted into being members of ethnic minorities and the religious Christian majority. Their memberships once more reversed upon returning overseas. Throughout their sojourns, they maintained a sense of a unified self even as their identities were socially modified.

Similar to Pak's research findings, Toomey et al. found that their bicultural participants (such as the Asian-Caucasians who took part in their study) demonstrated both an "oppositional bicultural identity" and a "compatible bicultural identity" simultaneously. In other words, participants integrated both the discontinuity of their bicultural identities while, at the same time, maintaining the continuity of their bicultural identities. This "double-swing" construction of identity construction models the conceptualization of a "fluid integrative identity."[78] Migration accentuates this yin-yang of identity construction insofar as it increases the number of cultural introductions to diverse symbols of meaning.[79]

The continuity and discontinuity of identity is also noticed in one's conversion to Christ, in sanctification, and in Christ's return (2 Cor 5:17). When one is adopted into Christ's body, one's previous constitution is not lost but redeemed. One's individual personality and talents are not

77. Jenny Pak, interview by author, recorded by phone, Dallas, TX, November 11, 2011. See also Smith, *Moral, Believing Animals*, 63–78.

78. Toomey et al., "Bicultural Identity Negotiation," 127.

79. Ibid., 120.

abandoned or forfeited, as if absorbed into anonymity; one's previous identifications continue. The uniqueness of that person—one's self-conceptions,
roles, traits, and skills—becomes sourced in Christ. The discontinuity of
identities, however, is also visible in this verse. What is old, that is, the first
nature of sinful desires, is dislocated. One's new location in Christ disrupts
one's identities, and each previous conception a person holds about oneself
must be re-evaluated in light of one's new identity in Christ (Rom 6:1–7,
20–22; 1 Cor 6:9–12). Becoming a new creation in Christ and being remade
into the likeness of Christ requires identification with increasing holiness;
one becomes someone one once was not (Rom 12:1–2; Eph 4:23–24; Col 3:
9–10; 1 John 3:3). At the judgment of Christ, certain self-views and acts will
be preserved and saved as continuous. Other identifications that were once
thought precious before one's transformation in Christ will be ruptured
from one's existence in discontinuity (1 Cor 3:9–15; 13:12; 1 John 2:17; 3:2).

How could one conceptualize a process of identity formation that
illustrates both the continuity and the discontinuity of identity? Volf, for
example, discusses that the self must de-center from its previous center in
order to allow for a christological re-centering. Given this project's focus on
migration, a better description may be to describe one's self as a road that
is intersected by two-way roads at every point. This image represents a less
confined journey of identity formation than a circle illustration. The road
illustrates the discontinuity of identity in the sense that it can turn, fork,
backtrack, and sidestep but still illustrates the continuity of identity because
the path is still one plotline if viewed from behind (as the person), with
the future still unknown. Thus, instead of an image that depicts a stationary point in the center, a path illustrates the dynamism of identity in its
movement (in any direction or elevation). In the case of Christian identity,
at some point on this road an individual meets, acknowledges, and invites
Christ to join oneself and then receives God's Spirit as a companion and
guide on life's journey.[80]

Contestation and Reconciliation of Identity

When Paul repeats God's orders to Israel in Isaiah 52:11 to the early Christian church—"Come out from their midst, and be separate," says the Lord,
"and touch no unclean thing, and I will welcome you," one can imagine the
conflict this presented in one's family and social interactions (2 Cor 6:17).
One's transformation as a believer in Christ means a reordering of one's

---

80. Rowan Williams and Volpe recognize the nonlinear path of Christian identity.
Volpe, *Christian Identity*, 59.

identities. Considering Volf's separating and binding in identity construction elaborated in chapter 3 and self's false desires and deception described in chapter 6, identity formation involves a process of contestation and reconciliation. Certain reconfigurations will disrupt not only one's personal self-understanding but will likely impinge upon those who disagree with them. Identities are disputed, and migration to diverse cultures complicates the negotiations of individual identities. Migration, as it introduces and disorients its subjects to differing public repertoires, chisels new sites for identity contestation and reconciliation.[81]

The contestation of identities in migration does not merely occur in new locations. Considering my international sample, these migrants, although they were cultural insiders in their home countries, were often perceived as outsiders upon their return overseas. Furthermore, because these international graduates were insiders as members of evangelical Christianity while remaining national and ethnic outsiders, they offered insights into U.S. cultural practices, particularly those within the North American evangelical community, as detailed earlier.

Mobility, furthermore, can accentuate the alienation of the self which impedes the processes of identity contestation and reconciliation. If the self is not grounded in a community—which is more arduous to attain during transition and resettlement—it can drift into an isolation that goes beyond the physical and grows out of the absence of social accountability. When one is not deeply known by others in relationship, the self is alienated from a social (and thus spiritual) point of reference. Chapters 3–6 each emphasize the necessity of being in relation for healthy identity formation. One can become a stranger even in a familiar land if not grounded in such a community. So too, if connected to a community, a stranger in a hostile land can find rest.[82] As two migrants explained in their transition to the United States:

> Having that connection and knowing that it's a Christian environment and knowing that people that we knew were really committed to help us and stand along us in the process helped. If I would go to a school and not have that context, I would think twice more than I did in first context. #5

> When I came here, my security foundation was shattered. I could not even do some of the normal things. I could not really go out on my own. I didn't have all the friends that I had. My

---

81. Park elaborates on such contestations from a sociological point of view in Park, "Ethnic and Religious Identities," 20.

82. Hauerwas and Willimon, *Resident Aliens*, 138.

family was not here at that time. So the only thing I did, was every Saturday, I would fast and kneel down, just spend time with the Lord. That strengthened me so much. #6

With such alienation, if not related, these participants might have missed the helpful identity contestation they described that migration brings.

In the construction of identities, humanity has seemed lost in its journey since the Garden. Given Goodin's description of the human condition as a vacillation between striving and settling, humanity seeks to discover peace and yet remains restless. God's intention for the culmination of human identity has been made clear: "God made the one who did not know sin to be sin for us, so that in him we would become the righteousness of God" (2 Cor 5:21). God's intended destination for humanity's journey or *telos* is the reconciliation to God in Christ by being made righteous (v. 20). The act of migration, then, is God's pursuit of reconciliation; God in Christ pursued humanity. Those who are in Christ are called to migrate within their own self-understanding in identification with the other for this same hope of reconciliation.[83]

Migration offers a pathway to identity reconciliation. Emmanuel Katongole underlines the importance of Christian identity as a pilgrimage and states that the goal of such a journey is reconciliation. When Christ toppled the divisions between people, those who were once separated became "fellow travelers" (Eph 2:14, 19). Since the Christian's call in one's new identity in Christ is to seek and find "unexpected gifts of friendship, community, and signs of new creation on the other side of our usual 'tribal' identities," migration extends this opportunity for a reconciliation of identities.[84] Identity formation for the Christian is a continual re-orientation and transformation to one's understanding of what one's identity in Christ means. Chapter 8, for example, describes how migration aided such understanding in that these graduates learned how others interpreted their Christian identity differently.

Migration serves as a "metaphor of faith" in the contestation and reconciliation of identity.[85] Physical journeys take a variety of routes to their destinations: linear, round-about, curved, backtracked, winding. Other variables (weather, economic factors, road conditions, parties involved) can

83. Ting-Toomey's identity negotiation theory is helpful here in "intercultural boundary-crossing," bearing in mind its ten key assumptions. Ting-Toomey, "Matrix," 216.

84. Katongole, "Journeyer."

85. Hanciles's metaphor of faith refers to Abraham's migration to obey God. Hanciles, *Beyond Christendom*, 43.

also affect the journey. In leaving and moving one demonstrates a certain degree of faith that one will reach the hoped-for destination. Similarly, in the construction of identity, Christians are called to move out from themselves in relation to another (Luke 6:27–36; Phil 2:3–4). The varying routes by which this might be accomplished hold as many variables as a physical journey. Migrating and making a movement toward another, however, requires tremendous faith, which is enacted not only by believing in the existence and request of God, but by believing that one's obedience to move toward improved relations will be honored. Because God has forged a path for humanity's reconciliation, it is not lost in its physical journey or in its self-configuration.

Migration of Identity: Identity Negotiation

The nature of Christian identity requires a negotiation, a migration. This includes the migration of identity in its interdependent identification and interdependent determination.

Interdependent Identification

Christian identity must include a self-construal that identifies with the other, as I relay in chapters 3 and 6. Further, what I term interdependent identification is critical to a theological assessment of identity construction in migration. The boundary construction of identity, the concept of the *imago Dei*, one's location in Christ, and the process of migration illustrate this principle for a theology of Christian identity in migration.

For the maintenance of Christian identity, one's boundaries of the self must neither be impervious nor overly yielding. Too exclusive a boundary creates an insulated identity; the person maintains a rigid distinction that results in a loss of influence and no engagement of the other. Denying the other in order to retain one's personal identity reflects an unhealthy management of identity. On the other hand, too absorbent a margin creates an indistinguishable identity. The person loses the distinction of identity and its influence; as a result, one does not engage with the other. Either extreme denies true engagement by forfeiting the tension between the distinction from the other and identification with the other. An individual's constituted identity must both be separate from and engage with the other. The naming of difference is not inherently evil.[86] One must identify the other as both

---

86. Hauerwas, *Approaching the End*. Hauerwas quotes Milbank on his view of

different from and similar to oneself. Peace is sustained when one is neither lost in the other (what Volf calls healthy differentiation), nor so isolated from identification with the other that violence results.

To use biological terminology, a semi-permeable membrane in cell construction illustrates both self-configuration and the process of identity formation. This barrier permits certain ions and molecules to enter the cell's interior while blocking others. It protects the cell from disintegration, deterioration, and invasion, yet also allows the passage of crucial supplies, such as nutrients that promote the health of the cell. This kind of discrimination is essential for the cell's continued survival and well-being. In much the same way, boundaries for human interaction should exist, but one's negotiated identities dictate, depending upon circumstances and individual choice, where those lines are drawn. Boundaries are both fixed and fluid. The prerogative, or rather the imperative, for a Christian identity is that it should allow room for the other into the self. The response should not be a passive one that permits room, but should actively "creat[e] space" in the self for the other.[87]

International migration illustrates the migration required in identity formation particularly well. As outlined in chapter 8, the international graduates from my study demonstrated such movement across boundaries to identify with multiple others. Despite significant cultural, historical, and political differences, they adjusted within themselves to identify with their host country's inhabitants. One student, for example, patiently attended a very conservative church, whose members predominantly identified as Republican. His fluidity to embrace them, despite some of their views, was balanced by his decision to write his thesis arguing that the U.S. "war on terrorism" was not just. Additionally, despite my interviewees' religious differences with those in their countries of origin, they determined to return and live in identification with their fellow nationals. For example:

> God used someone to make before me an opportunity to change my life and direction of my life. I am aware that I have the same opportunity. So I want to be available and accountable for this. #3

> I'm one of a kind of one-percenter who has a [PhD] education. If I used it here [in the U.S.], it would be one among one million, but if I used it in [country of origin], one in few. So you know, it's better used there than here. #6

difference in footnote 53.

87. Volf, *Exclusion and Embrace*, 64–68, 125–27.

One's construction of self-understanding must include both identification with and distinction from another. It is to say, you are in I am, but I am not you are. In personal terms, I cannot see myself without identifying with the other. In my marriage, for example, what happens to my husband happens to me. If I hurt him, I hurt myself. This identification does not deny one's individuation but does illustrate that identity-making is complex and thoroughly relational.

N. T. Wright explains that love adds space to allow the presence of the other while still distinguishing what is "you-are" from what is "I am." Wright maintains that God, in loving humanity, remains non-other and extends Godspace to include the other.[88] This image of God reiterates the necessary distinction between who is "I am" and who is "you are" in the formation of the self, a distinction reminiscent of Volf's theology of embrace of the other. "Embrace stands for reaching out to "others" and finding a place *within ourselves as individuals and cultures for "others" while still remaining ourselves.*"[89]

Secondly, the fact that humanity was created in the image of God supports an interdependent identification. The *imago Dei* is infrequently mentioned in the biblical text but has long been accepted as a concept by the church throughout its history (Gen 1:26–27; 5:1–3; Rom 8:29; 1 Cor 11:7; 2 Cor 3:18; Eph 4:22–24; Col 3:9–10; Jas 3:9). Of three primary views, the *functional view* defines the image of God as humans who reproduce the restorative activity of God.[90] The traditional *substantive or structural view* dictates that humans ontologically hold the image of God in their being and are uniquely set apart from the whole of creation because they bear God's image in their constitution.[91] The *relational view* defines the image of God in one's "being for others" as a relational participation between a person and God.[92] Michael Horton defines this image as moral "rectitude" that comes from being called into relationship and, as such, "ethical rather than metaphysical."[93] Regardless of which view one holds, the image of God that humanity shares in common supports an interdependent identification in the construction of Christian identity. Following Herman Bavinck,

88. This differs from Moltmann's description in which God lets the other into what is God. Wright, *Surprised by Hope*, 102.

89. Gundry-Volf and Volf, *Spacious Heart*, 10–11, original emphasis.

90. For example, Volpe, *Christian Identity*, 146, 155, 166.

91. The biblical text does not name which quality(ies) might define the image according to Erickson, *Christian Theology*, 498, 512.

92. Erickson summarizes Karl Barth. Ibid., 507.

93. Horton, *Christian Faith*, 381, 387, 394–95. In my view, the image of God may best be described as personhood.

a Dutch theologian (1854–1921), Richard Mouw believes that the image of God is only fully manifested on a collective scale rather than in one single person, and that each cultural group displays "different aspects of the divine image."[94] Mouw's view of a "God-created human commonness" based on the *imago Dei* supports my argument for interdependent identification.[95] This bond is supremely important in the construction of personal identity. One's identification with the image of God in others highlights the fact that all should depend upon one another to better understand themselves.

One's location in Christ further illustrates an interdependent identification in the construction of identity (2 Cor 5:17). All who are in Christ share Christ in common. One international migrant posed this particularly well:

> About identity, as Christ is shaping us into more Christ-like[ness] through the Holy Spirit's power, we become more like him who eventually doesn't belong to any country and belongs to all countries. #2

If one's Christian identity is found in the body of Christ, then that body collectively reflect Christ's total work (Rom 12:4–5).[96] Because of this, for example, the power of jealousy can be disarmed in me when I can enjoy the blessing of God in others through our mutual identity in Christ. Just as the persons of the triune God can enjoy one another's distinctive roles in mutual identification without identical possession, one can enjoy within one's own identity the fruit that others in Christ's body bear without resentment, justification, or infringement.[97] What is lacking in one's self is fulfilled in the body of Christ.[98] One is freed from having to be a certain way, from having particular items, or from pursuing assets that one may no longer be able to possess. Those mourning what they have lost can, in some part, powerfully identify with others in Christ who still possess it. From trivial matters to the most heart-breaking of circumstances, one's configuration of identity that includes an interdependent identification can experience with

94. Mouw, "Imago Dei," 265.

95. Ibid., 263.

96. Volf mentions the interdependence in the life of the body of Christ. Volf, *Free of Charge*, 86–87.

97. This principle can be extended to all who share the image of God. This principle does not legitimize injustice to persist; on the contrary, self-identification with their mistreatment should prompt one to act.

98. Volf reiterates Martin Luther's observation of this exchange between the believer and Christ, but neither specifically extends this to what members of Christ's body share together. Volf, *Free of Charge*, 81.

others what they themselves may have lost. In the same way, interdependent identification can lead individuals to identify with the hardships of others in their pain and the joys of others in their successes (Rom 12:15; 1 Cor 12:25–26).

In an interdependent identification, to seek the other *is* to seek one's self (Gen 1:26–28; Deut 6:5; 1 John 3:11; 4:21; Rev 21:3). The self with semi-permeable frontiers wills to not be without the other, for it sees identity relations as a covenant in light of the new covenant (Luke 22:20; 2 Cor 3:6; Heb 9:15; 12:24).[99] The integration of the self with the other, far from causing its dissolution, creates a culmination of relation. Human effort does not primarily forge this relationship; God's Spirit integrates the self with the other. Upon offering one's self to God and allowing itself to be reformed relationally, the self can be constituted in interdependent identification. Consider this graduate's explanation:

> I try to think, trying to put myself on their feet, trying to be a little more patient like Jesus would be patient with them, trying not to judge them. That is my initial reaction to things that are unknown or things that are different from what I am culturally used to, so it helps me to be able to give people the benefit of the doubt based on 1 Corinthians 13. I have to wait for everything. It helps me to listen more. It helps me to have a teachable heart every time I go to a new culture and just being able to think, "What do they have from God or from this culture that I can learn that is completely foreign to my own culture?" #7

A theology of Christian identity in migration not only refers to merely geographical movement but to a movement within the self *toward*. It is a move toward understanding one's self in terms of one's identification with different others. God migrated within the triune Self and became embodied to identify with those who were fundamentally different from the divine Self (Rom 5:6, 8; Heb 2:14–18). Christians likewise are called to seek those who are perceived as different from themselves. They must reach from within their own self-understanding to identify interdependently with all in the constitution of their identities. This identification requires the migration of one's thinking, one's behavior, one's possessions, and one's physical location (2 Cor 8:9). Who one is and how one knows oneself must take the other into account, not merely from those with whom one identifies easily but from those in perceived social outgroups (Luke 6:32–36). Christ's relational migration was not a quest for self-indulgence but rather for self-displacement

---

99. Volf, *Exclusion and Embrace*, 144–45, 257. Volf terms this idea a "will to communion."

(2 Cor 8:9; Phil 2:6–8). Similarly, Abraham, in obedience to God, faithfully inhabited a new identity. He no longer possessed an identity "for itself" but:

> Abraham opens himself as a refuge and advocate for many. . . . To be a child of Abraham, as Paul clearly saw (see Rom 4) is to be a child of a freedom supported on another, to be dispossessed and to live only by one's reference to another. Or, as Jesus suggests (see John 8:56), it is to keep oneself in hope and trust—the biblical form of identity—for the joy of the Day of the Lord.[100]

When one entrusts oneself to God, one is enabled to look beyond one's self to see the needs of others. Several of my research participants demonstrated interdependent identification with the marginalized in their societies and offered weekly care for them. One such graduate operated a food bank for foreign migrants to Italy. Others ran literacy programs for village children whose parents had not enrolled them in school. Another graduate embodied the migration of identity in serving a deaf community. She organized to have a school for deaf girls use the church's facility for additional activities. She remarked that these girls—being deaf, female, and "of no use" to their rural families—were sent to this urban boarding school. Many families could not afford or did not wish for their daughter's return over the weekends. The school allowed them to stay but had no weekend programs. Each Sunday, while her husband led the church service, she held a special class for the girls and their interpreter. She stated:

> I feel badly for these girls. This at least gives them something to look forward to on the weekend. #11

The identification of one's self-conception with the other involves several steps. One must first possess an awareness of and secondly acknowledge the other. Thirdly, the self pursues an understanding of the other, one that cannot be obtained from the outside. The other, or others who are similar to the original party, must share this information directly. The last step in remaking one's self-conception to be inclusive of the other is by demonstrating compassion in a proactive movement toward the other. The necessary risk one takes with this kind of movement is that one's attempt to identify with the other may not be reciprocated. While both communicators are needed for a successful identity negotiation, the efforts of one individual are sufficient to begin the communicative process.[101]

---

100. Susin, "A Critique," 88.

101. Ting-Toomey, "Matrix," 218.

Interdependent Determination

Another aspect of performing Christian identity in migration is one's willingness to be determined by another in interdependent determination. The individual creates one's self-views in the context of other relationships. One's identities are forged by acting on, reacting to, and receiving the reactions of others. Chapters 3–6 describe how the construction of one's self-imaging relies upon interaction with the other to form its identities. One's rebirth in Christ and the boundary making of the self further invite this other-determination of the self.

The liberation that is gained by one's identity being in Christ is not an unchecked, uninhibited freedom, but a call to interdependent determination. Membership in the body of Christ emphasizes (as does the Decalogue) a relational component among other members as part of one body. Being *in* Christ means a belonging to one another, much like two siblings, who are related to one father, are related to each other. Thus, one's new creation identity is intimately tied to Christ and to all who are in him. All Christians are instructed not only by Christ for the formation of their new identities, but also imperatively by one another (Heb 10:24–25; Jas 5:19–20). One severs a more thoroughgoing self-configuration when one cuts off one's relations in Christ. Volf critiques an "ecclesiological individualism" as the "denial of being conditioned by these relations and in the refusal both to enrich others and to allow oneself to be enriched by them."[102]

Walter Brueggemann describes that, in freeing the Israelites from their "brick quotas of the empire," Yahweh summoned them to serve a new master (Exod 5:1; 7:16; 8:1, 20; 9:1, 13; 10:3). The Exodus was a call out of slavery to "a new bonding" at Sinai (Lev 25:42). God delivered them from imperial oppression in order to invite them into a covenant relationship.[103] God offers the same freedom and relationship to the Christian today (Gal 2:19). God's liberation frees believers in Christ to walk in righteousness and allow themselves to be determined by others (Lev 11:44–45; 1 Pet 1:15–16; 1 John 2:5–6). Volpe quotes Rowan Williams in her assessment of Christian identity:

> Christian community is inseparable from the "self in construc-
> tion . . . whose good is understood in terms of a universally
> shareable good, and the self is not known adequately without
> a grasp of the inseparability of its good from the good of all."[104]

102. Volf, *After Our Likeness*, 281.

103. Brueggemann and Hanson, *Truth-Telling*, 53–55.

104. Volpe, *Christian Identity*, 60.

My interviewees and survey participants, based on their reported understanding of their purpose and call from God, allowed themselves and their personal journey to be determined in part by the need of and for the good of others in returning overseas. While roughly one-third of the quantitative graduate sample remained in the U.S. (a low stay rate compared to stay rates for graduates of other degrees), the majority departed and cited religious reasons to a statistically significant extent for doing so. Several elaborated:

> Because there are a lot of need in [country of origin]. . . . Less pastors are trained, and that's the reason we came—so that we can be useful to so many people. #10

> God has invested in us this education, and because of the lack of this kind of education . . . and because of also how much we understand the culture . . . I really feel that that's where we're most used right now. #13

> My reason for leaving the U.S. was primarily a combination of love for people in Europe and spiritual responsibility to them and God. #159 (survey participant)

An interdependent determination involves recognizing the beneficial role of the other in determining one's self, as well as how one is subject to the rest of the body of Christ. Despite the limitations imposed upon humanity by original and volitional sin, one recognizes the need for the other in order to rightly see oneself. Covenantal liberation figures directly into one's identity of interdependent determination. For, in relating to both God and the other, one's identity is determined by each. Rather than a polarizing stance of "oppressive conformity" or "destructive autonomy," God intends for his followers to pursue a "faithful covenanting" with one another.[105]

The boundary-making of the self also illustrates this interdependent determination in identity configuration. One cannot set independent boundaries in a social vacuum, for, if an individual cordons oneself off, these lines are pushed, pulled, and disputed by others in a process of self-configuration. One cannot determine oneself without taking into account the assessments of others. Physical migration, for the international graduates who drew and redrew boundaries around their various identities, broadened their discernment of where boundaries might be placed in the process of identity negotiation. Where self-boundaries should be drawn is a process of discernment, and, for the Christian, this decision must be made within a community, as Hauerwas's communal dependence dictates.

---

105. Brueggemann and Hanson, *Truth-Telling*, 56.

Like the tension between self-distinction and interdependent identification with the other, a tension presents itself in interdependent determination. The self is determined by its orientation between the two poles of individuality and communality. Dan McAdams refers to these poles as "agency" and "communion" and explains that people strive for a balance between the two in their lives. Stella Ting-Toomey similarly refers to a pursuit of balance between "autonomy" and "connection."[106] As chapter 4 elucidates, historical narratives significantly impact the way one negotiates identities, and the pole a person veers toward depends upon one's level of exposure to cultural extremes. Pak, for example, found that first-generation Korean mothers expressed themselves more in relation to others (communality) than did their 1.5 and second generation Korean American daughters who had been raised from an earlier age in the United States.[107] Their daughters, however, reformulated their identities to support and honor others without yielding to self-erasure, exemplifying an interdependent determination.[108] To the extent that diverse cultural narratives intersect with one another, a person is less dependent on a single narrative.

Similarly, my single Asian participants, in particular, expressed the tension between their personal independence and fulfilling communal expectations. Of the three Asian single interviewees, all lived with their parents. Interviewee #14 lived alone upon her return, but when her father died, she stated:

> All my siblings were married, so there was a kind of expectation that I should bring my mother back to live with me . . . which I did. #14

Depending where on the spectrum between individualism and collectivism a culture stands, interdependent determination could be fostered or weakened for the individual migrant. For example, interviewee #16 described the most difficult part in returning was a lack of "personal space," and another interviewee from Asia shared:

> I think being away from my family for four years made me more independent emotionally. #18

The act of migration acknowledges the effect of interdependent determination because these sojourners' self-understandings were unavoidably shaped and reshaped by their cultural environment(s). For the Christian,

---

106. McAdams, *The Person*, 409–12; Ting-Toomey, "Matrix," 218, 220–21.

107. Pak, *Korean American Women*, 12–13, 215–17.

108. Ibid., 214–17.

the willingness to admit one's other-determination opens the Christian to seek God's purpose in the interchange. Jehu Hanciles exhorts that the heart of Christian mission can be seen in precisely such intentional border movement, which I extend to the movement between the self and the other, in the discovery of difference:

> Insofar as it involves human agency, mission inevitably requires cross-cultural movement, or the crossing of boundaries, in which the primary experience is of vulnerability and risk, a readiness to live on another's terms—features typified by migration and resettlement.[109]

As these graduates experienced this discovery, these differences in turn determined, in part, their self-understanding. This interaction is heightened in migration because of the greater number of social factors that are upended. A pilot interviewee captured his changing self-views in his conversion and migration experiences:

> I would place my identity in the historic creeds as the Apostles' and Nicene Creed. . . . To my family and society, I am an alien that is so strange right now that I didn't have to make any effort to leave them; when I became a Christian and began following Jesus, it just happened. . . . So I find my identity and its definition in the Christ's holy catholic church . . . and that defines who I am more than anything else as an individual who is a part of a country, culture, and a language . . . and as such a part of Christ's mystical body, and that excites me more than any other definition or discussion of identity. Pilot interviewee #2

Inviting others to determine one's identity in part can also help to correct one's self-image and images of others, including God. Hanciles emphasizes how cultural specificity furthers one's understanding of God since the diverse "particularities of culture" that express the varieties of human creativity make God known.[110]

The Roman Catholic Church offers a theological perspective on migration that exemplifies how an interdependent determination contributes to identity formation. This perspective particularly applies to how institutions of nation-states relate to migrants. *The Compendium of the Social Doctrine of the Church* challenges host communities to consider the predicament of those who seek entrance from less economically stable lands and to imagine

---

109. Hanciles, *Beyond Christendom*, 142. Hanciles draws from Andrew Walls's assessment that a missionary evidences exactly such an attempt (167–68).

110. Ibid., 141.

the benefits they bring with them.[111] Migrants, for example, often fill a labor shortage in countries where the current workforce is inadequate for or uninterested in certain occupations. At the same time, those nations who do receive migrants for this purpose must guard against their exploitation. The protection of these laborers is the path for their functional integration into their new society, and policies that hinder or encourage such protection reflect how well that community understands the validity of an interdependent determination for self-actualization.

Christian Identity as Witness: Foreignness

Identity as witness demonstrates another principle for a theology of Christian identity in migration: the necessary character of foreignness for the Christian. In the first part of the chapter, migration as witness exemplifies how God moves God's people to reflect God's identity. One's identity in Christ bears witness to certain foreignness; those who adopt a new self-understanding as a vessel of the living God will appear peculiar to society (1 Cor 6:19). One's Christian identity witnesses to the strange then in inhabiting otherness and appearing foreign, and the process of migration is particularly illustrative.

Pak's work discussed in chapter 4 importantly draws out how individuals construct their inner worlds narratively and configure themselves according to their historical and contextual narratives. In this way, the foreignness of any culture is somewhat arbitrary and is based on one's social location. This assertion deflates the presumption that the culturally different other is wholly unrelated to one's possible configuration of self. While individuals engage different cultural narratives by which to live, the commonality shared among them is the task of meaning-making.[112] This shared task relativizes the concept of foreignness and reveals the other's configuration of identity to not be exotic, but rather a similar process as one's own, albeit with varying content. Similarly, one of my interviewees observed:

> Talking to people, knowing some people, having a little bit more real conversations about life with some people, I think that people are the same, and they have the same struggles. It's not like you go there and—and any issue is gone—any problem is gone. That's what [nationals in my country] tend to think [about the U.S.], and that's why probably I emphasize that. #5

111. "Compendium," paragraphs 297–98.
112. Smith, *Moral, Believing Animals*, 63–87.

My research study also recast the idea of foreignness as more flexible and interchangeable in the configuration of identity. One might have expected that these internationals would have reported a greater sense of strangeness and that they were more frequently perceived as strange during their period of study abroad than they did. These students instead found that their host country offered paths of convergence with the people they understood themselves to be. More remarkably, they met new forms of resistance and alienation when they returned home and were often perceived as foreigners in their countries of origin.

Foreignness as otherness can be distinguished in three ways; first of all, otherness can represent how humanity differs from God as sinful. Humanity, for example, does not possess the divine nature of God, and God does not dwell in the presence of sin as humans do. Secondly, the concept of foreignness can also refer to otherness as merely the unknown, that is, the presence of difference as a quality (without the guilt accompanying the first description of foreignness above). These two ways of representing difference—as shameful and as benign—must be applied to the construction of Christian identity. Otherness as guilt represents humanity's foreignness from God through sin, and the culpability of otherness from God is shared by all of humanity.[113] Between human parties, however, otherness can represent the differences among human qualities, all of which are not inherently evil. This second type of foreignness constitutes what is different from or unknown about the other. Otherness as particularity between the self and the human other, then, is not intrinsically sinful. While foreignness justifiably holds a negative connotation in the God-human relationship, it does not necessarily do so between human partners.[114] A third sense of foreignness is a foreignness from sin. This foreignness—what Miroslav Volf calls the "catholic foreignness" that all Christians should share—is the purity and morality that Christians seek in the pursuit of holiness.[115] This pursuit creates new fractures between human partners as one's lifestyle choices change according to one's new manner of foreignness (1 Pet 2:11).

Foreignness as difference is compositional of one's identity through its quality of harboring the strange and unfamiliar within the self. Volf's theological work described in chapter 3 brings to light that one's self-understanding cannot and should not exist without the presence of the other. In other words, what is not-me also resides within what is me in both mutuality

---

113. This commonality is discussed in terms of migration in Groody, "Church on the Move," 39–40.

114. Sheldrake, "Human Identity," 58.

115. Gundry-Volf and Volf, *Spacious Heart*, 45.

and differentiation. The witness of foreignness within one's self is indispensable for a construction of Christian identity. Just as Christ identified with humanity, his followers should identify with the other in mutual foreignness. Until the self understands itself to be foreign, unknown, and even the enemy, it will not be able to identify with the other (Rom 5:6–8). All share this quality of otherness, and a Christian identity must be configured and re-configured to reflect this understanding.

Volf also emphasizes the location and centrality of Christ within each believer. For God to dwell within each human who has surrendered one's will to follow Christ—for God to be at home in each person as a place where God's Spirit dwells—is a very strange thing indeed (1 Cor 3:16–17; 6:19; 2 Cor 6:16; 1 Pet 2:4–5). This presence of holiness that resides within broken vessels serves as a constant reminder of the presence of something foreign, that which is God and not-me (2 Cor 4:7). An international graduate characterized this as:

> To be a Christian is to have personal experience with this personal God that He attracts—captures—your affections, and He becomes the most delightful thing in your life, and the one thing that you want the most is just to continue to experience that. That re-energizes you to be able to love and live in ways that you would never be able to live without His presence. #7

Self-formation requires this understanding of the foreign as constitutive of who one is. While the nature of foreignness is often considered to be what is "not me," the term must be redefined to signify that foreignness is part of who one is in one's self-constitution. This differentiation indicates a mutuality that reflects the doctrine of the image of God, the body of Christ, and the triune God's interrelationship. If the term foreign is taken in its usual sense of strange, then, one's Christian identity enables one to better identify with those who have been labeled foreign or strange. This identification allows the Christian to evaluate oneself as an outsider and to develop a self-understanding that is more attuned to the social plight of the marginalized. As a result the Christian may include the foreignness of the migrant, for example, within one's own self-constitution.

Foreignness as difference can also be seen in the internal struggle between the two natures that reside within the individual: self-will and Spirit-control (Rom 7).[116] An innate pull for independence from God remains within the Christian self even though the reborn self acknowledges its

---

116. Traditionally, these are termed flesh and spirit. I do not use the first term to avoid the misunderstanding that the flesh—the physical body and one's corporeal existence—is evil.

rightful dependence on God through Christ by the Spirit. This self-division illustrates that the old-me still resides within one's self-understanding but remains different from the new-me. One of my interviewees, for example, described this well:

> Because certain things I believe came out from me which was not really—I didn't know that I had that in me, like, for example, some negative thoughts and negative way of doing things. I didn't know I had this way of thinking. . . . Some incidents happened, and I was like, "What did I do? Why did I do it like that?" So those kind of incidents made me realize that really you got sin in you. Sin is still there. It's during these times when you are going through something [and] the stress level is high, you know, that comes out. #9

As I detail in chapter 5, Hauerwas asserts that Christians should possess power as a minority constituency and names the Christian identity as alien. What does this alien nature mean? For Hauerwas, it requires the practice of nonviolence and the participation in church life.[117] He also seems to suggest that this alien status could not be maintained if Christians possessed certain powers within the state.[118] Rather, the alien nature of Christian identity can be manifested in each age among different historical periods and various relations between church and state.[119]

The Christian, perhaps more than any other migrant, may feel the most out of place at times, but not necessarily for the reasons Hauerwas names. One's identity of departure which I offer in chapter 6 witnesses a departure from expected custom that creates difference. What God offers the world through the church is the body of Christ bearing witness to a message of transformation through redemption—the gospel—wherever members migrate. This witness lent a strangeness to the graduates that differed by degree according to the variety of cultures in which they were interpreted. As one graduate explained:

> I'm saying that fit in as a Christian in [country of origin], it's a challenge. You don't fit. It's not part of the culture, so you find resistance. I found resistance among my non-Christian friends, I found resistance on the street, you find resistance on the daily life, so you don't necessarily fit there. You're a little different. You are different because you are evangelical. I was especially different since I was a pastor. I wasn't just evangelical. I was someone

117. Hauerwas, *Christian Existence*, 1.
118. Hauerwas and Willimon, *Resident Aliens*, 17–18, 47–48.
119. For example, Englehardt, "Belligerent Kingdom," 197–99, 201.

that would consecrate his whole life to it, so I was even more different than the rest of the people. #7

The process of migration illustrates the witness of Christian identity as foreignness. While some Christians may migrate geographically, all in the body of Christ become spiritual pilgrims. A Christian's existence on this earth is migratory, and one's pilgrimage is not only a journey to a different dimension of reality, but it is also a spiritual migration of the self, an identity transformation, after which a physical transformation will take place. One's conformity to the image of Christ occurs through the daily grind of one's particular life experiences, and this identity transformation in embodied existence is the pilgrimage of discipleship.[120] Discipleship is the process of one's identification with Christ.[121] Because one's Christian identity is performed through one's bodily existence, the demonstration of one's being remade shows that they are not of this world. The migrant appears an oddity, different from one's surroundings in manner and speech. This migration does not indicate that either one's physicality or the present earth is evil (they are God's good creations) but that the Christian now operates according to a different authority.

Witnessing to the strange requires faithfulness to this new authority. Proclamation is by word and deed, some acts of which may not be readily apparent. Embodying Christian practices make one foreign from the ways of the world, as an Asian international graduate confessed:

> Am I using the money wisely or even like doing my tax with integrity? Like, especially in [country of origin], the taxation system is pretty loose compared to the States, so it's very easy to withhold a lot of income and then not telling the [tax] revenue department. Especially my wife's income, a large part of it is cash, so if not for our faith, we could just pretend as though we didn't receive those income and not necessarily telling the government. #17

For this difference, Christians may not only appear alien, but also may experience exile from society. When the present state of affairs does not reflect the order of the new earth, Christians must refrain from participation and accept their own foreignness as witness. In this sense, the migration of identity one experiences in one's pilgrimage of discipleship *should* lead to a sense of exile. Ben Quash urges that elements of Christian wisdom, in

---

120. Quash, *Abiding*, 152.

121. See also Volpe, *Christian Identity*, 239.

fact, can only be ascertained in exile.[122] Migration, then, can illustrate the identity of witness as foreignness for the Christian, as it did in the lives of my research participants.

Christian Identity as Blessing: Keeper

In addition to its continuity, discontinuity, interdependence, and foreignness, the nature of Christian identity includes keeping. The root of this word, which is taken from Genesis 4:9, will be delineated, first followed by how this biblical concept applies to the construction of personal identity in contemporary times and its relation to migration as blessing.

In Genesis 4:9, Cain defiantly challenges God's inquiries, retorting, "Am I my brother's keeper?" The term keeper (Heb. root, *shamar*) means to keep, to watch over, to guard. The New English Translation (NET) renders this term guardian, meaning that the verse can be literally translated as "the one guarding my brother [am] I?" In other words, was Cain keeping his brother? Despite Cain's sarcasm, he verbalizes God's expectation, and this injunction to care for the other is no less obligatory in the present day. The command to love, to keep, one's neighbor is repeated throughout the testimony of the Judeo-Christian Scriptures (Lev 19:18; Luke 10:27–37; 1 John 3:11).

When one becomes a new creation in Christ, one's identity is transformed, which allows one to do what Cain was not able to do for his brother. Cain was so filled with his own self-will that he had no room to consider Abel as Cain's self. The Christian, whose self-will is subject to Christ, begins to form a new identity in the same manner as Christ. A crucial part of this formation is a self-understanding that includes personal identification with the other and even assuming the role of the other's keeper. Cain could not accept God's challenge to be his brother's keeper. As Christ died for the world and not merely for his blood relatives or for the Jewish population, Christians are not just their siblings' keepers, they are their neighbors' keepers.

What does it mean to construct one's identity as a keeper? The identity of keeping is a self-configuration that tends and preserves humanity and nature. Because one has been adopted into Christ and one's citizenship is in heaven, one's call to care for God's creation is transnational. While citizenship may be limited by one's nationality, one's identification with God's keeping the world is not. How is this identification rooted in this life, in this earthly existence? One's reconfiguration of identity, rooted in God's purpose

---

122. Quash, *Abiding*, 153.

for the world, becomes living out God's life in this world. One's enactment of one's citizenship in heaven connotes "allegiance" rather than "residence" (Phil 3:20–21).[123] Heaven seems to be a literal dimension as well as the place where God fully reigns. In the coming age, God will recreate new heavens and a new earth, joining them together into a place where all of creation dwells in right relation to God (Rev 21:1–5). To the extent that one allows one's identity to be reconfigured in Christ and lives from this new identity as a member of the "resurrection people," one lives in light of the future.[124] International graduates from my study demonstrated this sense of keeping through their expressed migration patterns in light of others' needs. For example:

> When I finished my PhD, I was offered a teaching position in [U.S. university]. With all these things, I don't want to claim anything for myself. We will not bargain our studies and our degree to make our life better. We will not use it to bargain our pay scale or, you know, hop from one position to another position. . . . This degree is given to me by God for a particular reason. . . . It is a stewardship. #6

A tension, however, remains. One's role as a keeper can muddy the very boundaries of the identity one constructs for oneself. How this tension plays out in the twenty-first century is complex and unpredictable. Despite the enormous variance of cultural values, some examples of keeping for the Christian are:

- A commitment to care and protect the other regardless of location

- A desire to coexist with the other without retaliation, even in light of differences or disagreements

- An avoidance of discord for the Christian (Rom 12:14–21)

- A willingness to rewrite one's own identity to include a capacity for the other[125]

- A refusal to dehumanize the other in speech, thought, or action

The international graduates demonstrated the tenuous nature of keeping. The myriad of factors involved in determining one's self-understanding

---

123. Wright, *Resurrection*, 230.

124. *Surprised by Hope*, 30, 100–101. Wright references Col 3:1–4; Rom 8:9–11; and 1 John 3:1. Those who have died are held intermediately in heaven, not to *stay* there. Christ's return to earth will inaugurate this resurrection of believers for the enactment of their heavenly citizenship on earth. In view of the future, the one, whose identity is transformed in Christ, can live by that self-understanding in the present.

125. Volf, *Exclusion and Embrace*, 255.

in order to bless and to keep others is complicated, made more so in the process of migration. Many communicated a spiritual sense of obligation to return as described in chapter 8, attributing their return to the dearth of trained pastors or lack of resources in certain countries. In fact, of the graduates who responded to the survey question (Upon first arriving in the United States to study, what was your initial plan upon graduation?), only 2.3 percent reported that their initial plan was to remain in the U.S. 36 percent, however, did. 76.6 percent reported they had intended to leave the U.S. 13 percent were open to either scenario, and 7 percent were undecided at time of entry. 1 percent reported intending to remain for further education. Others remained in the U.S., for example, to care for their family or to pursue further education for themselves or their children). Some migrated to care for aging parents; some stayed to pastor ethnic congregations in the U.S. The range of the survey responses in answering why they remained in or departed from the States include:

> I always believe that my gifts and talent could be best used back [home] to help transform lives and my community. #21

> I had received a scholarship that required my return to my country, and I wished to honor this commitment, even though I had been offered a post in a church in the U.S. #87

> After serving home church for 10 years, my home church asked me to return to the States to serve at her daughter church for a few years. #261

> To answer God's call at home, and it was very clear. I was committed to going back home to serve God. #284

> After graduation, I returned to my home country and resumed ministry until I had to return to the U.S. to help care for my ailing father. #289

> My wife changed her mind about missions. I accepted an offer of employment that allowed me to stay here [in the U.S.] since that was her preference. #322

> God has called us to serve in our country. He has given us a great love for our countrymen, and the need here is great. #364

> My oldest child was ill and on treatment that made it impossible for us to return [overseas]. The Lord used that difficult situation in our family and opened a new door of ministry for us. We are now missionaries [based in the U.S.] reaching out to Portuguese-speaking people in several countries. #377

These graduates' choices regarding whom to keep and how to best keep them were far from obvious. Fashioning one's identity as a keeper is as unique as each individual's journey with God.

To identify oneself as a keeper means to acknowledge that one's identity is crafted by God to care for the other in showing love for God (1 John 2:3–5; 4:7–8, 12, 20–21). Despite the boundaries that have been devised by humanity, the goal of the Christian identity is to value, protect, and watch over the other as God does (Rom 12:14–21; Jas 1:27). Wherever migrants may sojourn, those who are kept are blessed through the service and care of God's followers. As the examples given recount, many Christians demonstrated such keeping of these international graduates during their study abroad and return overseas. Two shared:

> Financial support is definitely a very practical thing which I did get from a few different churches and from the school. So that was good. . . . I think accountability from abroad—like from home—is important, like whether I'm really on track with things, whether I'm doing what I'm supposed to do like study, from family and from the churches that support me. Of course, the support of the prayers that comes together. I think the local—people from the U.S.—is very important too, where a lot of life needs, like, in advice, support. Like for me, I didn't have a car, and sometimes I needed a ride, and people would be willing to give me a ride. Later when it's difficult for me travel to church to attend my internship, people even left their car—unused car—just let me drive it and then give it back to them after I graduate. It made very much easier, and the love they gave me was very hardcore. . . . I needed much more with the U.S. People give me leftover food. It would make it easy because I could just cook less and save time just to study more. #16

> I get a lot of assistance from the churches in [the U.S.]. So if God didn't lead me to the U.S. then I would have maybe have quit after the first few months. #17

This kind of stewardship guards, cares for, and preserves the other without seeking to overtake the other. Letty Russell's corrections to the misapplication of the doctrine of election are helpful. One's chosen status by God should not lead one to a sense of self-importance over the other, but to a heightened sense of keeping the other. One's chosenness should motivate one to demonstrate God's love toward the other just as one has received love.[126]

---

126. Russell et al., *Just Hospitality*, 39, 41.

The performance of such an identity requires maintaining one's own individuality without trespassing on the will of another.[127] The identity of the keeper shuns domination and requires self-donation (chapter 3) and an identity of displacement (chapter 6). With each, one seeks to make room for the other within one's self-construction and extend oneself toward the other to invite a relationship. When this invitation is not reciprocated, one respects the distance the other has created but remains at the ready, as will be described below in the parable of the prodigal son.

A desire to see the other flourish in spite of one's wrongdoing is necessary for a keeper (Luke 23:34; Acts 7:60). The Christian identity displaces one's own desires so as to prevent domination of the other and seeks one's restitution even when violence comes by the other's hand.[128] Is there a risk of losing one's self in this act of donation?[129] Yes and no. One's possessions, reputation, and physical life can be stolen, but one's identification in Christ means that the truest essence of who one is, is never lost by these things (Matt 10:38–39; John 12:24). Is self-donation an injustice? No injustice occurs when one gives oneself voluntarily; this is why God cannot be accused of injustice in Christ's crucifixion. In a gesture of personal identification with humanity and out of a desire to see it restored, God the Son offered himself *willingly* to be punished in humanity's stead. Therefore, the performance of Christian identity must embrace this willingness to forgive and even to suffer (Col 3:13). The embrace of suffering seems counterintuitive to a self that seeks self-preservation at all costs, but it typifies what it means to enact a Christian identity in keeping of the other—one who gives to protect (Matt 10:8b; Acts 20:35). Those who have received the gift of forgiveness are entrusted to demonstrate what they have been given to others. At the risk of sounding hagiographic, I respect each of the returnees in my study who gave up certain benefits to leave the U.S. and serve the people to whom they felt called to go.

In fighting for our rights (and I speak here to the U.S. Protestant evangelical community most of all), we misunderstand the nature of Christian identity. The construction of one's Christian identity is more about understanding the communality of the human condition and seeking the good

127. Volf, *Exclusion and Embrace*, 91–92.

128. For example, Célestin Musekura lost five family members including his father and sister, along with seventy members of his congregation who were killed when perpetrators attacked their prayer meeting in Rwanda in the revenge killings following the genocide. He forgave them and founded African Leadership and Reconciliation Ministries (ALARM) that now operates in eight African countries. See Musekura, *Assessment*, 1–2.

129. Self-donation can be misconstrued and oppressive. Ross, "Pioneering Missiologies," 26–27.

of our perceived enemy than in protecting some hard-won turf.[130] Conflict often involves mutually exclusive alternatives and ends with a losing side. Christians, however, must seek identification with the other to such a degree that they risk losing something in the exchange or risk an illegitimate victory. A theological construction of Christian identity in migration necessitates that outside of one's national citizenship, one must configure an identity as a keeper of the other. This choice figures a new manner of being, of seeing oneself, and of resistance to any form of domination.[131] It is through attachment to Christ and to others and by releasing personal ambition that the genuine self is found (John 12:24–26). The healthy self is preserved in giving to others, a movement dictated by God's design, for the purpose of bringing peace to the world.

Forming one's identity as a keeper does not only mean giving in a traditional sense; it may mean guarding oneself. Keeping the other may mean waiting or holding what one wishes to give in order to avoid dominating the other. The identity negotiation of the father in the parable of the prodigal son is instructive (Luke 15:11–32). The father does not send servants to retrieve his son or money to aid him. Identification between the self and the other involves a balance between separating and binding (to use Volf's terms), between differentiating and inviting. The father loves his son on the son's terms. When the son leaves, the father does not undermine the designated familial boundaries. The distance the son instigates continues as a result of the son's unwillingness to reside with his family and the father's refusal to accommodate his son's indulgences. He does not run after his son. This parable offers a powerful example that identity negotiation within oneself toward the other does not mean overpermissiveness or the ignoring of wrongs. When the son returns, he does not approach his father presumptuously; he recognizes that his actions require forgiveness (v. 18–19, 21). The father has a design for his son's character, but he neither forces nor looks the other way in unqualified support. The father giving of himself does not mean that he surrenders who he is or who he thinks his son should be, but he does endure a costly wait for the other.[132] The father's open arms of

130. Taking legal action to defend certain rights that one believes one has according to the country's laws is justifiable. One must discern carefully if this action is rather to maintain the benefits of a majority power enjoyed. One must evaluate what time and energy is spent to defend what one wishes to preserve for one's way of life in comparison to defending others in greater need.

131. Kang urges "decolonization" in theological education, which I argue for Christian identity. Kang, "Envisioning Postcolonial Theological Education," 36, 39–40.

132. Ting-Toomey encourages that even the effort of one party is beneficial in the process of identity negotiation. Ting-Toomey, "Matrix," 218.

acceptance do not precede the son's acknowledgment of his folly, the son's recognition that he has no claim to assert restoration, and his humble turn of repentance.[133] In this way, the father embraces the son while remaining true to his own identity.[134]

The Christian identification of the keeper adds a clarification to Ting-Toomey's identity negotiation theory. Identity negotiation involves speaking into one another's lives and should not result in indiscriminate affirmation.[135] Identity formation does not escape the difficult tension of defining what is harmful or beneficial for humanity. Achieving or maintaining harmony can only be accomplished dialogically. If censorship of belief or unquestioning avowal is proposed, either party could be harmed.

One's Christian identity to bless as a keeper bestows an inevitable vulnerability. The one who gives might be taken advantage of or might give in the wrong way. These are inherent dangers which warrant due caution. If part of being human is the giving of one's self, one should continue to love selflessly, to act justly, to fight on the behalf of those who are oppressed, and to entrust one's self to God to repay injustice. Christ, for example, gave sacrificially to the very point of death and presumably died feeling forsaken by God (Matt 27:45–46). It may seem safer (rather, the illusion of safer) to remain isolated from the different other. Cruz draws an "ethic of risk" from the Catholic Social Teaching themes of human dignity, human rights, the common good, and solidarity.[136] She argues that to extend oneself to care for the marginalized other necessitates a sacrifice on one's part—of personal rights, time, expense, or identity (Matt 20:25–28). Risk is a necessary part of keeping in the performance of Christian identity.[137]

CONCLUSION

In summary, while one's imagination is initially constrained to one's cultural context, God possesses the power to speak into one's identity configuration.[138] Because God, through migration, plants seeds of imaginative capacity that allow the self to widen its identity horizon to pursue creative exploration and new directions, one is never completely constrained by one's culture. The beauty of migration, despite its turmoil, is its transmission of new ideas

133. Bock, *Luke 9:51—24:53*, 2:1306–20.

134. Gundry-Volf and Volf, *Spacious Heart*, 11.

135. Ting-Toomey, *Communicating across Cultures*, 42, 47.

136. Cruz, *Theology of Migration*, 64. Sharon Welch presumably coined this term.

137. Ibid., 65–67. Luke 22:25–30.

138. Volf, *End of Memory*, 199.

that allows one to know God more fully by studying the diversity and unity of the world.

Throughout history God has used the migration of peoples to introduce new ways of living and thinking across the world. Since no one local context defines all of what it means to be human, God seems to superintend the construction of human identity over time and space through this process. Original and volitional sin have marred one's ability to know who one is.[139] Due to this rupture from God through sin, humanity has been disconnected from whose they are. The narrative of each life tells a story of seeking and searching in discovering who one is and *whose* one is. Migration is a tool in this process of discovery. Humans need one another in a wider context than even a local community of faith to learn who they are. The global discourse brought about by migration prompts this wider reconsideration of who one thinks one is.

Considering various biblical texts and my empirical data, I described five aspects of migration in an effort to show how God employs migration as a tool for the construction of identity and drew implications for a theological consideration of Christian identity. This contemporary social research project elicited identity configurations for a limited cohort (a voluntary migrant population educated abroad and attesting to an evangelical religious identity) and should not be generalized. Importantly, I described how migration develops a theological understanding of what Christian identity should entail. Each of my interlocutors—Volf, Pak, and Hauerwas—claim that identity construction is teleological in nature, as does migration as I argue. This teleological path, however, is not linear, and both kinds of journey evidence forward, backward, and circular movement. Migrants do not speak in terms of returning to the same circumstances that prompted them to leave their homes; they rather hope to achieve something in the journey itself, with change in a forwardly direction. The construction of Christian identity is both a process and a destination. As creatures designed for relationship, people will continue to change dynamically and their identities, embodied in physical existence, will be formed and reformed. The dynamic formation of identities will continue in a movement without end.[140]

Active human migration will endure from creation to its final consummation. God gave the first movement mandate in Eden (Gen 1:28), and

139. Volpe, *Christian Identity*, 9–10, 42–43, 63–67.

140. Human identity is "an eternal process of formation" (ibid., 228). "The desire that is rightly oriented toward God is never satiated because each new vision of God's beauty incites the desire for more, and God's beauty is infinite" (165). So too, based on God's infinity, the construction of identity will continue as desire yields new discoveries in God, yielding new space for eternal growth.

movement appears throughout the biblical text. It seems to be intentionally related to making God's identity known and bringing the earth's people back to God (Gen 12:1–2; Exod 19:4–6; Ezek 20:42). When Christ inaugurated the new creation, another movement mandate was issued—the spreading of God's people throughout the earth as witnesses to God's identity (Matt 28:18–20). In the consummation of the re-creation, this mandate will not cease (Rev 21:3; 22:3, 5b).[141] Without migratory experiences, the construction of Christian identity is stunted. The dynamism of life leads us to our continuing identity in Christ.

---

141. The term "reign" in Rev 22:5b reflects a similar injunction to the dominion God gave the first couple in the Garden of Eden.

10

Applications and Conclusion

IN THE LAST FEW decades, the construction of self and identity—particularly Christian identity—has been heartily debated. In this interdisciplinary work, I consider Christian identity in light of the works of Miroslav Volf, Jenny Hyun Chung Pak, and Stanley Hauerwas. In his discussion of the centering and sociality of the self, Volf draws a compelling theology of identity. He considers both the creation account and the Trinity's interrelationship in affirming the duality of identity formation—how it differentiates yet binds—as well as the necessity of boundaries and non-exclusionary judgments. Volf's theological contribution to the construction of identity is profoundly applicable to contemporary issues of social violence and reconciliation. Pak, for her part, offers a narrative, psychological, and intercultural approach to the study of identity. Her work in the acculturation and identities of immigrant women particularly aided this study. Hauerwas, finally, contributes a philosophical and theological perspective in his discussion of the nature of the self in general and Christian identity in particular.

Both Volf and Hauerwas explicitly agree on the dependency of the self on God while Pak and Hauerwas both discuss the narrative nature of self and identity. Hauerwas's unique emphasis on the self's dependence on the church for its identity is an important addition to a theology of identity. Drawing upon the work of these scholars, I propose six components of a theology of identity in chapter 6 and argue that the theological nature of the self is given, related, and divided. I also consider the construction of Christian identity and three identities: the identities of departure, of belonging, and of displacement.

In my consideration of the construction of identity in migration, I conducted a research study that involved 405 participants—evangelical and voluntary migrants who had departed their countries of origin, pursued programs of study in the United States, and graduated from these programs. While oversimplifications should not be made from such a specific participant group, chapter 8 describes my findings regarding the relationship between religion and the construction of personal identity, the relationship between religion and individual migration, the negotiation of multiple identities for this educated migrant population, and the relationship between international migration and the individual. The interviewees from this study described themselves in terms of their religious calling, and this portrayal in part addresses and extends my earlier call for further research on how individuals organize themselves in terms of a calling.[1] They moreover described themselves as stewards of the biblical narrative, locating themselves within it as well as continuing it. Furthermore, their religious faith was associated with their migration decisions, especially for those who decided to leave the United States. Regarding the three identities examined in particular (religious, ethnic, and national), participants showed a favorable disposition toward each yet negotiated among them. They perceived their religious identities to be the most significant and often narrated their ethnic and national identities in terms of their religious identities. Interestingly, their rated significance of national identity was significantly greater than their ranking of ethnic identity. The internationals' perceptions of how U.S. citizens negotiate their multiple identities are also included. For the migrants who returned overseas, new tensions among their identities are discussed, and findings are presented detailing how international migration altered these migrants' self-understanding as well as how it dissolved and created partnerships, networks, and trajectories for them.

In chapter 9, I offer a theological reflection on Christian identity in an exploration of the premise that God shapes human identity through migration for its reconstruction and development. I describe how God uses migration as a tool to shape human identity in order to elicit more properly what a Christian identity should entail, based on my research study and sections of biblical narrative. From these, I recommend six principles for an initial theology of Christian identity in migration. I affirm the continuity and discontinuity of identities and introduce the interdependent identification and interdependent determination of a Christian identity. I describe the concepts of foreignness and keeper as central to a Christian

---

1. Williams, "God's Global Professionals," 192.

self-configuration. Finally, I discuss how migration is a tool for reconciliation in identity configuration.

In this concluding chapter, I offer possible applications for religious and educational leaders to consider when working with their respective constituencies. I then suggest several areas for further research and close with a few final remarks.

SUGGESTED APPLICATIONS

Since the United States receives the greatest number of foreign students,[2] religious and educational institutions can better prepare their constituents if more is understood about the identity crises these students face. How can seminaries in particular help their international religious leaders navigate a sense of self as well as the prejudices they might encounter during their theological education and cultural transitions? From this theoretical review and research field study, I suggest several possible applications for those in pastoral ministry, religious organizations, and educational institutions.

Correcting the Racialization of Identities

While cognitive categorization may be inevitable and even appropriate in the construction of identity[3], any categorization that leads to a form of dehumanization must be challenged. In this study, participants conveyed instances in which they were poorly treated because of their ethnicity and/ or their religious faith. Educational institutions should continue to introduce ways to offer its population a wider range of diversity, thinking, and membership to address these recurring wounds. U.S. religious organizations and its members are especially called upon to seriously consider the implications of these comments for their ministries.[4]

Renegotiating Categories: Neighbor, Stranger, Enemy

Many now live in a globally connected world—going, coming, returning, staying—that is hinged together by technology and transnationalism. One should not lapse into the old dichotomies of home/foreign, resident/ alien, host/migrant, in/out, neighbor/stranger, us/them. How easily can

2. "Open Doors."
3. Reicher et al., "Social Identity Approach" 20–22.
4. A starting point would be Emerson and Smith, *Divided by Faith*.

one's language and mentality construct social walls of separation, and the contingency of human existence begs all to hold their apparent security or place loosely. Categories, then, must be renegotiated to accurately reflect our ever-changing social contexts.

Theologically, all are born strangers before God. One's inability to identify with the other is a result of how poorly one knows its own self as a stranger.[5] When one recognizes this strangeness in oneself, one can rene- gotiate the distancing categories one gives to the other. For the striving self- focused nature within us, however, others can be made enemies. Enmity rises within individuals' chests to take from and war with and pilfer from one another. God bestowed, however, a kinship of creation on all people. This makes all neighbors, even brothers and sisters. This neighboring does not erase the existence of the other, as if the other is melted into one's self.[6] Williams elaborates, "A neighbor [is] inescapably an other. . . . The neighbor is not I, and loving my neighbor is not a matter of loving some conveniently familiar version of myself."

Loving one's neighbor is more broad and inclusive and yet more con- crete and demanding than it is often understood to be. Consider Martin Luther's statement regarding a Christian's responsibility during one of the besieging waves of the bubonic plague in Wittenberg in 1527. He states:

> If it were Christ or his mother who were laid low by illness ev- erybody would . . . gladly become a servant or helper. . . . If you wish to serve Christ and to wait on him, very well, you have your sick neighbor close at hand. Go to him and serve him.[7]

With a Christian theological understanding of self and identity, one can love the stranger, neighbor, and enemy as one loves oneself, and all can love each other as Christ has loved them (Matt 22:37–39; Mark 12:29–31; Luke 10:27–28; John 13:34). Identifying oneself as the enemy is perhaps the most crucial aspect of understanding how to love. Christ instructs his disciples to "love your enemies" (Matt 5:43–44). Christ indicates that people love preferentially but calls his followers to demonstrate the love of God. God loves all. God causes the "sun to rise on the evil and the good and sends rain on the righteous and the unrighteous" (Matt 5:45; see also Lev 19:15; Luke 6:35; Acts 14:17). Christians are called to "be perfect," which means

---

5. Hauerwas and Coles, *Christianity*, 5.

6. Williams, "Assimilation and Otherness," 253.

7. Lull and Russell, *Martin Luther's Writings*, 479.

to love perfectly, and perfect love loves all (Matt 5:48). This perfect love of non-preference leaves no place for fear to reside (1 John 4:18).[8]

Renegotiating Possessions: A False Premise of Ownership

During the writing of this book, I experienced a major transcontinental move within the United States, having spent nearly twenty years in North Texas. In the course of packing, leaving, losing, and gaining, I recorded several personal experiences that are pertinent to three points given here. My first admonition to those who have remained stationary in one locale for years is to *consider the quantity of your possessions.* In making my one-thousand-mile trek across the United States, I was often tempted to abandon the majority of our possessions and leave with only four pieces of luggage. Instead we opted to hire a moving company. When the moving company failed to deliver our belongings for almost one month, however, and we lived on what we had brought in one car, I realized how very little is needed to live well. With only an air mattress, two camping chairs, a small table, and two laptops, we experienced a foreign simplicity. I asked myself, "Why have I not lived more like a migrant?" I was also struck by how few essential items are needed to survive, namely, clean water, daily nourishment, employment, and shelter. What was I doing to help those who need these critical items?

My second advisement is to *count which blessings matter.* Humanity was created for relation and not possession, yet much of identity construction consists of what possessions or titles one can amass. In this pursuit one can lose one's identity or self-view. My third is to *relinquish your mass of personal possessions for the material good of another.* It is a countercultural practice to give up what one possesses. The false premise of ownership leads one to believe in the illusion that one is in control (Jas 1:10–11). On the contrary, Christians recognize that neither their lives nor their material possessions belong to them. The identity of possession for the Christian is far looser; the labels mine and yours are replaced by God's. Christians who understand themselves as stewards rather than owners offer a point of connection to the traveling stranger. Christ liberates his followers from false baggage so that they may cultivate something far more demanding: serving others before themselves.[9] God's identity forms Christian identity. Individuals who have been bestowed with God's provision are in turn to

---

8. The giver does not demand reciprocal love and knows that brutality instead might be returned. Gabrielson, "Paul's Non-Violent Gospel," 58.

9. Hauerwas and Willimon, *Resident Aliens*, 61.

emulate the identity of God by *giving*. May Christians follow Paul's example in this pursuit:

> But *as God's servants*, we have commended ourselves in every way, with great endurance, in persecutions, in difficulties, in distresses . . . by purity, by knowledge, by patience, by benevolence, by the Holy Spirit, by genuine love, by truthful teaching, by the power of God . . . regarded as impostors, and yet true; as unknown, and yet well-known; as dying and yet—see!—we continue to live; as those who are scourged and yet not executed; as sorrowful, but always rejoicing, as poor, but making many rich, as *having nothing, and yet possessing everything*. (2 Cor 6:4–10 NET, emphasis added)

Ministry of Remembrance

I submit that individuals' inhumanities to one another stem from a lack of identification with the other. The failure of Cain, for example, to identify with Abel does not suggest that, had he done so, his actions would have been different. The practice of identifying with the other, however, can avert evildoing because it offers the *possibility* of following a righteous path. This identification requires practice and forms a ministry of remembrance, which involves intentionally looking for, recalling, and acting upon the commonalities between two individuals. The greater task is to identify with another's different point of view. This compassionate imagining allows individuals to think outside of themselves and see the world through another's eyes. While it may not be theoretically possible to fully undergo another's experiences, simply attempting to understand the other's perspective may improve one's ability to approximate the other's view more closely than before.

For Christians, this remembrance of identification with the other is perhaps best illustrated by receiving communion. Receiving Christ's body offers a time for confession in self-reflection. It is an opportunity to remember how Christ identified with his enemies at great personal sacrifice. It is a remembrance of how all would earn the same harsh fate were it not for the other identifying with them. The act of taking communion reminds one of one's belief in the suffering, death, burial, and resurrection of Christ on one's behalf and one's likeminded identification with Christ in these events. I recently visited a Protestant church where communion was served differently than to what I was accustomed, and my experience relates directly to this point of discussion. After each received an individual wafer of bread, the audience was instructed to break it in half as the minister read the pertinent biblical passage aloud. When I broke mine, I was struck anew with the betrayal of Christ in his very body. This breaking is what Christ asks us to endure for others. Identification with the other makes one vulnerable and will, at times, include personal suffering and even betrayal. The sacrament's act of remembrance re-enacts the migration Christ requires from God's people. Identification with the other, at times, requires significant personal cost (Rom 8:17; Phil 1:29; 3:10; 2 Tim 1:8; 1 Pet 4:13, 19).

Ministry of Mutuality

In a theology of identity in migration, all parties identify with one another in a ministry of mutuality. A just partnership between parties discussed in 2 Corinthians 6:11–13 is an appropriate aim in this discussion. Others have cautioned that hospitality in terms of a host benefiting a stranger poses inherent difficulties.[10] What if hospitality could be separated from the contractual designs of commerce and framed as relational mutuality?[11]

Gemma Tulud Cruz defines God as the only appropriate host and both migrants and citizens as simultaneously guests and strangers. She writes, "Seeing God as the provider of hospitality destabilizes the usual roles (with the migrant as the usual guest and the citizen as the usual host) and the unbalanced order of relations these roles spawn."[12] Both parties, then, give and receive, sharing from that which God has given. Campese recovers the relational element of hospitality when he describes it not as doing or giving but being with another.[13] Hospitality is also a disservice if it is considered to be temporary, for the migrant is also an inhabitant and, quite possibly, a permanent resident.[14] Hospitality is neither unidirectional nor short-lived.

One ought not to approach the other before carefully inspecting one's self. This *a priori* evaluation may forestall at least some premature or inappropriate movements from the individual toward another. One must first consider one's place in the hierarchy of power relations as well as the historical place of one's group.[15] One must ask if one is perpetuating a colonial mind-set and, if so, in what ways. Even in self-displacing service to another,

---

10. Namely, paternalism. Cruz, *Theology of Migration*, 94.

11. Padilla, "Expanding Space," 55.

12. Cruz, *Theology of Migration*, 95.

13. Campese, "Irruption of Migrants," 28–29.

14. Ruiz, *Reading*, 138–39.

15. The historically overshadowed interpretations of those who have been moved, even subjugated, should be heeded. Cruz, *Intercultural Theology*, 157.

one must guard against how one's "[zeal] could blur the lines between giving oneself and sacrificing the 'other.'"[16]

The will to embrace, using Volf's terminology, opens an avenue for friendship and peaceful coexistence with the perceived other. When applied to the construction of identity, embracing the stranger in good will expresses an opening of oneself to the other and an inviting into one's life. It also suggests a closing—a commitment that the other has been allowed in and that the embracer desires to join the stranger's space. The hospitality of an embrace is, therefore, a negotiation between parties.

As mentioned earlier, assigning the labels of host and foreigner has its deficiencies. It is better to think of two parties as distinct partners who might share in a ministry of mutuality. It is difficult to express what is required without some use of categories for the delineation of differentiated advice. Given that this research study considered international students in the United States, the following briefly exemplifies several opportunities for inhabitants, whether recent or otherwise, to participate in a ministry of mutuality.

For Established Inhabitants

- Consider how to connect international students to their desired religious networks to support their cultural adjustment.[17] Of the participants who answered the question, over one-third (34.1 percent) cited their local church as the most important factor in their cultural adjustment during their time of study abroad, and over one-quarter of participants cited their personal religious faith as the most important factor in their cultural adjustment (27.3 percent).

- Consider the significance of religious symbols on display and what these symbols may mean to newer inhabitants. For example, consider how a national flag hanging prominently in a worship service might be perceived.

16. Gabrielson, "Paul's Non-Violent Gospel," 148.

17. Approximately 11.5 percent cited their own ethnic group living in the U.S. as the most important factor, whereas 10.4 percent cited their school's administrative staff as the most important factor. Approximately 9.9 percent cited their friends from school or previous networks as the most important factor. A small percentage of participants cited relatives in the U.S. (3.1 percent) or relatives overseas (0.5 percent) as the most important factor. Lastly, a small percentage stated that another factor was most important (1.3 percent), or that the question was not applicable (1.8 percent).

- Consider how one's sense of national identity is intertwined with one's religious identity. Since religion has long been used to legitimize the monopoly of power for questionable practices, consider how political maneuvers, especially if they strengthen those already in power, might sacralize military movements for the amplification of power.

- Remember the loss of connection to a particular location that migrants will experience in migration and help them devise new opportunities for remembrance.

For Recent Inhabitants

- More recent inhabitants bring a unique perspective upon entering a new cultural scene and can vocalize what is observed. This kind of feedback is vital for Christian communities.

- Maintain a "consciousness of weakness" in learning how to adapt and live in a religiously pluralistic context.[18] New neighbors who have experienced living as a minority in other political, religious, and ethnic contexts can help U.S.-born Christians in this pursuit.

- Allow six months to culturally adjust to a new environment.

- Consider the regional cultural differences of the United States upon migration. Also, words may have different definitions from what is culturally familiar. Words, such as friend, time, and soon, may be used much more loosely in the U.S. than in a new inhabitant's home country.

AREAS FOR FURTHER RESEARCH

Given the interdisciplinary nature of this project, multiple suggestions for further investigation are possible. Much research on international student migration remains to be accomplished. Researchers must seek to understand the push factors that lead some to migrate and not others. While social factors such as the presence of family abroad or education have been studied, the push factors that stem from personal characteristics have not. The present study should also be expanded to include the study of non-Christian international students. How does the salience of the various identities for Muslim students compare? Do Buddhists, Mormons, and those of other faiths cite religious reasons for their migration decisions to the same extent?

18. See also Hanciles, *Beyond Christendom*, 380, 391.

It will also be useful to inquire what percentage of current international students enrolled had parents who were international students themselves. Is being a child of an international student statistically related to later becoming one? This analysis would be useful in promoting the sustainability of international student enrollment among host universities.

Since the graduates in my research study deemed their religious identity to be the most salient, membership in a religious minority in a familiar, although religiously different, culture offers another interesting dynamic for further consideration of the identity negotiation process. Perhaps the spiritual aspect of relating to a divine being and/or their newfound transnational social networks gave these graduates the support they needed to mitigate their feelings of insecurity, distrust, separateness, and identity chaos as members of a religious outgroup. If narratives, especially in migration, allow for pulling from a plurality of options,[19] then why did these graduates maintain a traditional religious identity as a religious minority? The fact that the strength of these graduates' identities was not measured longitudinally creates an avenue for further research. One should ask, which identities remain salient over time with physical distance and under what circumstances?

In light of McAdams's psychological work, a comparison between the type of religious narrative in which individuals locate themselves with the type of life story they describe would be an interesting area for future study. Does Christianity, for example, elicit an increased association with the redemptive life story as a "characteristic narrative of selfhood"?[20]

International migrants, students or otherwise, also offer transnational and intercultural dynamics to further develop narrative and identity negotiation theories. Because people are interdependently determined by their contexts and relationships, the ways that migration expands or contracts personal identities also could be explored. In the development of a theology of Christian identity in migration, research should be conducted for both voluntary and involuntary sojourners in an investigation of how people see themselves in their changing global and local contexts. Research in countries that have experienced high rates of out migration should be conducted to assess how those who remain view themselves and what factors relate to their positive and negative self-views.

Finally, the initial principles for a theology of Christian identity in migration that I have drawn need to be further explored, contextualized, and

---

19. Park, "Ethnic and Religious Identities," 161.
20. McAdams, "Redemptive Self," 95–97.

applied to specific contemporary examples of social interaction between individuals and between groups.

CONCLUDING REMARKS

This project uniquely contributes to the identity literature and multicultural research currently available. It also adds to the theological discussion of what Christian identity is and how it is constructed. Christian identity is the practice of imitating the likeness (identity) of Christ. A Christian identity is a vulnerable identity, as the following example illustrates. One of my Haitian friends once explained to me the Creole word for compassion: *konpasyon*. Compassion can also be translated as *ke nan men*. This means literally "your heart in your hand," carrying the idea that when the heart moves, the hands act and do good to others. To hold one's heart in one's hand is to be deeply, personally moved, extending the most vulnerable part of one's self, even one's life, to another. May this compassion, exemplified fully by the triune God, define the identity of all those who understand themselves to be Christian.

Appendix 1

INTERVIEW PARTICIPANTS

To ensure confidentiality of interview respondents, ages are grouped by decade, and individuals' countries of origin are grouped into three categories. Field research and interviews were completed in these geographical areas: Catholic and former Communist Europe and South and Southeast Asia. Below are the number assignments for and demographics of interviewees.

Interviewees

1. Male, 40–49, Former Communist Europe

2. Male, 40–49, Former Communist Europe

3. Male, 40–49, Catholic Western Europe

4. Male, 30–39, Former Communist Europe

5. Male, 30–39, Former Communist Europe

6. Male, 40–49, South and Southeast Asia

7. Male, 30–39, Catholic Western Europe

8. Male, 30–39, South and Southeast Asia

9. Female, 40–49, South and Southeast Asia

10. Male, 40–49, South and Southeast Asia

11. Female, 30–39, South and Southeast Asia

12. Male, 30–39, South and Southeast Asia

13. Female, 30–39, Former Communist Europe

14. Female, 50–59, South and Southeast Asia

15. Male, 20–29, South and Southeast Asia

16. Male, 20–29, South and Southeast Asia

17. Male, 40–49, South and Southeast Asia

18. Female, 30–39, South and Southeast Asia

Pilot Interviewees (PI)

PI 1. Female, 20–29, East Asia

PI 2. Male, 30–39, Middle East

PI 3. Male, 50–59, East Asia

PI 4. Male, 40–49, East Asia

PI 5. Male, 50–59, Africa

Appendix 2

INTERVIEW QUESTIONS

1. What is your country of origin?[1]

2. What year did you come to the U.S.?

3. How many years did you live in the U.S.?

4. What is your current occupation?

5. What term would describe your current religious affiliation?[2]

6. What was your life like before you came to the U.S.?

7. What was your life like in the first 6 months in the U.S.?

8. Can you think of an image or visual picture that describes how you felt as an international student?

9. Knowing what you know now, what would you tell your younger self before you studied abroad?

10. How did you come to move to study in the U.S.?

11. What do tell your family and friends back home about the U.S.? A story?[3]

---

1. This question is adapted from Q27, Kosmin et al., "American Religious Identification Survey."

2. This question is adapted from question 4.2, Park, "Ethnic and Religious Identities," 194.

3. This question is adapted from Appendix I, Section: Culture and Society, question 3, Williams, "God's Global Professionals," 195.

12. Were you changed during your time in America? How? Have you an example of how living in the U.S. has influenced how you do things in a way that is different from back home?[4]

13. Have any of your cultural or political views changed since studying abroad?

14. Is there anything (spiritually, theologically) that you learned in the U.S. that you adopted?

15. Were there any values or practices you observed in the U.S. that you could not adopt?

16. Was there anything hard about living in the U.S.?

17. Is there anything you would call a blind spot of the U.S.? Has it infiltrated the American church?

18. Did your faith help you in your transition to the U.S.? How? Example?

19. What does it mean to you to be (ethnicity/nationality)? An example? What was it like being (ethnicity) in America?[5]

20. How does living out your faith relate to your national sense of duty?

21. Can you think of an example?

22. How did you come to move back overseas?

23. Did your faith help you in your transition back overseas? How? Example?

24. When you returned home, how did people see you?

25. How have you been received (in society/church) as someone who has studied abroad?

26. Have you faced resistance in your return? From whom?

27. If you could correct one misconception (about you) among your friends and family, what would it be? Among your neighbors? Among your congregation?

28. Have you experienced any tension between who you were in America and who you are expected to be now that you are back home?[6]

29. In what ways do you feel like you "fit in" this present society?

30. Have you ever felt "out of place" here? An example?

4. Ibid., Culture and Society, question 4.
5. Ibid., Culture and Society, question 2.
6. Ibid., Culture and Society, question 5.

31. Do you face challenges in your society for being a Christian? How do you deal with them?

32. An instance where you struggled to make a personal choice involving your faith between difficult options?

33. How do you decide between your national or civic responsibilities and personal convictions?

34. If your child were to ask, "Why can't we go back to America?", what would you say?

35. Do you worry about what your children lack here as compared to the U.S.? (educational resources, certain opportunities)?

36. Is there anything hard about living in (home country)?

37. [If female, ask] Have you experienced any difficulties as a woman? Gender issues?

38. If you were to describe what "identity" means to you, what would you say?

39. What does it mean, to you, to be a Christian?[7] Especially in migrating between different cultures? Is there an example you can give me to illustrate that?

40. What did you need most when you studied abroad?

41. What did you need most when you returned overseas?

42. Is there anything else you would like to share on these topics?

---

7. Ibid., 194., Beliefs and Practices, question 4.

Appendix 3

QUESTIONNAIRE

Directions: Since responses will be group averages, YOU WILL NOT BE IDENTIFIED INDIVIDUALLY from the information you provide. Your responses are completely confidential. Please answer each question.

1. What is the total time you have lived in the United States?[1]
0 to less than 2 years
2 years to less than 3 years
3 years to less than 4 years
4 years to less than 5 years
5 years or more

2. When you first studied in the U.S., of which country were you a citizen?

3. What is your age?

4. What is your gender?
Female
Male

---

1. Multiple questionnaire items were adapted from other research surveys. The source for each pertinent question is noted. This question is adapted from Gareis, "Intercultural Friendship."

5. What is your current marital status?
Single, never married
Married
Separated
Divorced
Widowed

6. In what year did you start your studies at Dallas Theological Seminary (DTS)? (Please select year from drop-down menu below.)

7. Did you begin studies in the U.S. on an F or J student visa?
Yes
No
I don't know

8. What was your religious background prior to your current faith?[2]
Animist or Spirit Worship
Atheist
Buddhist
Hindu
Muslim
Nominal Christian (Catholic, Orthodox, or Protestant)
Practicing Christian (Catholic, Orthodox, or Protestant)
Other (please specify): _____

9. How important, currently, is your religious identity in your life?[3]
Not important at all
Not very important
Moderately important
Very important
Extremely important

2. Adapted from Litton, "Negotiating Religious Identity," 186.
3. Park, "Ethnic and Religious Identities," 187.

10. I feel strong ties to other members of my religious faith.[4]
I strongly disagree
I disagree
I somewhat agree
I agree
I strongly agree

11. To what extent did your faith and/or religious beliefs play a part in determining your location after graduation?
Not at all
Not very much
Somewhat
A considerable amount
Very much

12. What is your ethnic/racial background? (Select all that apply.)[5]
Arab/West Asian (e.g., Armenian, Egyptian, Iranian, Lebanese, Moroccan)
Black (e.g., African, Haitian, Jamaican)
East Asian (e.g., Chinese, Japanese, Korean)
South Asian or South East Asian (e.g., East Indian, Sri Lankan, Cambodian, Indonesian)
Latin American/Hispanic
White/Euro-Caucasian
Other (Please specify):_____

13. How important, currently, is your ethnic group in your life?[6]
Not important at all
Not very important
Moderately important
Very Important
Extremely Important

4. Talebi, "Does Religion Matter?," 70.
5. Ibid., 71.
6. Park, "Ethnic and Religious Identities," 187.

14. I feel strong ties to other members of my ethnic group.[7]
I strongly disagree
I disagree
I somewhat agree
I agree
I strongly agree

15. Overall, being a member of my ethnic group has very little to do with how I feel about myself.
I strongly disagree
I disagree
I somewhat agree
I agree
I strongly agree

16. Considering your country of origin, how important, currently, is your national identity in your life?
Not important at all
Not very important
Moderately important
Very Important
Extremely Important

17. To what extent do you feel strong ties to other citizens of your nation of origin?[8]
Not at all
Not very much
Somewhat
A considerable amount
Very much

18. Overall, being a citizen of my country of origin has very little to do with how I feel about myself.[9]
I strongly disagree
I disagree
I somewhat agree
I agree
I strongly agree

7. Talebi, "Does Religion Matter?," 71.
8. Schildkraut, "Defining American Identity," 613.
9. Talebi, "Does Religion Matter?," 71.

19. What, if any, are the challenges that you face for being a Christian in your country of origin? (Select all that apply.)
Civil discrimination
Job discrimination
Physical threat
Lack of material resources
Lack of physical comfort
Lack of organization (e.g., efficiency)
Tension with relatives/friends due to your Christian faith
None
Other (Please specify):_____

20. How concerned are you about the opportunities (e.g., economic, educational, social) available to your children in your country of origin?[10]
Not concerned at all
A little concerned
Somewhat concerned
Very concerned
Extremely concerned
Not applicable. I don't have children.

21. [IF APPLICABLE] If you are concerned about your children's educational opportunities, how do you deal with this concern? (Select all that apply.)
Accept the tension (allow children to grow up in the tension)
Parental commitment to educate children personally
Pursue in-country private education for children
Pursue education abroad for children
Trust that God is at work in this country
I am not concerned
Other (Please specify):_____

22. Are people, based on a Christian religious identity or activity, currently discriminated against in your country of origin?[11]
Not at all
Not very much
Somewhat
A considerable amount
Very much

10. Schildkraut, "Dynamics," 76–77.
11. Finke and Grim, "Data from Arda."

23. [OPTION ORDER RANDOMIZED] Which of the following is most important to you?[12]
Your nationality
Your religious faith
Your ethnic group
Other (Please specify):_____

24. How many times did you visit your country of origin during your studies in the U.S.?
None
Once
Twice
Three or more

25. Which of the below was the MOST important factor to assist you during your cultural adjustment to the U.S.? Choose ONE.
Ethnic group living in the U.S.
Local church
Personal religious faith
Relatives in the U.S.
Relatives overseas
School staff
Fellow students
Other (Please specify):_____

26. Upon first arriving in the United States to study, what was your initial plan upon graduation? (Choose the best option that describes you.)
My plan initially was to return overseas.
My plan initially was to remain in the U.S.
I was open to either returning overseas or remaining in the U.S.
I was undecided at that time.
Other (Please specify):_____

27. What did you need the most when you studied abroad?
Cultural Translator (to help explain how to do things in a new environment)
Encouragement
Friendship
Funding
Ministry Mentor
Other (Please specify):_____

12. Syed et al., "Pakistan Religious Identity."

28. Do you currently live in the U.S.?[13]
Yes
No

29. [IF RESIDENCE U.S.] Why did you primarily stay in the U.S.? (Choose the best option that describes you.)[14]
Offer of employment
Religious/spiritual reason
Educational reasons concerning your children
Marriage to a U.S. citizen
Other family reasons
Love for the U.S. culture
Generally for a better life
Other (Please specify):_____

30. [IF RESIDENCE NOT U.S.] Why did you primarily leave the U.S. after graduation? (Choose the best option that describes you.)[15]
Offer of employment
Religious/spiritual reason
Previous organizational agreement or contract
Marriage to a non-U.S. citizen
Other family reasons
Love for home country culture
Generally for a better life
Other (Please specify):_____

31. [IF RESIDENCE NOT U.S.] What did you need the most when you returned overseas?
Encouragement
Finding housing
Funding
Friendship
Ministry mentor
Ministry network (of local Christian churches, leaders, groups)
Other (Please specify):_____

13. "European Social Survey," 18.
14. "2012 Asian American Survey," 256.
15. Ibid.

32. In what way, if any, has studying abroad changed your thinking the most? (Choose one.)
Appreciating teamwork
Encountering a different worldview
Learning new ways of interacting with people
Saying "No" is important in some situations
Thinking critically
Thinking creatively
Other (Please specify):_____

33. In what way, if any, has studying abroad changed your behavior the most? (Choose one.)
I relate to people differently.
I have new values I did not live by before.
I have become more patient.
I have become more tolerant.
I have become a better citizen.
Other (Please specify):_____

34. Would you describe yourself as an evangelical Christian?[16]
Yes
No
Other (I would describe myself as . . .) _____

35. What is the denomination of the church in which you currently participate?[17]
I am not participating in a church at this time.
Catholic
Anglican or Episcopal
Baptist
Evangelical
Lutheran
Presbyterian
Pentecostal/Assemblies of God
Methodist/Wesleyan
Nondenominational
Reformed
Other (Please specify):_____

16. Ibid., 236.
17. "European Social Survey," 15.

36. Is there anything else you would like to share about these topics?

Bibliography

"2012 Asian American Survey." Pew Research Center, 2013. http://www.pewsocialtrends. org/files/2013/04/asian-americans-updated-topline-03-2013.pdf.

Abdelal, Rawi, et al. *Measuring Identity: A Guide for Social Scientists*. Kindle ed. Cambridge: Cambridge University Press, 2009.

Al-Ali, Nadje, and Khalid Koser, eds. *New Approaches to Migration? Transnational Communities and the Transformation of Home*. London: Routledge, 2002.

Altheide, David L., and John M. Johnson. "Reflections on Interpretive Adequacy in Qualitative Research." In *The Sage Handbook of Qualitative Research*, edited by Norman K. Denzin and Yvonna S. Lincoln, 581–94. Thousand Oaks, CA: Sage, 2011.

Alwin, Duane F., et al. "Measuring Religious Identities in Surveys." *Public Opinion Quarterly* 70/4 (2006) 530–64.

Ammerman, Nancy T. "Religious Identities and Religious Institutions." In *Handbook of the Sociology of Religion*, edited by Michele Dillon, 207–24. Cambridge: Cambridge University Press, 2003.

Aslanbeigui, Nahid, and Veronica Montecinos. "Foreign Students in U.S. Doctoral Programs." *The Journal of Economic Perspectives* 12/3 (1998) 171–82.

Baggio, Fabio M., and Agnes Brazal. *Faith on the Move: Toward a Theology of Migration in Asia*. Quezon City: Ateneo de Manila University Press, 2008.

Baggio, Fabio, and Laura Zanfrini, eds. *Migration Management and Ethics: Envisioning a Different Approach*. Milan: Polimetrica, 2009.

Baker, Jill L. "1 & 2 Kings." In *The IVP Women's Bible Commentary*, edited by Catherine Clark Kroeger and Mary J. Evans, 184–213. Downers Grove, IL: InterVarsity, 2002.

Balmer, Randall Herbert. *Encyclopedia of Evangelicalism*. Waco, TX: Baylor University Press, 2004.

Bamberg, Michael, et al. "Discourse and Identity Construction." In *Handbook of Identity Theory and Research*, edited by Seth J. Schwartz, et al., 178–99. New York: Springer, 2011.

Bauerschmidt, Frederick Christian. "Thomas Aquinas: The Unity of the Virtues and the Journeying Self." In *Unsettling Arguments: A Festschrift on the Occasion of Stanley Hauerwas's 70th Birthday*, edited by Charles R. Pinches, et al., 25–41. Eugene, OR: Cascade, 2010.

Beath, Andrew L. "Migration." In *Globalization for Development: Trade, Finance, Aid, Migration, and Policy*, edited by Ian Goldin and Kenneth A. Reinert, 151–92. Basingstoke, NY: World Bank, 2007.

Bebbington, D. W. *Evangelicalism in Modern Britain: A History from the 1730s to the 1980s*. Winchester, MA: Allen & Unwin, 1988.

Bediako, Kwame. *Theology and Identity: The Impact of Culture Upon Christian Thought in the Second Century and in Modern Africa*. Oxford: Regnum, 1992.

Bender, Courtney, et al. *Religion on the Edge: De-Centering and Re-Centering the Sociology of Religion*. Kindle ed. New York: Oxford University Press, 2012.

Berry, J. W. "A Psychology of Immigration." *Journal of Social Issues* 57/3 (2001) 615–31.

Bevans, Stephen B., and Cathy Ross. *Mission on the Road to Emmaus: Constants, Context, and Prophetic Dialogue*. London: SCM, 2015.

Bock, Darrell L. *The Bible Knowledge Word Study: Acts-Ephesians*. Colorado Springs: Victor, 2006.

———. *Luke 9:51—24:53*. Vol. 2. Grand Rapids: Baker Academic, 1996.

Bonikowski, Bart. "Research on American Nationalism: Review of Literature, Annotated Bibliography, and Directory of Publicly Available Data Sets." RSF working paper. 1–19. New York: Russell Sage Foundation, 2008.

Bowie, Fiona. "Trespassing on Sacred Domains: A Feminist Anthropological Approach to Theology and Religious Studies." *Journal of Feminist Studies in Religion* 14/1 (1998) 40–62.

Brannen, Julia. "Working Qualitatively and Quantitatively." In *Qualitative Research Practice*, edited by Clive Seale et al., 282–96. London: Sage, 2004.

Braun, Willi. "Religion." In *Guide to the Study of Religion*, edited by Willi Braun and Russell T. McCutcheon, 3–20. London: Cassell, 2000.

Breen, Michael. *The Koreans: Who They Are, What They Want, Where Their Future Lies*. New York: Thomas Dunne, 2004.

Brown, Chris. "Review of *Exclusion and Embrace*: A Theological Exploration of Identity, Otherness and Reconciliation, by Miroslav Volf." *Millennium—Journal of International Studies* 29/3 (2000) 920–22.

Brubaker, Rogers. *Ethnicity without Groups*. Cambridge, MA: Harvard University Press, 2004.

Brueggemann, Walter. *Truth-Telling as Subversive Obedience*. Edited by K. C. Hanson. Eugene, OR: Cascade, 2011.

Bryman, Alan. *Social Research Methods*. 4th ed. Oxford: Oxford University Press, 2012.

Burns, Stephen, and Clive Pearson. *Home and Away: Contextual Theology and Local Practice*. Eugene, OR: Pickwick, 2013.

Burrell, David B. "Can We Be Free without a Creator?" In *God, Truth, and Witness: Engaging Stanley Hauerwas*, edited by L. Gregory Jones et al., 35–52. Grand Rapids: Brazos, 2005.

Buzo, Adrian. *Making of Modern Korea*. London: Routledge, 2002.

Campbell, William S. *Paul and the Creation of Christian Identity*. London: T. & T. Clark, 2006.

Campese, Gioacchino. "The Irruption of Migrants: Theology of Migration in the 21st Century." *Theological Studies* 73/1 (2012) 3–32.

Carroll R., M. Daniel. *Christians at the Border: Immigration, the Church, and the Bible*. Grand Rapids: Brazos, 2013.

Carson, D. A. "Contrarian Reflections on Individualism." *Themelios* 35/3 (November 2010). http://www.thegospelcoalition.org/publications/35-33/editorial-contrarian-reflections-on-individualism.

Cartwright, Michael G. "Stanley Hauerwas's Essays in Theological Ethics: A Reader's Guide." In *The Hauerwas Reader*, edited by John Berkman and Michael Cartwright, 623–72. Durham, NC: Duke University Press, 2001.

Cavanaugh, William T. "Migrant, Tourist, Pilgrim, Monk: Mobility and Identity in a Global Age." *Theological Studies* 69/2 (2008) 340–56.

Chan, Kwok Keung. "The First Mark of Mission: To Proclaim the Good News of the Kingdom of God." In *Life-Widening Mission: Global Perspectives from the Anglican Communion*, edited by Cathy Ross, 13–30. Eugene, OR: Wipf & Stock, 2012.

Charry, Ellen T. "The Crisis of Modernity and the Christian Self." In *A Passion for God's Reign: Theology, Christian Learning and the Christian Self*, edited by Miroslav Volf, 89–112. Grand Rapids: Eerdmans, 1998.

Cheah, Pheng, et al. "The Future of Sexual Difference: An Interview with Judith Butler and Drucilla Cornell." *Diacritics* 28/1 (1998) 19–42.

Chen, Carolyn. *Getting Saved in America: Taiwanese Immigration and Religious Experience*. Princeton: Princeton University Press, 2008.

Choi-Kim, Grace. "Continuing Gender Issues for Second-Generation Korean-American Women in the Home and in the Church." 2011. http://old.religiouseducation.net/member/01_papers/Choi_Kim.pdf.

Chow, Patricia, and Rajika Bhandari. "Open Doors 2010: Report on International Educational Exchange." New York: Institute of International Education, 2011.

———. "Open Doors 2014: Report on International Educational Exchange." Institute of International Education. http://www.iie.org/en/Research-and-Publications/Open-Doors/Data/International-Students/Infographic.

Christofferson, Ethan J. *Negotiating Identity: Exploring Tensions between Being Hakka and Being Christian in Northwestern Taiwan*. Kindle ed. Eugene, OR: Pickwick, 2012.

"Compare Nations." Association of Religion Data Archives (ARDA). http://www.thearda.com/internationalData/multicompare.asp?c=3&c=48&c=106&c=108&c=180&c=115&c=201&c=185.

"Compendium of the Social Doctrine of the Church." Pontifical Council for Justice and Peace. 2004. http://www.vatican.va/roman_curia/pontifical_councils/justpeace/documents/rc_pc_justpeace_doc_20060526_compendio-dott-soc_en.html.

"CPI (Maoist) Included in List of Terrorist Organizations to Avoid Any Ambiguity." India Ministry of Home Affairs. June 22, 2009. http://pib.nic.in/newsite/erelease.aspx?relid=49325.

Cresswell, Tim. *Place: A Short Introduction*. Malden, MA: Blackwell, 2004.

Cruz, Gemma Tulud. "Between Identity and Security: Theological Implications of Migration in the Context of Globalization." *Theological Studies* 69/2 (2008) 357–75.

———. *An Intercultural Theology of Migration: Pilgrims in the Wilderness*. Leiden: Brill, 2010.

———. *Toward a Theology of Migration: Social Justice and Religious Experience*. New York: Palgrave MacMillan, 2014.

Davies, Oliver. *Theology of Transformation: Faith, Freedom, and the Christian Act*. Oxford: Oxford University Press, 2013.

De Groot, Christiana. "Genesis." In *The IVP Women's Bible Commentary*, edited by Catherine Clark Kroeger and Mary J. Evans, 1–26. Downers Grove, IL: InterVarsity, 2002.

"Defining Evangelicalism." Institute for the Study of American Evangelicals. http://www.wheaton.edu/ISAE/Defining-Evangelicalism/Defining-the-Term.

"Defining the Term in Contemporary Times." Institute for the Study of American Evangelicals. http://www.wheaton.edu/ISAE/Defining-Evangelicalism/Defining-the-Term.

Denzin, Norman K., and Yvonna S. Lincoln. *The Sage Handbook of Qualitative Research*. Thousand Oaks, CA: Sage, 2011.

Donald, Stephanie, and Robert Benewick. *The State of China Atlas*. Berkeley: University of California Press, 2005.

Ecklund, Elaine Howard. *Korean American Evangelicals: New Models for Civic Life*. New York: Oxford University Press, 2006.

Elsie, Robert. *A Dictionary of Albanian Religion, Mythology, and Folk Culture*. New York: New York University Press, 2001.

Emerson, Michael O., and Christian Smith. *Divided by Faith: Evangelical Religion and the Problem of Race in America*. Oxford: Oxford University Press, 2000.

Englehardt, H. Tristram, Jr. "The Belligerent Kingdom." In *God, Truth, and Witness: Engaging Stanley Hauerwas*, edited by L. Gregory Jones et al., 193–211. Grand Rapids: Brazos, 2005.

Erickson, Millard J. *Christian Theology*. Grand Rapids: Baker Academic, 1990.

"European Social Survey Round 6 Questionnaire." Centre for Comparative Social Surveys, City University London. http://www.europeansocialsurvey.org/docs/round6/fieldwork/source/ESS6_source_main_questionnaire.pdf.

"Faith on the Move: The Religious Affiliation of International Migrants." Washington, DC: Pew Research Center, 2012.

Ferdinando, Keith. "Christian Identity in the African Context: Reflections on Kwame Bediako's Theology and Identity." *Journal of the Evangelical Theological Society* 50/1 (2007) 121–43.

Finke, Roger, and Brian J. Grim. "Data from the Arda National Profiles, 2005 Update: Religion Indexes, Adherents and Other Data." Association of Religion Data Archives (ARDA). http://www.thearda.com/Archive/Files/Descriptions/INTL2003.asp.

Finn, Michael G. "Stay Rates of Foreign Doctorate Recipients from U.S. Universities, 2011." Oak Ridge, TN: Oak Ridge Institute for Science and Education, 2014.

Fisher, Mary Pat, and Robert W. Luyster. *Living Religions*. Englewood Cliffs, NJ: Prentice Hall, 1991.

Flyvbjerg, Bent. "Five Misunderstandings About Case Study Research." In *Qualitative Research Practice*, edited by Clive Seale et al., 390–404. London: Sage, 2004.

Francis I. "Migrants and Refugees: Towards a Better World." http://w2.vatican.va/content/francesco/en/messages/migration/documents/papa-francesco_20130805_world-migrants-day.html.

Gabrielson, Jeremy. "Paul's Non-Violent Gospel: The Theological Politics of Peace in Paul's Life and Letters." PhD diss., University of St. Andrews, 2011.

Gareis, Elisabeth. "Intercultural Friendship: Effects of Home and Host Region." *Journal of International and Intercultural Communication* 5/4 (2012) 309–28.

Geertz, Clifford. *The Interpretation of Cultures*. New York: Basic, 1973.

Global Christianity: A Report on the Size and Distribution of the World's Christian Population. Washington, DC: Pew Research Center, 2011.

The Global Religious Landscape: A Report on the Size and Distribution of the World's Major Religious Groups as of 2010. Washington, DC: Pew Research Center, 2012.

Goffman, Erving. *The Presentation of Self in Everyday Life.* Garden City, NY: Doubleday, 1959.

Goodin, Robert E. *On Settling.* Princeton: Princeton University Press, 2012.

Gorospe, Athena E. *Narrative and Identity: An Ethical Reading of Exodus 4.* Leiden: Brill, 2007.

Greene, Jennifer C. *Mixed Methods in Social Inquiry.* San Francisco: Jossey-Bass, 2007.

Greer, Rowan A. "Sighing for the Love of Truth: Augustine's Quest." In *God, Truth, and Witness: Engaging Stanley Hauerwas,* edited by L. Gregory Jones et al., 13–34. Grand Rapids: Brazos, 2005.

Grenz, Stanley J. "The Social God and the Relational Self: Toward a Theology of the Imago Dei in the Postmodern Context." In *Personal Identity in Theological Perspective,* edited by Richard Lints et al., 70–94. Grand Rapids: Eerdmans, 2006.

Groody, Daniel G. *Border of Death, Valley of Life: An Immigrant Journey of Heart and Spirit.* Lanham, MD: Rowman & Littlefield, 2002.

———. "Church on the Move: Mission in the Age of Migration." *Mission Studies* 30 (2013) 27–42.

———. "Crossing the Divide: Foundations of a Theology of Migration and Refugees." *Theological Studies* 70/3 (2009) 638.

———. "Homeward Bound: A Theology of Migration for Fullness of Life, Justice, and Peace." *The Ecumenical Review* 64/3 (2012) 299–313.

———. "The Spirituality of Migrants: Mapping an Inner Geography." In *Contemporary Issues of Migration and Theology,* edited by Elaine Padilla and Peter C. Phan, 139–56. New York: Palgrave Macmillan, 2013.

Gundry-Volf, Judith, and Miroslav Volf. *A Spacious Heart: Essays on Identity and Belonging.* Valley Forge, PA: Trinity, 1997.

Gutiérrez, Gustavo. "Poverty, Migration, and the Option for the Poor." In *A Promised Land, a Perilous Journey: Theological Perspectives on Migration,* edited by Daniel G. Groody and Gioacchino Campese, 76–86. Notre Dame: University of Notre Dame Press, 2008.

Haar, Gerrie ter. *Strangers and Sojourners: Religious Communities in the Diaspora.* Leuven: Peeters, 1998.

Hamd, Robert T. "Migrant Domestic Workers, the Church, and Mission." PhD diss., Fuller Theological Seminary, 2013.

Hanciles, Jehu. *Beyond Christendom: Globalization, African Migration, and the Transformation of the West.* Maryknoll, NY: Orbis, 2008.

Hauerwas, Stanley. *Approaching the End: Eschatological Reflections on Church, Politics, and Life.* Grand Rapids: Eerdmans, 2013.

———. *A Better Hope: Resources for a Church Confronting Capitalism, Democracy, and Postmodernity.* Grand Rapids: Brazos, 2000.

———. *Christian Existence Today: Essays on Church, World, and Living in Between.* Durham, NC: Labyrinth, 1988.

———. "Christianity: It's Not a Religion, It's an Adventure." In *The Hauerwas Reader,* edited by John Berkman and Michael Cartwright, 522–38. Durham, NC: Duke University Press, 2001.

———. "The Church as God's New Language." In *The Hauerwas Reader*, edited by John Berkman and Michael Cartwright, 142–64. Durham, NC: Duke University Press, 2001.

———. "Church Matters." In *Revisioning, Renewing, Rediscovering the Triune Center*, edited by Derek Tidball et al., 343–60. Eugene, OR: Wipf & Stock, 2014.

———. *A Community of Character: Toward a Constructive Christian Social Ethic*. Notre Dame: University of Notre Dame Press, 2005.

———. *Hannah's Child: A Theologian's Memoir*. Grand Rapids: Eerdmans, 2010.

———. *The Peaceable Kingdom: A Primer in Christian Ethics*. Notre Dame: University of Notre Dame Press, 1983.

———. *Performing the Faith: Bonhoeffer and the Practice of Nonviolence*. Grand Rapids: Brazos, 2004.

———. "Reflection on Dependency: A Response to the Responses to My Essays on Disability." In *Critical Reflections on Stanley Hauerwas' Theology of Disability: Disabling Society, Enabling Theology*, edited by John Swinton, 191–97. Binghamtom, NY: Haworth Pastoral, 2004.

———. "Stanley Hauerwas in Conversation with John Milbank and Luke Bretherton: Theological Reflections on Being a Theologian and the Task of Theology." King's College London, 2010. http://podcast.ulcc.ac.uk/accounts/kings/Social_Science/ Milbank_Hauerwas_Bretherton.mp3.

———. *With the Grain of the Universe: The Church's Witness and Natural Theology*. Gifford Lectures, 2001. Grand Rapids: Brazos, 2001.

Hauerwas, Stanley, and Romand Coles. *Christianity, Democracy, and the Radical Ordinary: Conversations between a Radical Democrat and a Christian*. Eugene, OR: Cascade, 2008.

Hauerwas, Stanley, and L. Gregory Jones. *Why Narrative? Readings in Narrative Theology*. Grand Rapids: Eerdmans, 1989.

Hauerwas, Stanley, and Jean Vanier. *Living Gently in a Violent World: The Prophetic Witness of Weakness*. Downers Grove, IL: InterVarsity, 2008.

Hauerwas, Stanley, and William Willimon. *Resident Aliens: Life in the Christian Colony*. Nashville: Abingdon, 1989.

Healy, Nicholas M. *Hauerwas: A (Very) Critical Introduction*. Grand Rapids: Eerdmans, 2014.

Heide, Gale. *System and Story: Narrative Critique and Construction in Theology*. Eugene, OR: Pickwick, 2009.

Heyer, Kristin E. *Kinship across Borders: A Christian Ethic of Immigration*. Washington, DC: Georgetown University Press, 2012.

Hiebert Meneses, Eloise. *Love and Revolutions: Market Women and Social Change in India*. Lanham, MD: University Press of America, 2007.

———. "No Other Foundation: Establishing a Christian Anthropology." *Christian Scholars Review* 29/3 (2000) 531–50.

Hiebert, Paul G. "Critical Contextualization." *International Bulletin of Missionary Research* 11/3 (July 1987) 104–12.

Hieronymus, Sophronius Eusebius, and Andrew Cain. *St. Jerome: Commentary on Galatians*. Washington, DC: Catholic University of America Press, 2011.

"History." World Evangelical Alliance (WEA). http://www.worldea.org/whoweare/ history.

Hofstede, Geert. "National Culture Dimensions." http://geert-hofstede.com/dimensions.html.

Horton, Michael Scott. *The Christian Faith: A Systematic Theology for Pilgrims on the Way*. Grand Rapids: Zondervan, 2011.

House, Paul R. *1, 2 Kings*. New American Commentary. Nashville: Broadman & Holman, 1995.

Howell, Brian M., and Jenell Williams Paris. *Introducing Cultural Anthropology: A Christian Perspective*. Grand Rapids: Baker Academic, 2011.

Hunter, James Davison. *To Change the World: The Irony, Tragedy, and Possibility of Christianity in the Late Modern World*. Oxford: Oxford University Press, 2010.

Jenkins, Richard. *Rethinking Ethnicity: Arguments and Explorations*. London: Sage, 2008.

Kang, Namsoon. "Envisioning Postcolonial Theological Education: Dilemmas and Possibilities." In *Handbook of Theological Education in World Christianity: Theological Perspectives, Regional Surveys, Ecumenical Trends*, edited by Dietrich Werner et al., 30–42. Eugene, OR: Wipf & Stock, 2010.

———. "Han." In *Dictionary of Feminist Theologies*, edited by Letty M. Russell and J. Shannon Clarkson. Louisville: Westminster John Knox, 1996.

Katongole, Emmanuel M. "Hauerwasian Hooks and the Christian Social Imagination." In *God, Truth, and Witness: Engaging Stanley Hauerwas*, edited by L. Gregory Jones et al., 131–54. Grand Rapids: Brazos, 2005.

———. "Journeyer." http://emmanuelkatongole.com/journeyer.

Keifert, Patrick R. *Welcoming the Stranger: A Public Theology of Worship and Evangelism*. Minneapolis: Fortress, 1992.

Keil, Carl Friedrich, and Franz Delitzsch. *Commentary on the Old Testament*. Vol. 1. Grand Rapids: Eerdmans, 1975.

Kim, Ai Ra. *Women Struggling for a New Life*. Albany: State University of New York Press, 1996.

Kim, Hyejeong, and Jenny Pak. "Journeys toward Spiritual Maturity among Korean Immigrant Women in Midlife." *Journal of Psychology and Christianity* 32/1 (2013) 3–19.

King, Nigel, and Christine Horrocks. *Interviews in Qualitative Research*. Los Angeles: Sage, 2010.

Kosmin, Barry A., et al. "American Religious Identification (Aris) Survey 2001." http://commons.trincoll.edu/aris/surveys/aris-2001/aris-2001-codebook.

Koyama, Kosuke. "Extend Hospitality to Strangers—A Missiology of Theologia Crucis." *International Review of Mission* 82/327 (1993) 283–95.

Lash, Nicholas. "'An Immense Darkness' and the Tasks of Theology." In *God, Truth, and Witness: Engaging Stanley Hauerwas*, edited by L. Gregory Jones et al., 257–79. Grand Rapids: Brazos, 2005.

Lawler, Steph. *Identity: Sociological Perspectives*. Cambridge: Polity, 2014.

Lee, Matthew T., et al. *The Heart of Religion: Spiritual Empowerment, Benevolence, and the Experience of God's Love*. New York: Oxford University Press, 2013.

Lei, Xiao-Xiao. "Forgiveness in Confucianism and Christianity." MA thesis, Trinity International University, 2002.

Lelkes, Yphtach, et al. "Complete Anonymity Compromises the Accuracy of Self-Reports." *Journal of Experimental Social Psychology* 48/6 (2012) 1291–99. doi:10.1016/j.jesp.2012.07.002.

Levitt, Peggy, and B. Nadya Jaworsky. "Transnational Migration Studies: Past Developments and Future Trends." *Annual Review Sociology* 33 (2007) 129–56.

Lieu, Judith. *Christian Identity in the Jewish and Graeco-Roman World.* Oxford: Oxford University Press, 2004.

Lincoln, Yvonna S., et al. "Paradigmatic Controversies, Contradictions, and Emerging Confluences, Revisited." In *The Sage Handbook of Qualitative Research,* edited by Norman K. Denzin and Yvonna S. Lincoln, 97–128. Thousand Oaks, CA: Sage, 2011.

Litton, Chad. "Negotiating Religious Identity at Borden State College." PhD diss., University of Wisconsin-Milwaukee, 2002.

Long, Burke O. *2 Kings.* Grand Rapids: Eerdmans, 1991.

Longacre, R. E. "Joseph." In *Dictionary of the Old Testament: Pentateuch,* edited by T. Desmond Alexander and David W. Baker, 469–77. Downers Grove, IL: InterVarsity, 2003.

Lull, Timothy F., and William R. Russell, eds. *Martin Luther's Basic Theological Writings.* 2nd ed. Minneapolis: Fortress, 2005.

Luo, Wangshu. "Returning Overseas Students on the Rise." *China Daily,* 2013. http://www.chinadaily.com.cn/china/2013-12/28/content_16265529.htm.

Luther, Martin. *The Freedom of a Christian.* Edited by Mark D. Tranvik. Minneapolis: Fortress, 2008.

Luther, Martin, et al. *The Bondage of the Will.* Old Tappan, NJ: Revell, 1957.

Mandryk, Jason, and Patrick J. Johnstone. *Operation World.* Colorado Springs: Biblica, 2010.

Marx, Karl. *Selected Writings.* Edited by David McLellan. Oxford: Oxford University Press, 1977.

Mason, Jennifer. *Qualitative Researching.* London: Sage, 1996.

McAdams, Dan P. "Narrative Identity." In *Handbook of Identity Theory and Research,* edited by Seth J. Schwartz et al., 99–115. New York: Springer, 2011.

———. *The Person: A New Introduction to Personality Psychology.* Hoboken, NJ: Wiley, 2006.

———. "Personal Narratives and the Life Story." In *Handbook of Personality: Theory and Research,* edited by Oliver P. John et al., 242–62. New York: Guilford, 2008.

———. "The Redemptive Self: Narrative Identity in America Today." In *The Self and Memory,* edited by Denise R. Beike, et al., 95–116. New York: Psychology, 2004.

———. *The Stories We Live By: Personal Myths and the Making of the Self.* New York: William Morrow, 1993.

McGrath, Alister E. *Theology: The Basic Readings.* Oxford: Blackwell, 2008.

McGuire, Meredith B. *Religion: The Social Context.* Long Grove, IL: Waveland, 2008.

McKenna, Thomas F. "No Generic Spirituality: Ethnicity and the Spiritual Journey." In *Ethnicity, Nationality and Religious Experience,* edited by Peter C. Phan, 209–19. Lanham, MD: University Press of America, 1995.

"Meet Miroslav Volf, Whose Allah Is a Path to Peace." Read the Spirit. http://www.readthespirit.com/explore/meet-miroslav-volf-whose-allah-is-a-path-to-peace/.

Milton, John Peterson. *God's Covenant of Blessing.* Rock Island, IL: Augustana, 1961.

Mitchel, Patrick. *Evangelicalism and National Identity in Ulster, 1921–1998.* Oxford: Oxford University Press, 2003.

———. "Evangelicals and Irish Identity in Independent Ireland: A Case Study." In *Irish Protestant identities,* edited by M. A. Busteed et al. Manchester: Manchester

University Press, 2008. http://www.ibi.ie/resources/evangelicals-in-ireland/evangelicals-and-irish-identity-in-independent-ireland-a-case-study.

Moltmann, Jürgen. *The Spirit of Life: A Universal Affirmation.* Minneapolis: Fortress, 1992.

———. "Theology in the Project of the Modern World." In *A Passion for God's Reign: Theology, Christian Learning and the Christian Self,* edited by Miroslav Volf, 1–22. Grand Rapids: Eerdmans, 1998.

Mooney, Margarita A. *Faith Makes Us Live: Surviving and Thriving in the Haitian Diaspora.* Berkeley: University of California Press, 2009.

Morris, Leon. "Evangelical." World Evangelical Alliance (WEA). www.worldea.org/whoweare/evangelical.

Morris, M. J. "Hagar." In *The Lexham Bible Dictionary,* edited by John D. Barry and Lazarus Wentz. Bellingham, WA: Lexham, 2012.

Mouw, Richard J. "The Imago Dei and Philosophical Anthropology." *Christian Scholar's Review* 41 (2012) 253–66.

Musekura, Célestin. *An Assessment of Contemporary Models of Forgiveness.* New York: Peter Lang, 2010.

Musschenga, Albert W. "Personalized Identity in an Individualized Society." In *Creating Identity,* edited by Hermann Häring et al, 23–30. London: SCM, 2000.

Nahm, Andrew C. *Historical Dictionary of the Republic of Korea.* Asian Historical Dictionaries 11. Metuchen, NJ: Scarecrow, 1993.

Net Bible: New English Translation. Spokane, WA: Biblical Studies, 2001.

Nguyen, vanThanh, and John M. Prior. *God's People on the Move: Biblical and Global Perspectives on Migration and Mission.* Eugene, OR: Pickwick, 2014.

Niditch, Susan. "Genesis." In *The Women's Bible Commentary,* edited by Carol A. Newsom and Sharon H. Ringe, 13–29. Louisville: Westminster John Knox, 1992.

O'Neill, William. "'No Longer Strangers' (Ephesians 2:19): The Ethics of Migration." *Word and World* 29/3 (2009) 227–33.

"Open Doors: International Students in the U.S." Institute for International Education (IIE). http://www.iie.org/Who-We-Are/News-and-Events/Press-Center/Press-Releases/2010/2010-11-15-Open-Doors-International-Students-In-The-US#.UuVevLQpDIU.

Overland, P. B. "Hagar." In *Dictionary of the Old Testament: Pentateuch,* edited by T. Desmond Alexander and David W. Baker, 376–79. Downers Grove, IL: InterVarsity, 2003.

Owens, Timothy J. "Self and Identity." In *Handbook of Social Psychology,* edited by John D. DeLamater, 205–32. New York: Kluwer Academic/Plenum, 2003.

Owens, Timothy J., and Sarah Samblanet. "Self and Self-Concept." In *Handbook of Social Psychology,* edited by John D. DeLamater and Amanda Ward, 225–49. 2nd ed. New York: Springer, 2013.

Padilla, Elaine. "Expanding Space: A Possibility of a Cavernous Mode of Dwelling." In *Contemporary Issues of Migration and Theology,* edited by Elaine Padilla and Peter C. Phan, 53–72. New York: Palgrave Macmillan, 2013.

Padilla, Elaine, and Peter C. Phan, eds. *Contemporary Issues of Migration and Theology.* New York: Palgrave Macmillan, 2013.

———. *Theology of Migration in the Abrahamic Religions.* New York: Palgrave Macmillan, 2014.

Pak, Jenny Hyun Chung. "Acculturation and Identity of Korean American Women." Paper presented at the American Psychological Association Annual Conference, Chicago, August 22–25, 2002.

———. "Cultural Differences in Alliance Formation During Group Supervision." Paper presented at the American Psychological Association Annual Conference, Washington, DC, August 4–8, 2000.

———. *Korean American Women: Stories of Acculturation and Changing Selves.* New York: Routledge, 2006.

Pak, Jenny Hyun Chung, et al. "The Life Histories of Ten Individuals Who Crossed the Border between Community Colleges and Selective Four-Year Colleges." Los Angeles: University of Southern California, 2006.

Park, HiRho Yoon. "Practices of Ministerial Leadership of Korean-American United Methodist Clergywomen: Toward a Wesleyan Ecclesiology in a Global Context." PhD diss., Boston University, 2011.

Park, Jerry Z. "The Ethnic and Religious Identities of Young Asian Americans." PhD diss., University of Notre Dame, 2004.

Pearson, Owen. *Albania in the Twentieth Century: A History.* London: Centre for Albanian Studies, 2004.

Phan, Peter C., ed. *Ethnicity, Nationality and Religious Experience.* Vol. 37. Lanham, MD: University Press of America, 1995.

———. "The Experience of Migration as Source of Intercultural Theology." In *Contemporary Issues of Migration and Theology*, edited by Elaine Padilla and Peter C. Phan, 179–210. New York: Palgrave Macmillan, 2013.

Phinney, Jean S. "A Three-Stage Model of Ethnic Identity Development in Adolescents." In *Ethnic Identity: Formation and Transmission among Hispanics and Other Minorities*, edited by Martha E. Bernal and George P. Knight, 61–80. Albany: State University of New York Press, 1993.

Polkinghorne, Donald. *Narrative Knowing and the Human Sciences.* Albany: State University of New York Press, 1988.

Ponce, Albert. "Racialization, Resistance, and the Migrant Rights Movement: A Historical Analysis." *Critical Sociology* 40/1 (2014) 9–27.

Population Division, Department of Economic and Social Affairs. "International Migration 2013 Wall Chart." United Nations. http://www.un.org/en/development/desa/population/publications/migration/migration-wallchart-2013.shtml.

Quash, Ben. *Abiding: The Archbishop of Canterbury's Lent Book 2013.* London: Bloomsbury, 2012.

Rainey, Lee Dian. *Confucius and Confucianism: The Essentials.* Oxford: Wiley-Blackwell, 2010.

Rasmusson, Arne. "The Politics of Diaspora." In *God, Truth, and Witness: Engaging Stanley Hauerwas*, edited by L. Gregory Jones et al., 88–111. Grand Rapids: Brazos, 2005.

Razon, Na'amah, and Karen Ross. "Negotiating Fluid Identities: Alliance-Building in Qualitative Interviews." *Qualitative Inquiry* 18/6 (2012) 494–503.

Reicher, Stephen, et al. "The Social Identity Approach in Social Psychology." In *The SAGE Handbook of Identities*, edited by Margaret Wetherell and Chandra Talpade Mohanty, 45–62. London: Sage, 2010.

Reinders, Hans S. "The Virtue of Writing Appropriately." In *God, Truth, and Witness: Engaging Stanley Hauerwas*, edited by L. Gregory Jones et al., 53–70. Grand Rapids: Brazos, 2005.

Richardson, Neville. "What's Going on in the Church in South Africa?" In *God, Truth, and Witness: Engaging Stanley Hauerwas*, edited by L. Gregory Jones et al., 229–53. Grand Rapids: Brazos, 2005.

Ricoeur, Paul. *Figuring the Sacred: Religion, Narrative, and Imagination*. Minneapolis: Fortress, 1995.

Riessman, Catherine Kohler. *Narrative Methods for the Human Sciences*. Los Angeles: Sage, 2008.

Ritchie, Jane, and Jane Lewis. *Qualitative Research Practice: A Guide for Social Science Students and Researchers*. London: Sage, 2003.

Rivera-Pagán, Luis N. "Xenophilia or Xenophobia: Towards a Theology of Migration." *The Ecumenical Review* 64/4 (2012) 575–89.

Roberts, W. "Homilies by Various Authors." In *The Pulpit Commentary: Genesis*, edited by H. D. M. Spence-Jones and Joseph S. Exell, 446–49. Grand Rapids: Eerdmans, 1950.

Rosenlee, Li-Hsiang Lisa. *Confucianism and Women: A Philosophical Interpretation*. New York: State University of New York Press, 2006.

Rosenthal, Gabriele. "Biographical Research." In *Qualitative Research Practice*, edited by Clive Seale et al., 48–64. London: Sage, 2004.

Ross, Cathy. "Pioneering Missiologies: Seeing Afresh." In *The Pioneer Gift*, edited by Jonny Baker and Cathy Ross, 20–38. Norwich: Canterbury, 2014.

Rubin, Herbert J., and Irene S. Rubin. *Qualitative Interviewing: The Art of Hearing Data*. London: Sage, 2004.

Ruiz, Jean-Pierre. *Readings from the Edges: The Bible and People on the Move*. Maryknoll, NY: Orbis, 2011.

Russell, A. Sue. *Conversion, Identity, and Power: The Impact of Christianity on Power Relationships and Social Exchanges*. Lanham, MD: University Press of America, 1999.

Russell, Letty M., et al., eds. *Just Hospitality: God's Welcome in a World of Difference*. Louisville: Westminster John Knox, 2009.

Salih, Ruba. *Gender in Transnationalism: Home, Longing and Belonging among Moroccan Migrant Women*. London: Routledge, 2003.

Sarot, Marcel. "Trinity and Church: Trinitarian Perspectives on the Identity of the Christian Community." *International Journal of Systematic Theology* 12/1 (January 2010) 33–45.

Schildkraut, Deborah J. "Defining American Identity in the Twenty-First Century: How Much "There" Is There?" *Journal of Politics* 69/3 (2007) 597–615.

———. "The Dynamics of Public Opinion on Ethnic Profiling after 9/11 Results from a Survey Experiment." *American Behavioral Scientist* 53/1 (2009) 61–79.

Schreiter, Robert. "Ethnicity and Nationality as Contexts for Religious Experience." In *Ethnicity, Nationality and Religious Experience*, edited by Peter C. Phan, 9–28. Lanham, MD: University Press of America, 1995.

Seigel, Jerrold E. *The Idea of the Self: Thought and Experience in Western Europe since the Seventeenth Century*. Cambridge: Cambridge University Press, 2005.

Sellers, Robert M., et al. "Multidimensional Model of Racial Identity: A Reconceptualization of African American Racial Identity." *Personality and Social Psychology Review* 2/1 (1998) 18–39.

Sheldrake, Philip. "Human Identity and the Particularity of Place." *Spiritus: A Journal of Christian Spirituality* 1/1 (2001) 43–64.

Shim, Eun Jung. "Marital Maintenance among Korean Young Married Couples from the Wives' Perspectives." PhD diss., Rosemead School of Psychology, Biola University, 2010.

Shortt, Rupert. *God's Advocates: Christian Thinkers in Conversation.* Grand Rapids: Eerdmans, 2005.

Sider, J. Alexander. "Friendship, Alienation, Love: Stanley Hauerwas and John Howard Yoder." In *Unsettling Arguments: A Festschrift on the Occasion of Stanley Hauerwas's 70th Birthday*, edited by Charles R. Pinches et al., 61–88. Eugene, OR: Cascade, 2010.

Smilde, David. *Reason to Believe: Cultural Agency in Latin American Evangelicalism.* Berkeley: University of California Press, 2007.

Smith, Christian. "Critical Realism." Paper presented at the Fashioning Faith with Scholarship in Sociological Research, Princeton University, June 21, 2013.

———. "Future Directions in the Sociology of Religion." *Social Forces* 86 (2008) 1561.

———. *Moral, Believing Animals: Human Personhood and Culture.* Oxford: Oxford University Press, 2003.

———. *What Is a Person? Rethinking Humanity, Social Life, and the Moral Good from the Person Up.* Kindle ed. Chicago: University of Chicago Press, 2010.

Smith, Stelman, and Judson Cornwall. *The Exhaustive Dictionary of Bible Names.* North Brunswick, NJ: Bridge-Logos, 1998.

Snodgrass, Klyne. "Paul's Focus on Identity." *Bibliotheca Sacra* 168/671 (July-September 2011) 259–73.

Soerens, Matthew, and Jenny Hwang. *Welcoming the Stranger: Justice, Compassion and Truth in the Immigration Debate.* Downers Grove, IL: InterVarsity, 2009.

Somers, Margaret R. "The Narrative Constitution of Identity: A Relational and Network Approach." *Theory and Society* 23/5 (1994) 605–49.

Song, Young I. "A Woman-Centered Perspective on Korean American Women Today." In *Korean American Women: From Tradition to Modern Feminism*, edited by Young I. Song and Ailee Moon, 3–10. Westport, CT: Praeger, 1998.

Stanley, Brian. *The Global Diffusion of Evangelicalism: The Age of Billy Graham and John Stott.* Downers Grove, IL: InterVarsity, 2013.

"State & County Quick Facts." United States Census Bureau. http://quickfacts.census. gov/qfd/states/48/48113.html.

Susin, Luiz Carlos. "A Critique of the Identity Paradigm." In *Creating Identity*, edited by Hermann Häring et al., 78–90. London: SCM, 2000.

Swann, William B., Jr. "Identity Negotiation: Where Two Roads Meet." *Journal of Personality and Social Psychology* 53/6 (1987) 1038–51.

———. "Self-Verification Theory." In *Handbook of Theories of Social Psychology*, edited by Paul A. M. van Lange et al., 23–42. Los Angeles: Sage, 2011.

Swann, William B., Jr., and J. K. Bosson. "Identity Negotiation: A Theory of Self and Social Interaction." In *Handbook of Personality: Theory and Research*, edited by Oliver P. John et al., 448–71. New York: Guilford, 2008.

Syed, Faria, et al. "Pakistan Religious Identity Online Survey 2012." http://www.scribd. com/doc/81787529/Pakistan-Online-Religious-Identity-Survey-2012.

Talebi, Miki. "Does Religion Matter? The Role of Ethnic and Religious Identity and Social Support in the Resilience of Canadian Immigrants." MA thesis, Carleton University, Canada, 2009.

Tanner, Kathryn. *Theories of Culture: A New Agenda for Theology.* Minneapolis: Fortress, 1997.

Taylor, Charles. "The Politics of Recognition." In *Multiculturalism: Examining the Politics of Recognition,* edited by Charles Taylor and Amy Gutmann, 25–74. Princeton: Princeton University Press, 1994.

Taylor, John Brian. *The Theology of Blessing in the Hebrew Scriptures.* Milton Keynes: Open University Press, 1992.

TeSelle, Eugene. "Exploring the Inner Conflict: Augustine's Sermons on Romans 7 and 8." In *Engaging Augustine on Romans: Self, Context, and Theology in Interpretation,* edited by Daniel Patte and Eugene TeSelle, 111–46. Harrisburg, PA: Trinity, 2002.

Ticciati, Susannah. *Job and the Disruption of Identity: Reading Beyond Barth.* London: T. & T. Clark, 2005.

Tihanyi, Laszlo, et al. "The Effect of Cultural Distance on Entry Mode Choice, International Diversification, and Mne Performance: A Meta-Analysis." *Journal of International Business Studies* 36/3 (2005) 270–83.

Ting-Toomey, Stella. *Communicating across Cultures.* New York: Guilford, 1999.

———. "Communicative Resourcefulness: An Identity Negotiation Perspective." In *Intercultural Communication Competence,* edited by Richard Lee Wiseman and Jolene Koester, 72–111. Newbury Park, CA: Sage, 1993.

———. "Identity Negotiation Theory: Crossing Cultural Boundaries." In *Theorizing About Intercultural Communication,* edited by William B. Gudykunst, 211–33. Thousand Oaks, CA: Sage, 2005.

———. "Interpersonal Ties in Intergroup Communication." In *Intergroup Communication,* edited by William B. Gudykunst, 114–26. London: E. Arnold, 1986.

———. "The Matrix of Face: An Updated Face-Negotiation Theory." In *Theorizing About Intercultural Communication,* edited by William B. Gudykunst, 71–92. Thousand Oaks, CA: Sage, 2004.

Toomey, Adrian, et al. "Bicultural Identity Negotiation, Conflicts, and Intergroup Communication Strategies." *Journal of Intercultural Communication Research* 42/2 (2013) 112–34.

Tsolidis, Georgina. *Migration, Diaspora and Identity: Cross-National Experiences.* Dordrecht: Springer, 2014.

Tull, P. K. "Methods of Interpretation." In *Dictionary of the Old Testament: Historical Books,* edited by Bill T. Arnold and H. G. M. Williamson, 682–93. Downers Grove, IL: InterVarsity, 2005.

Turner, Jonathan H. *Contemporary Sociological Theory.* Los Angeles: Sage, 2013.

Velloso da Silva, C. Rosalee. "The Politics of Scripture: Exile and Identity in Jewish and Christian Readings of Jeremiah." PhD diss., Duke University, 2003.

Vertovec, Steven. *Transnationalism.* London: Routledge, 2009.

———. "Transnationalism and Identity." *Journal of Ethnic and Migration Studies* 27/4 (2001) 573–82. http://www.tandfonline.com/loi/cjms20.

Vignoles, Vivian L., et al. "Introduction: Toward an Integrative View of Identity." In *Handbook of Identity Theory and Research*, edited by Seth J. Schwartz et al., 1–27. New York: Springer, 2012.

Voas, David. "Surveys of Behaviour, Beliefs and Affiliation: Micro-Quantitative." In *The Sage Handbook of the Sociology of Religion*, edited by James A. Beckford and N. J. Demerath, 144–66. Los Angeles: Sage, 2007.

Volf, Miroslav. *After Our Likeness: The Church as the Image of the Trinity*. Grand Rapids: Eerdmans, 1998.

———. *Against the Tide: Love in a Time of Petty Dreams and Persisting Enmities*. Grand Rapids: Eerdmans, 2010.

———. *Allah: A Christian Response*. New York: HarperOne, 2011.

———. "Being as God Is." In *God's Life in Trinity*, edited by Miroslav Volf and Michael Welker, 3–12. Minneapolis: Fortress, 2006.

———. *Captive to the Word of God: Engaging the Scriptures for Contemporary Theological Reflection*. Grand Rapids: Eerdmans, 2010.

———. *The End of Memory: Remembering Rightly in a Violent World*. Grand Rapids: Eerdmans, 2006.

———. *Exclusion and Embrace: A Theological Exploration of Identity, Otherness, and Reconciliation*. Nashville: Abingdon, 1996.

———. *Free of Charge: Giving and Forgiving in a Culture Stripped of Grace*. Grand Rapids: Zondervan, 2005.

Volf, Miroslav, et al. *A Common Word: Muslims and Christians on Loving God and Neighbor*. Grand Rapids: Eerdmans, 2010.

Volpe, Medi Ann. *Rethinking Christian Identity: Modern Theology and Christian Formation*. Chicester: Wiley-Blackwell, 2013.

Walker, Hugh Dyson. *East Asia: A New History*. Bloomington, IN: AuthorHouse, 2012.

Wallace, Daniel B. *Revisiting the Corruption of the New Testament: Manuscript, Patristic, and Apocryphal Evidence*. Grand Rapids: Kregel, 2011.

Walls, Andrew. "Missiology as Vocation." In *Walk Humbly with the Lord: Church and Mission Engaging Plurality*, edited by Viggo Mortensen and Andreas Østerlund Nielsen, 230–37. Grand Rapids: Eerdmans, 2010.

Walls, Andrew F. *The Missionary Movement in Christian History: Studies in the Transmission of Faith*. Maryknoll, NY: Orbis, 1996.

Walls, Andrew F., and Cathy Ross, eds. *Mission in the 21st Century: Exploring the Five Marks of Global Mission*. Maryknoll, NY: Orbis, 2008.

Wan, Enoch. "A Comparative Study of Sino-American Cognitive and Theological Pattern and Proposed Alternative." 2007. www.enochwan.com/english/articles/pdf/Sino-American%20Cognitive%20and%20Theological%20Pattern.pdf.

Wannenwetsch, Bernd. "Representing the Absent in the City." In *God, Truth, and Witness: Engaging Stanley Hauerwas*, edited by L. Gregory Jones et al., 167–92. Grand Rapids: Brazos, 2005.

Weber, Max, et al. *The Protestant Ethic and the "Spirit" of Capitalism and Other Writings*. New York: Penguin, 2002.

Wild-Wood, Emma. "Common Witness "in Christ": Peregrinations through Mission and Migration." *Mission Studies* 30/1 (2013) 43–63.

———. *Migration and Christian Identity in Congo*. Leiden: Brill, 2008.

Williams, A. N. "Assimilation and Otherness: The Theological Significance of Négritude." *International Journal of Systematic Theology* 11/3 (2009) 248–70.

Williams, Roman R. "God's Global Professionals: International Students, Evangelical Christianity, and the Idea of a Calling." PhD diss., Boston University, 2010.

Williams, Rowan. *On Christian Theology*. Oxford: Blackwell, 2000.

Wolff, Joshua R., et al. "Understanding Why Fathers Assume Primary Medical Caretaker Responsibilities of Children with Life-Threatening Illnesses." *Psychology of Men and Masculinity* 12/2 (2011) 144.

Wray Beal, Lissa M. *1 and 2 Kings*. Downers Grove, IL: InterVarsity, 2014.

Wright, N. T. *The Resurrection of the Son of God*. Minneapolis: Fortress, 2003.

———. *Surprised by Hope: Rethinking Heaven, the Resurrection, and the Mission of the Church*. New York: HarperOne, 2008.

Wuthnow, Robert. *Meaning and Moral Order: Explorations in Cultural Analysis*. Berkeley: University of California Press, 1989.

Yang, Fenggang. *Chinese Christians in America: Conversion, Assimilation, and Adhesive Identities*. University Park: Pennsylvania State University Press, 1999.

———. "Religious Conversion and Identity Construction: A Study of a Chinese Christian Church in America." PhD diss., Catholic University of America, 1996.

Yangarber-Hicks, Natalia, et al. "Invitation to the Table Conversation: A Few Diverse Perspectives on Integration." *Journal of Psychology and Christianity* 25/4 (2006) 144–57.

Yin, Robert K. *Case Study Research: Design and Methods*. Los Angeles: Sage, 2009.

Zelinsky, Wilbur. *The Enigma of Ethnicity: Another American Dilemma*. Iowa City: University of Iowa City Press, 2001.

Zimmer, Heinrich. *Myths and Symbols in Indian Art and Civilization*. New York: Harper, 1962.

www.ingramcontent.com/pod-product-compliance
Lightning Source LLC
Chambersburg PA
CBHW071845270326
41929CB00013B/2108